TALES OF THE MIDWEST

Growing Up and Growing Old in Rural Small-Town, U.S.A.

An Anthology

By

John Eric Vining

Major Contributions by Robert E. Vining

Final Short Story by Marianna Fetters

Compiled and Edited by John Eric Vining

Order this book online at www.trafford.com
or email orders@trafford.com

Most Trafford titles are also available at major online book retailers.

Print information available on the last page.

ISBN: 978-1-4907-6357-6 (sc)
ISBN: 978-1-4907-6356-9 (e)

Trafford rev. 08/21/2015

 www.trafford.com

North America & international
toll-free: 1 888 232 4444 (USA & Canada)
fax: 812 355 4082

CONTENTS

Prologue ix

Robert E. Vining.. xi

John Eric Vining xiv

Part I: Growing Up in the Rural Midwest:

The Fergie (1952-2006)…and Beyond? 3

The Hayfork Incident.. 6

Déjà Vu All Over Again: David versus Goliath, Circa 1964......... 9

The Palm Sunday Tornado... 16

The Train in the Night... 21

Missy 23

These Kids Are Special 27

Junior High Gorillas.. 35

The Carnie and the Princess 38

Put Me in the Game, Give Me the Ball, and We'll Win! 42

The Pull 47

Medals in the Attic 50

Yesterday's Titan.. 53

The Kids Who Saved a City 57

Amos, the Peasant Prophet 66

The Herod Dynasty 72

Are We Gambling With Our Life? (And Afterlife?) 78

The Nature of the Ghosts: Five Ways to Categorize Them 83

Part II: Growing Up in the Rural Midwest:

The Russian Revolution: Its Causes and Results 95

Is the Government Covering Up Too Much Information? 107

Nuclear Common Sense 114

Afterward 122

The Years of Jubilee 123

2013 Postscripts:
  "Nuclear Common Sense" and "The Years of Jubilee" 129

Tactical Aircraft for the 1990s 141

Postscript: Why Didn't Events Occur in the 1990s as John
  Projected? 161

The Rise and Fall (And Rise Again) of OPEC 163

Postscript: The (Rise Again) of OPEC 186

Book Review: "American Capitalism" 192

William O. Douglas 198

Major General John E. Wool 200

2nd Lieutenant Frank Luke, Jr.: Clearing the Controversy 218

A Tale of Two Eras 228

Background to: The Russian Invasion of Czechoslovakia 231

The Russian Invasion of Czechoslovakia 237

A Short History of the U.S. Labor Movement 239

In Defense of the World War II
  Allied Strategic Bombing Campaign 262

A 150-Year Evolution:
  Mounted Militia to Mechanized Infantry - 1790 to 1940 264

American Super-Frigates 270

The Lion of the West 274

Get a Good Look at the Basket 277

Part III: Growing Old in the Rural Midwest:

The Beauty and the Beast 301

Tux & Olivia 305

But, Gee, All I Have On My Team is a Bunch of Rookies! 310

The Superstar 314

God Is In Control 320

The Rest of the Story 325

Epilogue 329

PROLOGUE

"At 20, you care what *everybody* thinks about you.
    At 40, you don't care what *anybody* thinks about you.
        At 60, you realize *nobody* was thinking about you."

I heard this memorable and humorous quote many years ago, probably about the time I was approaching 20-years-old. Little did I know how true it really was, and how my brother's and my lives would come to resemble the reality of this quote. As I approach my 60th birthday, this reality hits home.

I continued to contemplate this quote, and I realized it would be a great structural format for publishing the many short stories Bob and I had written over the years. Some of the stories tell about our lives growing up. More of the articles tell of our interests and consciousness of the world around us as we matured. And finally, some of the stories tell of the life lessons we learned and the things that were important to us as we grew older. Thus, the articles and short stories in this book will be [roughly] arranged in three parts:

"Part I: Growing Up- 'At 20, you care what *everybody* thinks about you.'"
"Part II: Growing Up- 'At 40, you don't care what *anybody* thinks about you.'"
"Part III: Growing Old- 'At 60, you realize *nobody* was thinking about you.'"

When I was little, my mother had a book called "*A Book About A Thousand Things*" by George Stimpson (New York and London: Harper & Brothers, 1946). It was really just a compendium of unorganized but interesting facts, phrases, and short informational paragraphs. I used to pull this book down off the bookshelf and read it when I had a few moments to spare. The collection of short stories you are about to read is something similar, except it is less than "a thousand things" and more short-story oriented. Another inspiration for this collection was *"Twice Told Tales,"* a conceptually similar compendium completed by Nathaniel Hawthorne in the 1830s and 1840s.

The book is organized roughly chronologically, starting with some of the first episodes that I can remember. This is not a hard and fast rule; for example, some of my first memorable activities as a young adult will still be considered part of the early "growing up" phase. In like manner, our first forays into writing about wider-world, or "social issues," occurred in our late teens. However, these were the awakenings of more mature thought, and so these are included in the "middle-aged" portion of the collection.

Finally, I realized some of the stories and groups of stories might need the provision of a little foreknowledge to be meaningful to you as readers of the collection. Therefore, throughout the book, you will find sections entitled "Setting the Stage for…" to provide this needed foreknowledge.

The reality is these are stories of the lives and interests of two boys growing up in rural America. I hope many are quite interesting to you. Perhaps some of the stories might not interest you. If these do not, what I hope they *will* do is stir some fond memories of *your* lives and interests during certain periods of *your* life.

I do believe there is something for everybody in this collection. I hope it will provide an enjoyable diversion for you, as you share Bob's and my journey through this sojourn we call life.

John Eric Vining

ROBERT E. VINING

(1946-2006)

A summarization of his literary work.

Robert Vining (1946-2006) was an extremely intelligent individual, and was a product of the time of his coming of age – the turbulence of 1963 to 1970.

Bob wrote an outstanding senior history capstone project entitled _"The Russian Revolution – Its Causes and Results"_ in April, 1964. However, Bob was able to think and talk intelligently on a variety of different subjects. An example of the breadth of his intelligence was the following anecdote during his time as a student at Ohio Northern University:

Bob took an advanced mathematics course, and sat for a mid-term examination. Approximately one week later, he got the test results back and was astounded to find that he received a "zero" on the exam. In looking through his answers he found that he had provided all correct ones. After class, Bob approached the professor to inquire why he had received a zero on the exam when all his answers were correct. The professor said Bob must have cheated since he did not show any of his calculations on the exam face. "I did all the work in my head," Bob replied.

"That's impossible," exclaimed the professor. "Nobody can do that on this exam."

"Just put together a new exam with similar questions, then you can stand and watch over my shoulder while I complete it," said Bob.

The professor did just that, watched Bob complete the entire new exam in his head, and gave him the 100% he deserved on the test.

Bob's intellectual life suffered somewhat from the student activist/intellectual syndrome of the '60s. He took nearly 25 years to complete his undergraduate bachelor's degree, including time spent at (at least) Huntington College, Ohio Northern University, Wright State University, Indiana/Purdue University-Ft. Wayne, Michigan

State University, and Central Michigan University. He steadfastly refused to apply his conventional genius and unconventional ability to "think outside the box" in a corporate or education institutional setting, instead preferring the rather non-conformist role of a simple, small, pseudo-organic farmer, and later truck driver. Given his understanding of Galbraithian economics, I think he would be gratified to be identified as rejecting the *"conventional wisdom."* Few people recognized the true brilliance of his thought processes.

Being a small farmer/truck driver did give Bob a lot of time to think, however. He completed the articles *"Nuclear Common Sense"* and *"The Years of Jubilee"* in the 1983-1985 time period, during the "social consciousness" period of his life. Bob was approximately 37 to 40 when he wrote them. The articles reveal his great ability to "think outside the box." They also reveal his social and political naivety in thinking that anybody would listen to a small farmer from rural Northwest Ohio who had not paid his dues by spending years in an institutional setting, thus establishing conventional credentials before recommending such sweeping macro-ideas.

Both of the above characteristics were typical of Bob Vining. Written many years ago, the papers are surprisingly prescient and enduring. They provide a good, deep read yet today.

A more diverse series of pieces were written by Bob later in his life, and reflect a different focus from his "social consciousness" period. In late-1985 Bob sold his farm and moved from northwest Ohio to the central Michigan area, originally to raise sheep there but eventually to finish his education at Central Michigan University. Bob's dream of raising a large sheep herd failed to materialize, and he suffered two failed marriages in the late 1980s and early 1990s. I believe he sensed his inability to influence others, and recognized some of the mistakes he had made, even his inability to fully manage his own life. (Bob once confided to our mutual friend, Bill Gamble: "I should never have left the farm. But my way of farming is gone forever, never to return.")

I believe by the 1990s Bob yearned for the simpler, happier times of his younger days – times spent in Northwest Ohio plus the time when he was fully free: serving in the Peace Corps in

Micronesia. Many of his younger days were spent with his brother John in northern Mercer County, Ohio: working on the farm, participating with, or observing John in sports. Thus in the 1990s Bob wrote the pieces *"The Palm Sunday Tornado"* (about events in 1965), *"These Kids Are Special"* (events in 1967), *"Put Me in the Game, Get Me the Ball, and We'll Win!"* (events in 1973), and *"The Kids Who Saved a City"* (events in 1982), plus the farcical fiction *"Get a Good Look at the Basket".* Also in this period under the pen name "Raymond Refoen," Bob published *"Micronesia's Never-Forgotten Island – Where Life is a Coconut"* (Virginia Pines Press, copywrite 2000), an account of his Peace Corps experiences from 1967 to 1969.

After his first heart problems in 2002, Bob sensed that time was short, and wrote of his survival of three massive heart attacks and his Christian conversion experience in the article *"God Is in Control"* (originally entitled *"Sweet Peace, The Gift of God's Love")*. With time running out, Bob (once again as "Raymond Refoen") melded his writing skills with his sense of social consciousness/responsibility; first to Native Americans in his novel *"Peace in the Valley"* (completed but unpublished), then to Mormons in *"The Long Journey Home"* (uncompleted at the time of his death).

The timeline of Bob's life was capped by the short article *"The Rest of the Story"* (written by our sister, Marianna Fetters). This was an epilogue to Bob's earlier article *"Sweet Peace,"* and told of his return to Northwest Ohio to spend his last hours with his family, culminating with Bob's death on October 17th, 2006, thirty-four days short of his 60th birthday.

Therefore, because this book is organized in roughly chronological order, according either to the event described or the focus of writing during a certain interval in the life of Bob or John, you will find his works scattered periodically throughout this series of short stories. Be sure to look for the author's name of the short story you are reading. Also note the unique, sometimes whimsical style that Bob used to tell his stories of growing up and growing old in the Midwest.

JOHN ERIC VINING

(1955-)

A summarization of his literary work.

John Eric Vining, like his brother Bob, was also somewhat a product of his time of coming of age: 1969 to 1977. Some demographers maintain that the "Baby Boom" generation (those born between 1946 and 1964) are actually two generations. Those born before 1955 are the activist "60s Kids" who believed that individuals could make a difference, and the way to make that difference was to band together, influence government, and create a common good. Those born after 1955 felt that government had betrayed them - that things were going to go "The Man's" way no matter what, because "The Man" had big government, big business, big power, and their attendant dirty tricks behind him. The best thing to do was to work hard (for your *own* good) when it was time to work, and play hard when it was time to play (remember the discos?).

What made the difference between the "two generations?" Watergate! Those who experienced Watergate during the tender "leaving home/establishing yourself year" of 19-years-old were jaded by the cover-up, the subsequent Senate hearings, the resignation, and "the pardon." From then on, the Baby Boomers did a "180 degree" about-face from "activism" to "feel-good-ism."

John was born in 1955 and consequently was 19-years-old in 1974 – the Watergate Year. Thus, he was on the fence: he had older "activist" Boomer siblings, yet his attitudes were seared by Watergate. He had some early activist tendencies, as noted in his senior capstone project *"Is The Government Covering Up Too Much Information?"* (1973), and a left-leaning 1976 book review of *"American Capitalism,"* by John Kenneth Galbraith. He had considerably more right-wing thoughts in *"The Russian Invasion of*

Czechoslovakia" (1975) and *"Tactical Aircraft for the 1990s"*, (1984). Perhaps no two works express John's ambivalence toward the political spectrum than *"William O. Douglas"* (2002) and *"A Tale of Two Eras"* (2003).

Vining had always been interested in religion and religious philosophy. Early on, this interest led to short pieces on *"Amos, The Peasant Prophet"* (1975), *"The Herod Dynasty"* (1975), and *"Are We Gambling with Our Life (and Afterlife)"* (1976).

John took a turn at literary criticism with *"The Nature of the Ghosts"* (1975), a review (with a religious emphasis) of a segment of Henry James' classic *"The Turn of the Screw."*

First and foremost, John always loved history and found vent to this love through writing. He was fascinated by an almost unknown general from the Nineteenth Century and wrote his story in *"General John B. Wool: First in War, First in Peace, and Forgotten the in Eyes of his Countrymen."* (2004), and an equally nearly forgotten *"2ⁿᵈ Lieutenant Frank Luke, Jr."* (1984). He wrote both technically and historically in *"The Rise and Fall (and Rise Again) of OPEC"* (1988) and *"The History of Labor Law."* (1990). John developed some works of military analysis with *"In Defense of the World War II Allied Strategic Bombing Campaign"* (1993), *"A 150-Year Evolution: Mounted Militia to Mechanized Infantry – 1790 to 1940"* (1997), and *"American Super-Frigates"* (2005). John even dreamed about history in a short fiction, set in the Civil War, entitled *"The Lion of the West"* (2002). His greatest historical work was published as *"The Trans-Appalachian Wars, 1790-1818: Pathways to American's First Empire."* (Trafford Publishing, copyright 2010), not included in this collection.

John, like Bob, tended to look back fondly on his formative years. He engaged in less "heavy" writing as he grew further into mid-life. Perhaps he, like Bob, realized he was not going to be able to change the world from his vantage point and station in life in the rural Midwest. This led to his writing of some of the experiences of his youth, such as *"The Train in the Night, "Yesterday's Titan," "The Carnie and the Princess," "The Fergie," "The Hayfork Incident,"*

"Déjà Vu All Over Again: David versus Goliath, Circa 1964," and the poignant stories *"Missy,"* and *"Medals in the Attic."*

As John grew older and the kids left home, he felt freer to indulge in some of the activities of his youth. A couple of these activities are outlined in *"The Beauty and the Beast"* and *"Tux & Olivia."*

Finally, in later life John realized that the only truly lasting legacy was the positive impact he had on others – particularly kids. Thus his short stories *"But, Gee, All I Have On My Team Is A Bunch Of Rookies"* and *"The Superstar."*

As of this writing, John still lives among the quiet grain fields of Northwest Ohio. He is planning more historical writing projects and has several manuscripts in various stages of completion.

I hope you enjoy John's stories of growing up and growing old in the Midwest.

PART I

Growing Up in the Rural Midwest:

"At 20, you care what *everybody* thinks about you."

THE FERGIE (1952-2006)...
AND BEYOND?

The Little Tractor that Could!

By

John Eric Vining

If there was one farm implement that symbolized the small 160-to-250 acre farms in Northwest Ohio where Bob and John Vining grew up, it was the Ferguson TO-30 utility tractor (the "Fergie"). It was ubiquitous in our area; we had a 1952 model, the neighbor across the road had one, the neighbor across the field had one, the neighbor who helped us bale hay had one. The neighbor down the road was especially lucky: He had the Ferguson 30's successor – the Massey-Ferguson 65!

The Fergie was small with a short wheelbase. You sat down in/amongst the Fergie, straddling the transmission and sitting just atop the rear-end gear housing – about like riding a horse. Power steering? You've got to be kidding! Even so, the Ferguson was pretty nimble and easy to handle. It was utilitarian in the extreme: four forward and one reverse gears. Three gauges: water temperature, oil pressure, and amperes - positive or negative. You want to know how much gasoline you have left? Open the hood, open the gas cap, and take a look in the tank!

Yet the Ferguson series was somewhat innovative in at least one respect: it had the very first controllable hydraulic three-point hitch system on the market. Now the downside: It was a "Series 2" three-point system and you couldn't hitch bigger equipment to it. That was okay, though – the hydraulic pump on the Ferguson had minimal capacity and wouldn't lift the big stuff anyway. Power-Take-Off (PTO) shaft? Yep, but again too small (it needed a condom-like conversion/extension to handle standard-sized power shafts). And "live" PTO (the ability to compress the clutch to stop the forward motion of the tractor without stopping the attached powered equipment)? Nope – this was several years in the future for the Ferguson utility tractor series. It could handle a two-bottom plow, a 7-foot disc, and an 8-foot spring-tooth harrow – and all at an underwhelming 24.37 drawbar horsepower. (To put this into perspective, my new 42-inch zero-turn-radius lawn mower has a 26-horsepower engine!)

Yet, for all its shortcomings, the Fergie was the mainstay of our farm from the beginning to the end. We plowed, disked, harrowed, planted, and sprayed with it. We cultivated with it. We mowed the hay, rolled the hay, and pulled the hay bailer with it. We pulled the combine and the corn picker with it. We hauled hay, hauled corn, hauled beans, hauled wheat, hauled feed, and hauled our butts from one farm to another on it. We even designed our new cattle barns with the Fergie's turning radius in mind so we could load manure with it. And then we'd hook the Fergie up to the manure spreader to haul nature's fertilizer out onto the fields with it.

The Fergie that was so much a part of my early life participated in my first "farm equipment" work experience, at the tender age of seven years old. My dad sat me on the tractor (with the disc attached), started the engine, let out on the clutch (which I couldn't reach with my foot), and jumped off. He told me to go 'round and 'round the field I was in until I had the field all disked, then turn off the motor and come get him. I did it: he came and moved the Fergie and me to another field and told me to do the same thing all over again!

I think my dad really loved that tractor. I was a seasoned, veteran tractor operator, all of 10 years old, when Dad sent the Fergie and me back to plow a field in the "Back 40" ("acres" to those city folks who are reading this!). I was near a recently cleared fencerow and I must have hit a particularly big root or stump, because all of a sudden I began to hear some pretty loud grinding and clanking coming from the bowels of the Fergie. I immediately stopped plowing and creeped back to the barn on the Ferguson.

This was a mistake: I should have stopped the tractor and turned it off right then and there. When Dad heard the sound of the Fergie's gears creaking and clanking, he almost cried. I think it must have been like one of his kids getting badly injured in a football game! The mechanic said I had broken off every other tooth of the main bull gear and broken several more gears in the transmission, as well as cracking the transmission housing. I don't think my dad ever fully forgave me for hurting (not "damaging," *hurting!*) his beloved Fergie!

But this was not the last time the Fergie would be beaten up or broken. The engine block cracked after some hard use, and forever after it sported a new, dull red engine block in contrast to its overall gray coloring. A wagon once got away from Dad and Bob and smashed into the front of the Fergie: we hammered out the hood and grill and put a new radiator on it. The barn fell on it after the tornado, and the Fergie sported dented, flattened rear fenders from then on. It was dinged, scratched, broken, welded, unbolted, rebolted, stripped, repainted, drilled, filled, supplemented, unwired, rewired, and held together with baling wire.

And it was loved. Other tractors came and went, but always the Fergie stayed. When we got out of farming in 1985, we didn't have the heart to let it go in the auction – the Ferguson stayed in my barn for several years thereafter. When Bob moved to Florida and started a vegetable and fruit garden, he came home to Ohio and took the Fergie back to Florida with him. He put a "Massey-Ferguson Red" coat of paint on it and used it right up until his death in 2006.

I lost track of the Ferguson after that. I like to believe the Fergie is soldiering on somewhere in Florida right now – its tough little 4-cylinder, many-times-rebuilt Continental engine still hammering out its distinctive, clattering roar - serving another master. Just like it served us, for all those years – all those years ago.

THE HAYFORK INCIDENT

Circa 1959

By

John Eric Vining

Let's face it; growing up on the farm is mostly all work and no play. One of my favorite quotes from my dad was this: Bob and I were up in the hayloft "mowing back" hay ("stacking/storing" for the uninitiated!), right up against the steel roof of the barn. It's late-June, 95 degrees with around 90 percent humidity, and it's about the fourth wagonload of 125-pound bales of hay we've unloaded that day. Bob and I start horsing around, like brothers nine years apart in age will do, and my dad yells up from the barn floor: "You guys quit screwing around up there or I'm going to put you to work!"

However, sometimes during the course of the grinding manual labor inherent to operating a small farm, something happens that is so funny that you can't help doubling over with laughter.

I can't remember much from when I was 4-years-old, but I do remember a few incidents: 1) Seeing my dad and grandpa, both of whom had fallen asleep in identical positions side-by-side on the couch in front of the television. 2) Some snap-shot mental images from a family vacation at Robinson Lake in north-central Indiana. 3) And a few scattered moments from a farm activity that I now term *The Hayfork Incident.*

Most of you probably don't know what a hayfork is. In fact, most of you who have grown up on a farm since the 1950s or '60s probably don't know what a hayfork is. Have you ever played that arcade game where a big glass box is about one-quarter filled with stuffed animals, and you control a four-tined grappling hook suspended on strings or small chains from the top of the box? The object is to reach down with the controllable grappling hooks and grab a stuffed animal. If you can do this and successfully maneuver the suspended stuffed animal over to a bin and drop it in there, you win the animal.

Well, an old-fashioned hayfork assembly is very similar in concept. A large, four-tine set of hooks is suspended via a block-and-tackle from a track and "car" that runs along the inside peak of the barn. The "car" runs back and forth along this track. You drove your wagonload of hay bales directly under the center of the barn where this car/block-and-tackle/hayfork assembly was located. The hayforks were lowered via the block-and-tackle to the wagon load of bales, the forks were inserted into 8 bales by one or two guys standing on the wagon, then the signal was given to pull on the free rope of the block-and-tackle. This was originally done with a team of horses. The hayforks and bales were lifted until the hayforks "caught the car" on the rail at the top of the barn. This triggered a car-release mechanism and the entire mass would roll to the haymow where another release mechanism would drop the bales into the mow. Then a couple more guys would "mow back" (i.e.: "stack") the hay for later usage.

It was pretty ingenious nineteenth-century farm technology. We didn't use horses anymore: we used our trusty Ferguson TO-30 tractor (the *"Fergie"*) to supply the power to lift the bales, "catch the car," and propel the accumulated mass into the haymow.

There was (both literally and figuratively) one "catch" to the whole operation. If you didn't lift the bales from the wagon to the roof fast enough to "catch the car" firmly, the hayforks would release and drop the bales right back down on the guys on the wagon.

So let's set the stage: A couple of local older teenage neighbor-boys are in the hay mow stacking the hay. My dad and another neighbor are atop the hay wagon, setting the hayforks into the bales on the hay wagon. A distant relative and also a neighbor, sixty-year-old Edgar Clouse, is more-or-less supervising the operation from the ground beside the hay wagon. Thirteen-year-old Bob Vining is operating the Ferguson tractor that is pulling on the free rope of the block-and-tackle, supplying the power for the whole operation.

Four-year-old John Vining is playing in the yard, watching, and yearning for the day when _he_ can help.

Things are not going well. Young-teenager Bob is afraid to supply the needed power for the forks to "catch the car" securely, for fear of wrecking the whole system. After three consecutive pulls where "timid Bob" has failed to set the hayforks so they catch in the car, and thus sending the entire eight bales cascading back down on my father, Dad's temper is rising. As he angrily sets the hayforks for the fourth time, he repeatedly spits out the following invective at Bob:

"Bob, you've got to _**hit**_ _that car_ with those hayforks! Now I want you to give that tractor the gas and _**hit**_ _that car with those hayforks!!!_"

The ever-obedient Bob does exactly as he is instructed: He yanks the gear-shift into fourth gear; drops the hammer on the throttle; and pops the clutch! Up scream the hayforks, bearing their half-ton load of bales, to crash loudly into the car at the top of the barn. Off to the left, like a blue/green streak, screams the car, hayforks, and bales on the rooftop rail. Faster than anyone can react, the assembled components reach the end of the rail, jump the track, and the entire mass leaps into space, demolishing the entire upper-left side of barn!

There is a moment of stunned silence. Then there is a tittering smirk from the haymow; followed by a snort; then a raucous round of full-blown laughter from everybody anywhere near the barn!

As if this was not funny enough, the spectacle of sixty-year-old Edgar Clouse is unforgettable. His is literally rolling around on the barnyard, laughing so hard he has to hold his sides, tears streaming from his eyes, and kicking his legs in the air like a six-year-old!

Dad (the only one who is not laughing) is once more howling: "No! No! _No_, Bob! Not like that! _Not like that!_"

"Oh yes, Gene!" Edgar manages to splutter between gales of laughter. "You told him to _hit that car with those hayforks_! Well, **_he hit that car with those hayforks!_**"

As I noted, there are very few things most people can remember from when they were four-years-old. _"The Hayfork Incident"_ is one of those stories that was told around our family Thanksgiving feast for years afterward. I can proudly say that I was there and I remember it.

Déjà Vu All Over Again: David Versus Goliath, Circa 1964

1964

By

John Eric Vining

Bob Vining slumped on the bench of the locker room beneath the Parkway High School gymnasium – elbows on knees and hands cupping chin. 'What have we gotten ourselves into this time?' he moaned silently to himself as he listened to the coach's pre-game harangue. 'We shouldn't even be on the floor with these guys!'

Bob had ample cause for concern. The Parkway Panthers boys basketball team's opponent this evening was the Celina Immaculate Conception High School ("ICHS") Spartans. The Spartans were 18-0 and currently ranked #1 in the Ohio High School Class A State Rankings. The Panthers were second to ICHS in the Mercer County League at 10-4.

This current ICHS squad was the proud representative of an impressive basketball tradition. Celina IC was the first school to represent the Northwest Ohio area in the state small school basketball tournament in Columbus way back in 1933. The Spartans had continued success throughout the 1930s and 1940s; they won the Mercer County Tournament in 1934 and 1936, and won league regular season titles in 1936, '42, and '46. They also had a well-deserved reputation for pulling stunning upsets in years when they had less than stellar squads. None was more impressive than the night of February 12th, 1952, when an 11-6 Spartan team stunned a 15-1 Fort Recovery squad in the opening round of the Mercer County League Tournament.

The 1964 ICHS Spartans were a team of legendary strength. The team was spearheaded by 1st Team All-Ohio and "1964 Ohio Class A Player of the Year" Lee Sutter. Also on the team was future (1965) 3rd Team All-Stater Tom Link. A budding superstar was sophomore Kerry Myers, who would go on to be two-time 1st Team All-Ohio and two-time "Ohio Class A Player of the Year" in 1965 and 1966. Ron Houts and Bill Reichert rounded out the starting five, while the bench was filled with capable substitutes. Even 48 years later, a local newspaper touted the 1964 ICHS Spartans as one of the greatest basketball teams the area had ever produced.

Parkway High School was only three years old in 1964. It was a consolidation of two small-town, rural high schools, and was still searching for an academic and athletic identity. However, one of the schools making up the newly-formed consolidation had achieved some basketball success in the fairly recent past. Willshire High School had made the small school state tournament finals in 1940, 1955, and 1956, being the state runner-up in 1955. One team that Willshire had beaten on the way to the state tournament only nine years earlier was a 15-8 Celina ICHS squad. In other words, the blood was in the water.

The 1964 Panthers had their share of athletes. Gerald Deitsch had led the team in scoring during the first half of the season and was a legitimate double-digit scoring threat. Duane Osborn was a slick ball-handling point guard, while his running mate at 2-Guard, burly Dennis Kuhn, was a lock–down defender. Parkway also had some size. Center Bob Vining, a 6'4" jumping-jack, was the team's leading rebounder. His specialty was the offensive rebound; he had collected more by himself on the season than had the rest of the team put together. Best of all was rugged 6'5" Forward Bill Stober - a gifted athlete who could shoot, rebound, and defend. Bill was a record-shattering quarterback on Parkway's football team, and would go on to a fine colligate career as a 3-year starter at tight end for Louisiana State University.

The tension in the air was electric as the teams took to the floor. The cool, confident Spartans ran their warm-up drills smoothly and efficiently. The herky-jerky, nerve-laden Panthers almost stumbled through theirs, constantly glancing at the other end of the court – seemingly in awe of the all-conquering ICHS Spartans.

The Panthers' nerves continued to plague them as the game began; ICHS ran out to a quick 8-0 lead just two minutes into the game. 'Oh sure,' the home Panther crowd sagged. 'We thought we could play with the big boys, but the cream is rising to the top!'

After a much-needed time-out, Bill Stober buried a long jumper from the corner, and the Panthers were on their way. They continued to chip away at IC's lead throughout the first quarter, and by its conclusion the Panthers were down by only two, 15-13.

Bob Vining slammed home an offensive rebound to start the second quarter, and the Parkway Panthers pulled even with ICHS. From then on, the teams traded game-tying baskets, until they were tied at 28 with 3:34 left in the first half. Denny Kuhn dropped in a jumper to give Parkway its first lead, and the Panthers' confidence soared. Vining came alive with two jumpers as the half waned, and Parkway had extended its lead to 36-32 when the halftime buzzer sounded.

Whatever Celina Immaculate Conception's coach said to his team in the halftime locker room worked, because the Spartans came out for the second half with fire in their collective eyes. They quickly scored thrice to tie the score at 38. The scoreboard seesaw resumed: Parkway scored...40-38; IC tied. The Panthers jumped ahead 42-40; ICHS retaliated. Vining tipped in a rebound; Sutter drilled a long jumper. On and on the teams battled until ICHS knotted the score once more at 46-46. Then Big Bill Stober decided it was time to play some basketball: scoring from every conceivable point on the court, he gave the Panthers a 51-46 lead as the third quarter came to a stirring close.

Bob Vining once again began a quarter with a vicious slam dunk off an offensive rebound. This seemed to be a turning point, as the Parkway fans, who had watched relatively passively as the teams had traded punches earlier in the half, now began to stir restlessly. Could the Panthers do it? Could they really pull off an upset of the mighty #1-ranked ICHS Spartans?

However, there was a reason why the Celina Immaculate Conception High School basketball team was undefeated this late in the season. Working carefully, running their offense with precision, and taking advantage of every opportunity, the Spartans battled back to a 54-54 tie. But this time, in the face of adversity, the Parkway faithful never wavered as they thunderously roared support for their gritty Panthers. A missed free throw broke the teams off potential ties, and back and forth the teams whipsawed from 55-54 – Parkway to 60-59 – ICHS.

Then a curious thing happened. For the first time in the 1963-'64 season, the Spartans were being challenged late in a game, and their invincible confidence cracked. They alternately missed shots and fouled the Parkway big men, as Houts and Reichert fouled out within moments of each other. Vining and Stober calmly sank their free throws to give the Panthers a 63-60 lead.

Now the confident façade was completely gone, and the increasingly desperate Spartans uncharacteristically fouled at will. The Panthers, an excellent free-throw-shooting team, took advantage of nearly every opportunity, and shot their way to a 70-64 lead with only 1:15 remaining on the clock.

The great Kerry Myers converted two free throws as the fading Spartans gathered themselves for one last weary attempt to rally for the victory. However, Gerald Deitsch intercepted an errant ICHS pass and drove the length of the court for an uncontested lay-up as the buzzer sounded. Final score: the upstart Parkway Panthers – 72; the humbled ICHS Spartans – 66.

Bob Vining jumped for joy at mid-court as Deitsch's lay-up slipped through the cords, fully displaying his prodigious vertical leaping ability. It was a fitting, enduring mental picture - the soaring, slashing Panther big men had dominated the game. Bill Stober tallied 9 field goals on his way to a game-high 24 points. Gerald Deitsch scored 11 points, including that final dagger into the Spartans' heart. And high-flying Bob Vining had the game of his life, scoring 23 points and "unofficially" grabbing 24 rebounds (rebounds were not officially tallied at the scorers' table in those days). Never before, and never again, would he ever have a game like this one. For one night – one night! – Bob, Bill, Gerald, Duane, Denny, and the rest of the Parkway Panthers were the best boys small high school basketball team in the state of Ohio. David had defeated Goliath – again…

Setting the Stage for *"The Palm Sunday Tornado,"* by Robert E. Vining,

And

"The Train in the Night," by John Eric Vining

It is not particularly surprising that both Bob and John Vining chose to write short stories about their experience with and survival of the April 11, 1965 "Palm Sunday Tornadoes." At the time, this was the biggest outbreak of tornadoes ever to hit the Midwest, and has only been superseded by one subsequent outbreak, that of April 3-4, 1974. The Palm Sunday Tornado was a defining moment in both Bob's and John's lives.

What is surprising is that neither Bob nor John knew the other had written on this subject. At his death, Bob never knew that John had written about the tornado, and John only found out that Bob had written about it when he went through Bob's papers after the latter's passing.

As you read these accounts, I think you will be struck by the similarities in the basics of the stories, despite some lapses in memories (and perhaps poetic license) of the details. The eerie, windy day; the stormy night; the rumbling in the darkness; the terse conversation; the terror as the brothers lay flat on the floor - all come through via stark verbal illumination.

The tornado that struck the Willshire, Ohio vicinity was labeled an "F4" on the Fujita Scale - the next to the largest and most damaging class of tornados. There was some speculation that, due to the early, crude methods of technical damage evaluation that was practiced in 1965, the Willshire tornado was in fact an "F5" - the biggest and baddest rating of them all.

To get a sense of the awe in which storm chasers hold an F5 tornado, watch the movie *"Twister"* (Warner Brothers, copywrite 1996). In a mid-movie scene in which the chasers are describing the various levels of tornados to a novice, the veterans speak in near reverential terms of the might and destructive power of an F5 tornado. It is moving, especially to someone who has lived through one!

So, strap in and prepare yourself to read about the ride of Bob's and John's lives: *"The Palm Sunday Tornado"* and *"The Train in the Night."*

THE PALM SUNDAY TORNADO

1965

By

Robert E. Vining

Palm Sunday, April 11, 1965, was the first hot day in Ohio since the previous fall. A strong southern wind driving this heat and high humidity into cold Arctic air created the perfect combination for the formation of thunderstorms and tornados.

Sunrise wasn't hot at all but crisp and cool. As usual, my family and I arose early in order to arrive at church on time. My dad, Gene, and I hustled to do the farm chores, then we ate breakfast with my mother, Rosella, my older sister, Marianna, and my younger brother, Johnny. Soon afterward, we scrambled to wash up and get dressed in our Sunday best. As usual, we ran late. As we tumbled into car we, again as usual, stared daggers at Marianna for taking too much time in the bathroom. Dad drove like a maniac and, as usual, we rushed into the church just as Sunday School began. As usual, about all the other church members were arriving at the same time we were. Most unusual, the church was packed. The day warmed up quickly. With no air conditioning, everyone was sweltering and drenched in sweat by the time the service was over.

"I don't like this weather at all," said Dad as we drove home. "It often breeds trouble."

"It's been hot like this before," answered Mom.

Dad shook his head. "Not this hot, not this early in the year, and not with this high humidity. It scares me."

What a pessimist, I thought. Whatever weather we have, it's not right to him. But Dad was only expressing the sentiments of most farmers. The weather was always too wet, too dry, too hot or cold, never just right. However, Dad was different from other farmers or anyone else I knew because he was the only reliable rainmaker in the area. When the weather turned dry, all Dad had to do was mow down a field of hay and sure enough, a storm would come and rain on his hay, ruining it. I remember years when it was so dry there were prayers, fervent prayers, uttered in church by the faithful for rain. And at the conclusion of these prayers, all the farmers in the congregation cast their eyes on Dad. I believe they were adding their own silent prayers of, "PLEASE, GENE, MOW DOWN SOME HAY!"

"When are you planning to make hay," I asked.

Dad tuned the car into the driveway. "Not for a while."

Then we aren't likely to have a storm, I thought.

Mom and Marianna prepared a delicious dinner. Afterward, Mom and Dad prepared to visit some friends in Indiana. They wouldn't return home until after church that night. Marianna, Johnny, and I were expected to go with them. Johnny and I protested that we had too much homework to do. We really didn't lie because we both were bookworms so we always had homework to do. Thus we always had a good excuse to weasel out of family obligations.

Poor Marianna had no good excuse. Frowning, her mouth in an upside down "U," she crawled into the car. So did Mom and Dad. Johnny and I, both smiling with "cat-ate-the-canary" grins and books in hand, waved goodbye.

Dad rolled the car window and looked at me. "Bobby, you do the chores tonight."

My smile disappeared; I grimaced. *What's wrong with telling Johnny to help me? Oops! I'd better keep my mouth shut or I'll be going to Indiana.* "Okay, Dad. I'll get them done."

Johnny and I buried our heads in our books all afternoon and we were unaware of how high the temperature rose. We lived in a sturdy log house and the thick walls were excellent insulation, keeping the house cool in summer and warm in winter. At 5:00 PM I decided to do the chores. As I stepped out of the house, the searing heat hit me. "Whew! Dad's right. This heat is no good."

I took my time doing the chores and thought about the upcoming planting season. I loved this time of year. I also thought about some of the jobs I'd probably end up doing. Outside our house were two sheds. One had been fixed up but the other was a dilapidated eyesore. Mom had been on the rampage for weeks about this building. She wanted it torn down as soon as the weather became fit. I was certain I'd be the one doing the work with very little help from anyone else. But in our family, if mama ain't happy, ain't nobody gonna be happy. Somehow I'd find the time to get the eyesore cleaned up.

Spring always brought another problem. I'd be the one taking the blame for all the tools which were lost because, unfortunately, I was the one that lost most of the tools. However, I thought the chewing outs I received from Dad because of these lost tools were uncalled for. Whenever one of our tractors broke down, it always broke down at the end of the field furthest from the garage where our tools were stored. Also, whatever tools we took with us in the tractor's toolbox were always the wrong tools. Since I was the best at repairing equipment, I'd walk to the garage and get the tools I needed, then walk back to the broken down tractor and fix it. I'd throw the tools somewhere on the tractor, and invariably, these tools would fall off and be covered up with dirt. Someone had to be blamed. I handled the tools last so that someone was me.

It's too bad we can't be lucky like our neighbor, Bill Gamble. His tractors always broke down near his shop and, like Batman, whatever tools he needed were always right at his fingertips. He had tools for everything, and most unbelievably, he never lost any of them. An amazing man, our neighbor.

I finished the chores by feeding the chickens, ducks, and geese. The geese made nests outside the chicken coop in various protected spots. I stayed as far away as possible from these geese because they were in a lousy mood this time of the year and would attack me if I got too close to their nests.

Back inside the house, Johnny and I continued to read. We didn't turn on the television or radio so we weren't warned of an approaching line of thunderstorms with embedded tornados.

The sun set. Soon the wind howled, lightning filled the sky, and thunder rumbled almost continuously. Torrents of rain fell. But the storm ended after about a half an hour and the wind died down to nothing.

I glanced up from my books and out the living room window. "Looks like the storm is over."

Johnny looked out the window too. "I think you're right. But what's that rumble in the distance?"

I spoke to Johnny like an authority: "It's the train."

Johnny shrugged. "Must be." But the rumble grew louder. Johnny put down his book. "It can't be the train because the train runs north of us. This rumble is coming from the west."

Again I talked like an authority. "You worry too much. What else could it be but the train?"

A minute later, the rumble had become a roar. Johnny threw down his book. "Something is really wrong!"

No more authority talk! "You're right!" I jumped out of my chair and gazed out the window. "Holy mackerel!"

"What is it?"

"TORNADO!" I grabbed Johnny and shoved him between the piano and the wall.

Johnny stammered, "What do we do now?"

"Pray!"

The lights went out. The tornado struck, and the old log house shook. Our ears popped. Glass shattered; it was over. I stood up. "That wasn't too bad. You stay here and I'll check things out. Okay?"

Johnny nodded. "Please don't be gone too long."

I opened the door. "Good grief!"

"What's wrong?"

"Everything is wrecked!" I stepped outside and scanned the farm. The shed Mom wanted torn down was gone. The garage with some of our tools was gone too, but our Ford Falcon car parked in it was still there. The barn stood but just barely. The fences, electrical wires, and poles were all down. I stepped back into the house and grabbed a flashlight, then went out back to see if any of our animals had been killed or injured. Miraculously only one animal had been killed and none injured. A goose had been lifted off her nest and smashed into our mailbox post.

I returned to the house to stay with Johnny until help arrived. About a half hour later some neighbors stopped by. They told me two people down the road had been killed and several injured. The tornado had been a monster a half a mile wide and left a path of destruction seventy-five miles long.

Within an hour, my parents returned home. Johnny and I rushed out to meet them. My mother ran to us. "Are you okay?"

"We're fine!" said Johnny.

I pointed to the shed. "You know that old shed you wanted torn down?"

"Yes."

"Well, it's torn down!"

Mom grimaced, "Don't joke at a time like this. Look at this place. It's a mess!"

Dad tumbled out of the car. "How about the livestock?"

I pointed to the dead goose. "Everything is alive accept that goose."

Dad blew out a sigh of relief. "That's a miracle."

"I know, but all the fences are down."

Dad rushed to the house. "I'll change my clothes. We've got to fix the fences or the cattle will be gone by morning."

Mom, Marianna, and Johnny left to spend the night with our relatives. Dad and I worked until 3:30 the next morning fixing fences. Dad did most of the work; I held the flashlight so he could see. As usual, wherever I shined the light, it was in the wrong place. But we fixed the fences good enough so the cattle would not get out.

The next morning, I was able to see the massive mess the tornado had caused. We worked a year rebuilding the farm. The tornado, though, did have a silver lining. For the next twenty years whenever Dad blew up at me for losing a tool, I would weasel out of this verbal onslaught by insisting that the tool had been lost in the tornado.

THE TRAIN IN THE NIGHT

1965

By

John Eric Vining

Palm Sunday, 1965, began much the same as many other Sundays before. April 11th was typical early spring day, which would have a not-so-typical ending. It would provide a defining moment in my life.

During the day, I was only vaguely aware that the sun's heat was much warmer than usual as it spread over the still-cool earth. Even less obvious was the increasing crescendo of the wind that tore furiously at the tenderly-leafed blossoming trees.

Our great aunt invited us to dinner that noon, as usual. The afternoon passed quickly, filled with conversation and TV. As evening approached and we journeyed home, the wind blasted our car on the flat midwestern landscape we were traversing. Arriving home, I found my schoolbooks still lying untouched where I had deposited them Friday night after school.

"I won't be able to go to church tonight," I said matter-of-factly. "Homework still needs to be done."

"Ok," Mom replied. "I know it has been a busy weekend."

My brother, then a freshman in college, also begged off for the evening; his studies were also demanding time. Mom and Dad left, and my brother and I cracked the books while the fast-fading daylight created lengthening evening shadows. The sky grew gray with clouds as books gave way to television. I was only dimly aware of the huge storm clouds gathering in the west, the angry thunderheads choking the evening into premature blackness.

Suddenly, the television snapped off, and the room was thrown into darkness. I was uncomfortably aware of a deathly silence – the wind was completely still. Off in the distance, a train rumbled in the night.

"I don't like this," muttered my brother, Bob. "I'm going outside to look around."

The train rumbled more resoundingly in the still air. A thought flashed through my mind – the nearest railroad was three miles away in a different direction. At precisely that moment, my brother burst through the door. He threw me to the floor under the piano and tumbled on top of me.

"John," he stated firmly, "We're in for a big blow, so keep your head down and your mouth shut." My brother's weight crushed me into the carpet as the sound of the train grew deafening.

"What is it?" I shouted.

"Tornado!" came the terse reply.

The beam of my flashlight pierced the darkness as the house shook and the glass flew. A tremendous crash in a rear bedroom indicated the house was breaking up. Was this the end?

Suddenly, it was over. The roaring and crashing faded into the distance to the east. A suffocating silence once more filled the house. We had made it!

Soon, probing headlights began creeping toward our house as curious and concerned neighbors converged on the area. Throughout the night, with our friends' help, we salvaged what was left of our belongings. It had been a very close call, and other friends and neighbors had not been so lucky.

My life was changed by the tornado. There were times before, and times after, but all events – for me – were marked by their relation in time to the passing of the tornado. Nothing was ever the same after hearing the terrifying rumble of the train in the night.

MISSY

1965

By

John Eric Vining

I guess the old saying "Every storm cloud has a silver lining" is true. In the case of the Vining family, this was almost literally true. For example, not all events associated with the Palm Sunday tornado that struck my father's farm on April 11, 1965 were uniformly bad. My dad loved to hunt wild game, and as a hunter, he maintained a group of hunting dogs whom he kept and trained to assist him. In 1965, he had several Beagles to hunt rabbits and also several Brittany Spaniels to hunt pheasants and quail.

One of Dad's best hunting dogs of all time was a female Beagle named Twinkle. Dad always maintained that the best "pair" of Beagles he ever owned was Twinkle and her mother, Nellie. He had previously owned several Beagles that individually were equal to or better than Nellie and Twinkle, but those two - working together tracking rabbits - were the best "pair" he had ever owned. Sadly, Nellie had grown aged and passed away about a year before the tornado hit our farm. But Twinkle was still in her prime in April, 1965.

At that time (April, 1965), Northwest Ohio still had good quantities of both pheasants and quail; accordingly, Dad had a pair of Brittany Spaniels named Lady and Gent, who were good, but not great, birddogs. Many of my fondest memories while I was growing up consisted of Saturdays spent in the woods and grasslands near our farm, hunting with my dad and the dogs.

Well, as fate would have it, our farm was directly in the path of the Palm Sunday tornado that passed south of Willshire, Ohio. Many buildings on our farm were destroyed, including several of the doghouses. And as fate *and* timing would have it, Gent's house was destroyed but he was fine…and Twinkle was "*in,*" as they say. Gent was a big healthy male, and despite the thorough frightening he had received, he was not so scared that he still didn't have the one thing on his mind that most big healthy males have on their minds. You can put two-and-two together. A few months later, Twinkle had a nice litter of puppies nestled snugly in the straw of her doghouse.

Dad thought this was a mixed blessing at best. Twinkle was a full-blooded Beagle, and Gent was a full-blooded Brittany Spaniel, but that still made their progeny ordinary cross-breeds. Even though they were from hunting-dog stock, this cross-breeding made them essentially worthless from a registration standpoint. We decided to give these puppies away to whoever wanted them. In those days, every farm kid in the area had a dog, and the combination of Beagle and Brittany Spaniel would make them relatively small and good-natured. We also made a somewhat fateful decision: we decided to keep the last one of the litter – essentially the one no one else wanted.

Weeks went by, and one by one the members of the litter went to friends and neighbors who wanted a free dog as a companion. Finally, only one was left: a short-haired female whose body was just about the size of an average Beagle, but whose legs were slightly longer and "musclier" than that of a Beagle. She was red and white, with Beagle coloring patterns, but without the characteristic black fur – Dad said her coloring was like that of a "throwback" Beagle. We named her Missy.

Missy had a particularly pleasant disposition with above average intelligence, and because of that we let her run free instead of chaining her. We could trust her to remain on our property and not cross the road where she might be hit. She was at my side constantly, and we became best friends.

Soon came the time when we would take Missy out into the fields with Twinkle to go hunting. With her high intelligence, she was a quick learner. We soon became astonished at Missy: she was a natural as both a rabbit dog *and* a bird dog. She had astounding eyesight and an exceptional nose; this, in combination with her long, powerful legs meant she could track rabbits much faster than the normal Beagles. Indeed, a few times, she literally *ran down* rabbits in first few yards after they had been kicked up. She could sense when birds were near; her demeanor would change and we could tell this from the way she acted in the rough ground. Missy would retrieve both rabbits and birds that had been shot. Dad eventually came to the conclusion that not only was Missy the best hunting dog he had ever owned; she was the best hunting dog he had ever *SEEN* – high praise indeed from a man who had been hunting since he was four years old.

For approximately three years, Missy ran free as our household pet and my best friend – she was always with me. Then Missy fell prey to her breeding; one day we got a call from the neighbor lady saying that our dog had gotten into her henhouse and had killed several of her chickens. Hey, these WERE birds – how was she to know? That was the end of Missy's freedom: from that day forward, Missy was sentenced to spend her remaining days at the end of a chain attached to a doghouse.

> "One gray night it happened; Jackie Paper came no
>   more,
> And Puff the mighty dragon, he ceased his fearless
>   roar.
>
> Without his life-long friend, Puff could not be brave,
> So Puff that mighty dragon sadly slipped into his
>   cave."
>
> From *"Puff The Magic Dragon,"* by Peter, Paul, and
> Mary

Missy's prison sentence came precisely as I was entering the seventh grade. Girls, sports, and cars soon came to dominate my thoughts, and I spent less and less time with my old friend. Finally, feeding Missy as well as all the other dogs was simply another chore - something I rushed through to get done - so I could go do the things all the other teenagers were doing. Missy watched day after day, year after year, as I raced past on my way to other things, with almost never a smile or even an acknowledgement from her old friend.

It is to my everlasting dishonor that I let poor Missy live the last nine years of her short life all alone at the end of a chain. How could she know that pursuing the thing her breeding led her to do, and for which she had received so many approving pats on the head, had cost her freedom and her best friend? Missy died alone in her doghouse on a cold November night in 1977. My brother let me know the news, and I barely shook my head in acknowledgment as I prepared to go out on the town for the evening.

Missy, if there is any part of your spirit that can still sense my thoughts after all these years, I want you to know how sorry I am that I abandoned you. I should have spent a lot more time petting you and taking you off your chain for one-on-one playing and romping. I want you to know that now, years and years later, I have a new pair of dogs that I love and cherish like I should have loved and cherished you. Perhaps in a few years, not too long from now, we can run and play on green, hilly pastures together, like we used to do before I became a thoughtless teenager and self-centered young adult.

Please forgive me, my little sweetheart and old friend…

These Kids Are Special

August 14, 1967

By

Robert E. Vining

The Willshire Reds baseball team had not been beaten all season, but now they faced their biggest challenge. It was the last game of the Monroeville Little League Tournament; Willshire would play the Decatur All Stars for the championship. The All Stars had a superb pitcher named Mike "No Hit" Faurot. He had an impressive record. For a twelve-year-old, he was a giant. He towered over most of the other players at about six feet tall, with a lean, lithe body. We had seen him in action two nights before. Spectacular! He threw a devastating hard ball and - not to my surprise – at the batters at times, too. On top of that, his curve ball was like a tornado – a real twister. He was right handed and his curve ball would break away from our right handed hitters. He was confident; it showed in every move he made. What control! We could be sure he was not going to walk many batters.

Like the All Stars, we had won two games in the tournament. We had saved our best pitcher for this one, and we hadn't even given the All Star coaches a chance to see him in action. He had a face like a clenched fist, and was built like a bulldog. He was short and stocky, with a cannon for a left arm. We called him "Spanky," not for the old "Our Gang" character, but for the way he "spanked" the opposing batters if they dared challenge him. Mike "Spanky" Schumm was his name. He threw so hard that our catcher, Alan Brandt, had to stuff foam in his mitt for extra padding – even then Alan's hand would be swollen to nearly twice its size after a game.

Game time was nearing. Coach Paul Ridenour stepped out of the dugout and motioned to our players to come to him. He looked across the diamond to where "No Hit" was warming up in the bullpen. "No Hit" was bigger than he was. Ridenour took off his baseball cap and brushed back his graying black hair with his hand. He put his cap back on, turned around and began speaking with a commanding voice.

"Boys," he said, "Tonight you're going to face a pitcher like you've never seen before. He throws hard and he'll throw at you. He's got a wicked curve ball and he's not going to beat himself with walks. But remember, not every pitch he throws is going to be perfect. If you hang in there, you'll get some pitches you can hit. But you can't bail out. If he knocks you down with an inside pitch, you've got to stand right back up there on the plate and dare him to do it again. You can't let this guy intimidate you. And when you get your pitch, you've got to pounce on it. Okay, let's go play some baseball and give this super team we're facing a run for their money." I ran down to the third base coach's box and took up my position.

"Play ball," yelled the home plate umpire.

Johnny Vining, my brother, was the first batter. He didn't have power, but he could hit the ball and knew how to run the bases. He looked down at me for the sign and I flashed "hit away." He stepped into the batter's box and glared defiantly at "No Hit" Faurot. Faurot wound up and threw a blazing fast ball right at him. Johnny hit the dirt and the ball just missed him.

"Ball one," bellowed the umpire.

Johnny got back up and looked down the third base line at me again.

"Come on, Johnny," I yelled. "Hang in there. You'll get your pitch."

Johnny stepped right on top of the plate again and dug in for the next pitch. Faurot wound up and threw another blazing fastball right down the middle of the plate. Johnny swung late and hit the ball foul down the first base line.

"Time out," I called to the ump and ran down the baseline to talk to Johnny. He ran toward me and we met between third base and home plate.

"Johnny," I said, "I think you ought to look for the curve ball all the way. I think he's going to throw it. Choke up on the bat, don't bail out, and hammer it."

"What if it isn't a curve?" asked Johnny.

"It'll only be strike two," I answered. "This kid we're up against is real good. We need to rattle his cage by showing him we can hit his curve."

All during the past week, I had been throwing curve balls to Johnny in batting practice in anticipation of this moment. Johnny stepped up to the plate, dug in again and waited for the next pitch. Faurot wound and delivered. The ball was heading right at Johnny, but he held in. When the ball was a few feet from him, it started to curve away and towards the plate. Johnny pounced on it, and drilled the ball into right-center field. Johnny was off like a rabbit, rounded first, and headed for second. The right fielder got to the ball and threw a line drive to second base. Johnny desperately gave a head-first slide.

"Safe!" yelled the second base ump.

I called time out and ran over to second base. I looked at "No Hit." He stalked around the pitching mound, hands on his hips, periodically kicking small clods of dirt – obviously unsettled. Johnny had hit his best pitch, and "No Hit" knew it.

"Good job, Johnny," I said. "You've got the green light to steal third. If you can get a good jump, do it!"

Johnny nodded, and I headed back to the third base coach's box. The next batter up was Alan Brandt, our catcher, and another right handed batter. The All Stars' pitcher wound and delivered a smoker.

"Strike one," shouted the ump.

Alan stepped out of the batter's box and looked down at me.

"He's gonna throw strikes," I yelled. "You can hit them."

Alan stepped back up to the plate. The next pitch was another heater right down the middle of the plate. Alan swung late and hit a foul ball down the first base line.

"You've got this guy measured, Alan," I shouted. "Now hammer one."

The next pitch was out of the strike zone. Johnny got a good jump on the pitch and raced to third. The catcher came up firing the ball. Johnny again hit the dirt head first.

"Safe!" shouted the ump.

Alan stepped back up into the batters box and waited. "No Hit" delivered another ripper right down the middle of the plate. Alan swung. CRACK– a hard line drive right at the first baseman. It hit him on his leg and spun off toward the second baseman. Johnny shot toward home as the catcher straddled home plate. The ball reached home plate first, but Johnny plowed right into the catcher, knocking him off the plate and the ball out of his glove. Brandt took second. The score - Reds: one; All Stars: zero.

"Way to go Johnny," I said. Johnny got up with a big smile on his face. The game wasn't even fifteen minutes old, and he had already hit the dirt so many times he looked like a ditch-digger.

We had one run and the way "Spanky" was pumped up to pitch, that might be enough to win. The song *Light My Fire* by "The Doors" echoed through the ball park from a nearby concert, and it seemed to fit "Spanky's" mood perfectly that night. Why not get more runs? "Spanky" stepped up to the plate, ready to clobber any pitch that came close. He batted from the left side, so the dreaded curve ball didn't work against him. He was going to get fast balls. Faurot wound and delivered a smoking fast ball right down the middle. "Spanky" swung and ripped a low line drive over the second baseman's head into right-center field. It took one bounce and was over the fence, a ground-rule double. Brandt came home to score. Reds: two runs, All Stars: zero.

The All Stars' manager had seen enough. He went out and talked to his pitcher, to try and settle him down. Faurot could throw hard, but not hard enough. Our batters were too good. "No Hit" had to mix up his pitches and his location. If he kept putting fast balls down the middle of the plate, our boys would tattoo his tail.

The All Star coach returned to the bench and "No Hit" immediately settled down. He began to pitch with finesse, and one out, two outs, three outs. The top half of the first inning was over.

Now it was "Spanky's" turn. During his warm up pitches, "Spank" threw slowly, just enough to warm up his left arm. The All Stars looked on with disbelief, and they glanced at each other with cocky smirks on their faces. They thought they were going to clobber this guy!

"Batter up," yelled the ump.

The first batter cockily flung an armload of bats toward his bench, retaining one to begin the slaughter. "Spanky" wound up and delivered. His left arm suddenly became a flame-thrower, and his pitch was like a jagged bolt of lightning as it smoked all the way into the catcher's mitt. The batter looked down at his third base coach, eyes wide as saucers, with a different kind of disbelief written all over his face.

"Strike one," yelled the ump.

"Spanky" wound up again and delivered even more heat. When Schumm threw like this, the baseball seemed to explode as it neared the plate, either twisting, or popping, or tailing away.

Three batters up; three strikeouts.

The game became a pitchers' duel. The All Stars' pitcher used finesse and was untouchable. Schumm threw nothing but blazing fast balls and couldn't be touched either. The question was whether "Spanky" could keep it up for six innings.

In the third inning, "Spanky's" fast ball had a little less heat, a little less pop. His control was not quite as sharp. Schumm began to struggle a little. The big All Star first baseman got a hold of one of "Spank's" fast balls and knocked it out of the park – a home run. Reds: two – All Stars: one.

"Spanky" Schumm had been hit. He was running out of gas. But this kid refused to fold. He reached way down inside himself and put all the energy he could muster back into his pitches. The heat came back. Schumm once more mowed down the All Stars' batters like a sharp scythe though grass.

The bottom of the sixth inning arrived. "Spanky" went out to the mound. He looked exhausted. Schumm had given everything he had. Could he last just one more inning?

"Spanky's" pitches still had a lot of heat, but he had lost his control. The first batter walked; the second batter struck out. The third batter walked; the fourth batter struck out. The fifth batter walked. The bases were loaded, and the All Star's center fielder was coming to bat. I called time out and walked to the pitcher's mound to talk to "Spanky."

"One more out," I pleaded. "That's all we need. Hang in there."

"This fella is gonna hit my fast ball," "Spanky" said. "I wanna throw curve balls."

"But 'Spank,'" I said. "You haven't thrown a curve all night. You got anything left? Can you control the curve?"

"What choice do we have?" replied Schumm. "There's no place to put this guy."

I motioned for catcher Alan Brandt to join us. When we were all together, I said to Alan:

"'Spank' is gonna throw curves. Whatever you do, block the ball. Don't let it get by you."

I went back to our dugout and Alan went back behind the plate. Schumm wound and delivered. The ball looped up, then came twisting down and curved over the plate. The astounded batter was caught looking.

"Strike one!" yelled the umpire.

Once again, "Spanky" wound and threw. The ball looped up, then down, twisting and curving over the plate. The batter swung and hit a foul ball just inches outside the base line. Strike two.

I called time and ran to the pitching mound. "Don't throw another curve," I pleaded. "He's got you measured."

"Well, what should I throw?" answered the "Spank."

"Try cutting your fastball – kind of a hard slider," I said.

"But I don't know how," stammered Schumm, as his voice shook ever so slightly.

"It's easy," I said. "I've seen you working on it a little in practice. Throw just off the outside corner of the plate – throw hard but give a little inward spin or 'cut' as you release. Hang in there, 'Spank.' We only need one more strike."

I returned to the dugout and watched Schumm closely. I wasn't sure who was more nervous – him or me.

"Spanky" wound and delivered. The pitch looked like an outside fastball, but as it approached the plate it slid in a few inches and just caught the outside corner of the plate – a perfect pitch.

"Strike three!" bellowed the ump.

We win! We win! Our players raced to the pitcher's mound, surrounded "Spank," and hugged each other. We were the champs!

These kids were special. They knew how to hang tough. They did whatever it took to win.

Junior high gorillas

JUNIOR HIGH GORILLAS

1967-'68 (written 1996)

By

John Eric Vining

The cartoon I have chosen to best represent the "wonderful confusion" of the junior high years was taken from "The Far Side" 1994 calendar. It is entitled, *Junior High Gorillas,* by Gary Larsen. Biology texts tell of birds that rank themselves according to the presence or absence of a large star on their stomachs. The birds with star-bellies have a high status. The birds with plain-bellies have low status. In the book *Animal Farm,* by George Orwell, pigs take over the classless animal society. They do this by altering one of their cardinal rules from "All animals are equal" to "All animals are equal – but some animals are more equal than others."

These animals, and the gorillas in this cartoon, are engaged in the process of social stratification. Through this cartoon involving gorillas, we can see a part of the social stratification structure that is taught us by our society and our peers. There are different areas of the social stratification process. These areas include income, power, and prestige. The cartoon simulates the prestige dimension. The younger gorillas are demonstrating social recognition, respect, and admiration for the newly developed "silverback" gorilla.

This cartoon is representative of a common experience of most boys and girls of junior high age – the locker room. Junior High is a time of maturing for most boys and girls. Typically, they are both fascinated with and frightened of the physical process by which they become men and women. This is a time of an uncomfortable mixed-feeling toward and self-consciousness of ourselves at a time when others are changing at a faster or slower pace. In our society, at this time of life, we are made to feel uncomfortable with ourselves if we do not develop at the same pace.

In the animal kingdom, this maturing process is much less dramatic and/or painful than it is for humans. Animals typically become physically mature at a much younger age than humans, and seem to "grow up" with their sexuality intact. Sex is a fact of everyday life for animals. However, for young boys and girls, it is a time of awkwardness, mixed emotions, and hormones "gone wild." These factors, for a time, affect their ability to maintain balance in life.

The humor of this cartoon is created by the placing of the gorillas in a human setting at this particularly emotional time of life. First, the newly developed "silverback" is larger than the two similarly-aged but less matured "observers." This parallels the human experience in which some boys have their "growth spurt" earlier than others. Boys of 13-14 are impressed with and intimidated by size at that time of life. Thus, the "observers" are viewing "the big guy" from a distance so as not to antagonize him.

Secondly, the "silverback" has obviously reached physical maturity earlier than the "observers." This is always a source of curiosity for teenaged boys. Yet again, they are observing from a distance and apparently in hushed tones. One must not be caught in making this natural comparison. This is also the age for name-calling if one is caught looking at another male – a truly uncomfortable experience for the fragile psyches of teenaged boys.

Finally, Larson captures the "wonderful confusion" of the "junior high years" in the expressions and postures of the observing gorillas. The gorilla in the foreground is sitting so his feet are not touching the floor – emphasizing his smallness and immaturity. The second observer is sitting with his legs crossed and hunched forward in a contemplative position. Both have expressions of wonderment on their faces.

All in all, the cartoon entitled *"Junior High Gorillas"* is very effective in finding humor in the absurdity and irrationality of the human male and female experience in the junior high locker room. This social stratification dimension is an area that we have all dealt with some time in our life. It is also a time at which we can look back and find humor, as Larson has done in this cartoon.

Setting the Stage for *"The Carnie and the Princess"*

Yes, there is such a thing as love at first sight! What small-town boy has not been smitten by that first teenaged love?

It was a warm, balmy Friday evening, June 16, 1972. A cool, refreshing breeze whispered through the freshly-leafed trees of The Park, in Willshire, Ohio. The Willshire Days celebration was in full swing. Crowds of new and old acquaintances laughed, joked, and told stories. Darkness had fallen, bands of stringed lights glowed over and around booths and games, and street-carnival rides whirled in the background.

All of a sudden, in the midst of a circle of high school friends, there she was! I'd known her all my life, but I'd never seen her like this before! Tall, slender, tanned, golden-brown sun-streaked hair, *those eyes* - she was the typical, yet definitely not typical, farmer's daughter. White sleeveless blouse, red short-shorts, and white sandals inlayed with gold. I began talking to her, and suddenly we realized we had been talking for hours – now it was time for her to go home. I asked if I could give her a ride to her parent's house, and she said…yes! A kiss goodnight just inside her front door, and it began.

Here, then, is a fanciful, timeless tale - of which virtually every Midwestern boy has experienced his own version - "boy meets girl - boy loses girl - boy swears to win her back again:" *"The Carnie and the Princess."*

THE CARNIE AND THE PRINCESS

1972

By

John Eric Vining

Billy Joe McMaster stared blankly as the *"Twister"* spun madly about its axis. What used to be so new and exciting about operating the noisy ride now seemed monotonous and routine. The towns, the kids, and the fairgrounds all looked the same. Billy Joe stared down at his rumpled clothes and scuffed Nikes. He wondered if his life back in southwest Georgia along the banks of the Chattahoochie River had been so bad after all. There didn't seem to be much of a future when he had run away from home at sixteen, but what did he have going for him with his life now?

Billy Joe sighed. There was going to be a parade later on tonight. This was something different than most county fairs. Maybe it would break up the suffocating boredom that now filled his life.

Precisely at six-thirty, Billy Joe heard the fire trucks leading the parade sound their sirens. As unit after unit passed, Billy Joe realized the parade provided no relief from the numbing sameness of the carnival atmosphere, and he felt anxiety rise in his chest. He shuffled up the roadside, moving toward the starting point of the parade – anything to get this over with.

Suddenly, the crowd parted, and a beam of hot, fading sunlight flooded a passing float. The float itself was no different than a dozen other "Chamber of Commerce" floats he had seen – it was the girl! *Maren Gentry, Chamber Princess* read the sign on the convertible. A slim, raven- haired seventeen-year-old with a flawless complexion and a beautiful smile waved gently to the crowd as the convertible on which she was seated moved sedately in the procession.

Billy Joe felt as if his world had suddenly changed. The raucous cacophony of the fair now seemed to be a melody in his heart. The close mugginess of the stifling evening now seemed to contain a comforting summer breeze, as the sun tenderly lay on the horizon. He had heard there was no such thing as "love at first sight," but Billy Joe now knew this was not true. He knew he had to meet this young lady!

He glanced once again at his clothes. I've got to get to the trailer *pronto*, he thought. He tore through the door and pulled on his best shirt and Levis. He flashed a comb through his flaxen hair and splashed soapy water on his sun-beaten face. "The best I can do," was his self-deprecating pronouncement as he took one final, rushed glance in the mirror.

Billy Joe raced to the parade terminus. He was not a moment too soon, as the "Chamber" float pulled into the disassembly area. Now what do I do, thought Billy Joe desperately. Boldly, he strode up to the door of the convertible and opened it for Maren.

"Hi. I'm William Joseph McMaster," blurted Billy Joe awkwardly. "I…I…uh, I saw you getting out of the car, and I didn't want you to tear your pretty dress. I thought I'd give you a hand." Billy Joe was miserable – what a terrible line!

"I rate that a *D-*," smiled Maren. "Not that I've heard that many, but that was a *bad* line. I'm Maren Gentry. *Billy Joe*, is it? You can't hide that accent!"

Billy Joe shifted uncomfortably. *William Joseph!* he thought. How *stupid* could I be?

"Nice to meet you, Billy Joe. Thanks for the gallant gesture, anyway," Maren said sweetly as she turned to walk away

"Hey, uh, can I…I'd really like to show you around the fair."

"Oh, I don't think so. I already know my way around the fair."

"Well, uh…I'd really just like to talk to you," stammered Billy Joe.

Maren half-turned with an amused smile on her face. "What have you got to say that I haven't heard before?"

"I don't…well…uh; you'll never find out unless you talk to me."

"OK, Billy Joe McMaster. How can I answer that one?" she answered brightly. "Let me change and I'll meet you by the Ferris Wheel."

That night was the best of Billy Joe's life. He was thrilled to find that Maren, for all her refinement, was totally unbiased toward his background and job. She was more interested in what he thought and how he felt than how he dressed or what he had. They talked about everything – the words seemed to flood out of his soul.

All too soon, Maren glanced at her watch. "Oh, it's a quarter 'til twelve. I promised my parents I'd be home at twelve. I've had a wonderful evening, Billy Joe McMaster." She placed her hands around his neck and gave him a soft kiss on the cheek. "You're not like the other boys I know."

"Maren, your friends say you were walking with a boy none of them knew. Want to tell me about it?" Maren's father questioned.

"He's just a boy from out of town," said Maren.

"I know exactly what he is, Maren," said Mr. Gentry sternly. "He's a carnie from the fair. Have you taken leave of your senses? Think! Why…"

"He's different, Dad!" interrupted Maren. "He's bright…he's witty…he's sensitive…"

"What girl has ever said differently of a boy 'from the wrong side of the tracks'"? Mr. Gentry retorted. "There will be no debate. You will not see him again."

Billy Joe stared out of the window into the streaming rain and pitch-black night, as the bus crossed the Georgia state line. Maren had said all the right things, but he knew the real reason she had grown cold. Maren was from a different station in life. Her father was a successful businessman, and Maren's family lived in a house on a hill. She had time to think it over, and she made the smart choice.

Billy Joe made a promise to himself as the bus rumbled toward the old farmstead on the Chattahoochie River. He would return to that Midwest county seat someday. He wouldn't go back as a drifter...he would be someone. Billy Joe knew in his heart he was different than the rest of the carnies – he had to prove it. He didn't know how, but he would build a life and return one day for the princess who glided past and changed his life forever.

Put Me in the Game, Give Me the Ball, and We'll Win!

January 29, 1973

By

Robert E. Vining

Parkway Panther reserve guard John Vining squirmed in his seat, trying to massage his aching backside. *"I'm a guard alright,"* he muttered to himself. *"Guarding the end of the bench!"* He looked up at the scoreboard for the fifth time in the last two minutes. Period 4; Time: 7 minutes, 32 seconds; Visiting St. Henry Redskins: 56; Home Parkway Panthers: 51.

John then glanced out on the court; the Redskins had the basketball and were whipping it around the perimeter of the Panthers' 1-3-1 zone defense. A quick cross-court pass caught the Panthers off guard. A Redskin player caught the ball and readied for a wide open shot. He launched the ball – just as a Panther guard, Stan "The Marksman" Minnich flew through the air and slammed it away.

"PSSSSTTT!" blew the referee's whistle. Stan "The Marksman" had also slammed into the Redskin guard. The ref pointed at Stan and shouted, "Foul on Number 10! Two shots!"

Stan looked down at the number on his gold jersey with black lettering, shook his head, and dejectedly raised his hand. The jubilant Redskin player clapped his hands while walking to the foul line, confident he would sink both shots.

John, head bent over, stared at the floor, then looked across the court at the Redskin coach, Frank Joubert. As usual, Coach Joubert had a smug, cocky smirk on his face that went well with his "superior than thou" attitude. It was an attitude born from the years of dominance his teams had enjoyed over the Panthers.

John slapped his hands over his face. "I can't look at this anymore!" he muttered to no one in particular. He then put his elbows on his knees, hands on the side of his head, and again stared at the floorboards between his feet. John's Panthers had already been beaten once by St. Henry High School this season, and it looked like the Redskins would win again.

John shook his head. *"How disgraceful!"* In fact, for the last two seasons in John's varsity career the Panthers had been the patsies of Mercer County, and it shouldn't be that way. The Panthers had talent. But teams would slough off the Panthers' guards and clog up the middle of the court. Stan "The Marksman" was supposed to keep that from happening by bombing away from the outside. Stan, though, was slow in getting his shot off. Defenders could get to him before he could fire away. This game was typical. Stan had only five points so far.

John looked up just in time to see the Redskin guard hit his first foul shot. "I've got to do something," he thought desperately. John zeroed his eyes on the Panthers' coach, Ron Niekamp. He concentrated while staring, trying to summon the power of mental telepathy. *"Put me in the game, get me the ball, and we'll win!"* He concentrated even harder. *"PUT ME IN THE GAME, GET ME THE BALL, AND WE'LL WIN!"*

The Redskin's second shot was also good, giving them a seven point lead. The Panthers called time out. John broke his concentration and looked away.

"VINING!"

John's eyes widened; he whirled around. Coach Niekamp pointed in his direction. John pointed a finger back at himself. "Who, me?"

Coach Niekamp nodded. "Yes, you! You're in the game!"

John hopped up, ripped off his warm-up jacket, and reported in at the scorer's table. He then returned to the Panthers' huddle.

A waiting Coach Niekamp looked right at him. "You're in for Stan. He's got four fouls and needs some rest. Just don't make any stupid mistakes like throwing the ball away. Just play defense and don't screw up. Okay?"

John nodded and the Panthers trotted onto the court. If Coach Niekamp had taken out a marksman in Stan, he had unknowingly put in a gunslinger in John, a streaky shooter who, win or lose, was going to draw quick and blast away.

John threw the ball inbounds to the Panthers' point guard. He then hustled up court and took a position outside the Redskins' sagging defense, some thirty feet from the basket. The point guard passed the ball to John, who in one lightning moment, caught the ball and readied it for a one-handed jump shot. John zeroed in on the basket while on the way up. The Redskin defender lurched at him, but...too late! John let it rip, rifling a bullet straight for the basket.

Coach Niekamp flew off his chair, a scowl on his face; this was *NOT* what he wanted from his sub. His hands shot up in the form of a "T" to call a time out, but was interrupted by the *SWISH* of the ball as it bore through the net; the Panthers were again down by five.

Coach Niekamp dropped his hands; the scowl disappeared, replaced with a smile. He sat back down and laughed with his players on the bench. "I knew he would do that," he said jokingly.

The Panthers retreated to the far court, but were now much tougher on team defense. John was an excellent defensive player – tall, quick, and agile. The Panthers extended their defense; the Redskins forced up a poor percentage shot and missed. The Panthers grabbed the rebound.

"The Gunslinger" again took his spot outside the Redskins' defense and once more blasted away. *SWISH!* John Vining may not have been the best shooter in the world, but when he was on one of his infamous streaky tears, these shots were like lay-ups to him.

Twice more John drilled in two pointers from downtown (these were the days before the three-point goal). The Redskins' coach had seen enough; he called time out. Joubert wiped the sweat from his eyebrow; the cocky smirk was gone. He had to do something about "The Gunslinger."

John jumped for joy while trotting to the Panthers' bench. He glanced at the scoreboard. The Redskins had only scored one bucket while he was on the court. The score – Redskins, 60; Panthers, 59.

There were grins all around when John bent down into the Panthers' huddle. He received pats on the back from his coach and teammates.

Then Coach Niekamp barked out his strategy. "The Redskins will come out of that sloughing 1-2-2 zone they've been in," he said. "Run your man-to-man offense until you can get the ball into the low post." He nodded to each player. "Get the ball to the low post and we'll win this game!" He thrust his hand out. The Panthers slapped their hands on top of his.

"Let's go!" they shouted in unison.

The Redskins took the ball out of bounds, pushed it up the floor, took another low percentage shot, and missed. The Panthers rebounded.

"The Gunslinger" again set up outside, but a Redskin defender was all over him. The Panther point guard flipped the ball to John, but unable to shoot, he bounce passed the ball back. The Panthers ran their pick-and-roll offense. John set a hard pick, then rolled to the basket. The ball came back to him, and he set to shoot… no; *a pump fake!* But the Redskin defender jumped at the fake and gave John the opportunity to bounce pass the ball under him to the Panthers' big center, 6'6", 230 lb. Randy Humerickhouse. Big Randy had out-muscled his defender and had posted up low under the basket. With a move that would never remind anybody of John Havlicek, Randy grabbed the basketball, lunged to the basket, and, dragging a couple of defenders up with him, laid the ball in. There was absolutely nothing the Redskins could do to stop him. The Panthers took the lead, 61 to 60.

The Redskins did their best to stay in the game, but the Panthers were now the stronger team on the court. John "The Gunslinger" became John "The Team Player," which was his real game; defense, setting picks, and passing. The Panthers went on to win easily.

In the span of a few moments on a wintry January night in 1973, John Vining helped turn around a team and a season. No longer a patsy, the Panthers went on to be the hottest team in Mercer County, and had their first winning season in nine years. Did John "The Gunslinger" lead the attack? No. Even though he started every subsequent game, he scored very little. He didn't have to because after the St. Henry game, no team dared slough off Parkway's guards on defense.

First year Coach Ron Niekamp learned several lessons about basketball that season. First, defense keeps a team in basketball games. Second, a team's best shooter doesn't necessarily score a lot of points. Third, basketball is a team sport; savvy players can make up for what they lack in talent by using their heads. And when Coach Niekamp finally discovered the right combination of players, placed in their proper team roles, he developed one of the savviest teams ever to play in Mercer County.

THE PULL

1975

By

John Eric Vining

A significant portion of life growing up on a small farm in Northwest Ohio was centered on farm animals and farm equipment. As I was growing up, farmers in our area were starting to assemble bigger farms to take advantage of economies of scale. (We didn't do this because my dad was primarily a livestock farmer who didn't foresee the coming demise of the small livestock farm.) As the size of the farm acreages grew, so too did the size of farm implements to work them and farm tractors to pull the implements. Our neighbor, Bill Gamble, kept up with this trend and was one of the first farmers in the area to buy tractors in the 100-horsepower range, which was a big tractor for that day. I remember Bill purchasing an Oliver Model "1850" in 1966, and a Minneapolis-Moline "G1000" in the early 1970s.

As this trend grew, a rural motorsport, "Tractor-Pulling," became very popular. When this sport started out when I was a kid, it was basically just farmers taking their field tractors to the pull and hitching them to a pulling sled. The sled was an interesting contraption: It featured a weight transfer device that mechanically transferred an enormous weight from over the wheels of the sled forward over a flat sled-pan toward the drawbar of the tractor. Correspondingly, the sled became tougher and tougher for the tractor to pull as the combined tractor and sled progressed down the hard-packed dirt track. Most individual pulls ended with the tractor's rear-wheel-drive, oversized, cleated tires spinning furiously as the tractor stopped when approaching the end of the track. Pull officials measured the distance the tractor/pulling sled combination had progressed down the track: the farmer who had pulled the sled the furthest was the winner of the pull, and perhaps just as importantly, got local bragging rights as owning the most powerful tractor in the area.

As an almost natural consequence, some farmers decided (in the winter months) to build tractors designed specifically for pulling. These tractors featured high-performance automobile racing engines, beefed up transmissions, and exotic weight placement schemes (unlike auto drag racing [which tractor-pulling resembled], more weight on the tractor was *good* for pulling). Soon, tractor pulling became a flashy event, with high-revving racing engines shooting flames from header exhaust stacks, clouds of dust and dirt spewing from the huge, spinning, cleated tires, and occasionally, pieces of engines and/or transmissions flying from the tractor as it ground violently to a halt mid-pull.

Obviously, it was not long before the regular farm tractors became hopelessly outclassed by these fire-breathing, specialized pulling monsters. Tractor-pull promoters quickly organized the pullers into two classes: the "stock" class for relatively standard farm tractors, and the "modified" class for the dedicated pulling tractors.

This didn't mean that the local farmers abdicated all the excitement to the flashy "modified" pulling tractors. The local "stock" pullers tried to emulate the sound and fury of modifieds by "taching-up" the engine before the flag fell, "popping the clutch" on the transmission to race down the track at the drop of the starting flag, rearing the front end of the stock tractors off the ground as the drivers fought to control machines not designed for this effort, and the smoke-belching, wheel-spinning completion of the pull, virtually always short of the "full-pull" marker at the far end of the dirt track.

This was all great fun, and one sunny July day, some friends and I traveled to a nearby village to attend a pull which was rumored to attract some of the best pullers from several states. The pull began with several sleek modifieds roaring and tearing down the track before inevitably spinning out well short of a full pull. Then came the stockers; same result – sound and fury as they tore down the dirt track, but no full-pulls.

I was surprised to see the next tractor pull onto the track, then back up to attach to the pulling sled: it was my neighbor, Steve Gamble, competing with his dad's new Minneapolis-Moline G1000. Steve caught the hook, pulled the tractor into low gear, gave the big Minnie some throttle, and slowly but firmly released the clutch as the starting flag fell. The big Minnie crept forward. The crowd in the stands stared incredulously, then broke into gales of laughter at the unfamiliar sight of tractor and sled virtually inching down the track.

On and on Steve and the Minnie crept - Steve steadily opening the throttle as the weight on the sled shifted forward. The laughter subsided as Steve moved closer and closer to the "full-pull" flag. The jeers turned to cheers as Steve crept past the full-pull flag and completely out the end of the pulling track – the only competitor to do so all day! We had all been sheepishly quiet as Steve had started his pull; now we were slapping each other with high-fives and shouting, "Hey, we know that guy!"

Steve Gamble and his slow-revving Minneapolis-Moline G1000 had the last laugh of the day. It was Steve who hoisted the "stock pulling tractor" championship trophy into his truck-trailer as the daylight faded to darkness and we all headed home from a fun afternoon at the local tractor-pull.

MEDALS IN THE ATTIC

1976

By

John Eric Vining

Sometimes, the most interesting and poignant discoveries about the nature of those we love happen almost by accident. Imagine a hot, mid-summer day. A chore is assigned to a ten-year-old son – clean the attic, because the boy is the only one small enough to crawl into the corners to dust and sweep. Soon follows the discovery of an old jewelry box, almost buried by the long-discarded refuse of a typical, middle-class family. Certainly doesn't seem a likely scenario for a huge lesson in life, does it? Yet, this seemingly innocuous incident provided the backdrop for me to discover that my dad was a great human being.

The first years of my life were typical of many small-town, Midwestern farm boys. My dad worked two jobs – for a telephone company during the day and as a farmer in the evenings and weekends. My mother was an elementary school teacher. I worked on the farm – tending the livestock and working in the fields. As was similar with most of the earlier generation in our community, my parents grew up during the Great Depression. The Depression was cruel to our area of the Midwest, and my parents reflected the lessons of their time – you worked hard, you were loyal to your friends and neighbors, you saved and "made do" with what you had. But most of all, you did not whine or complain about your lot in life. Others had it just as bad or worse.

Most of my parent's generation also fought or worked at supporting the fighting of World War II. These twin catastrophes – the Great Depression and World War II, left an indelible imprint on my parent's generation. The Greatest Generation, Tom Brokaw

50

called it. I began learning something about the Greatest Generation that day in the attic.

Dad boosted me up into our small, claustrophobic attic one hot July afternoon in 1965. I scrambled over relics of days gone by, periodically asking Dad if this or that piece of memorabilia was still important. As I rummaged in a corner of the attic, I came upon a dusty old jewelry box. I opened the box, and in it I saw several tarnished medals, each attached to a faded red, white, and blue ribbon. I pointed my flashlight into the box, carefully scrutinizing the medals. They were old military medals, awarded for gunnery excellence.

"Hey, what are these?" I shouted to Dad, across the attic and through the attic door.

"Bring them over and let me see them," Dad called back.

I made my way over to Dad and handed them down. He opened the box and peered at the medals. Then he stared past me for several moments – I noted a haunted, far-away look in his eyes.

"Dad, what is it? Are you OK? What are those medals?" I asked quizzically.

Dad snapped back to reality. "Nothing – put these back over in the corner with the other stuff," he stated firmly.

That was the end of that. I never spoke of the medals again, and neither did he.

Life went on. Junior high years came and went, then high school; finally, off to college. Dad and I hunted together on winter Saturdays – I was amazed at his abilities with a shotgun. He often saw and shot rabbits before I could even get my gun to my shoulder. I commented on this several times, but with that same haunted look in his eyes, Dad invariably turned away and said nothing.

Then came that call in 1976, during my junior year in college. "Come quickly - Dad had a heart attack! If you want to see him, you must come right away," my brother said tersely into the phone.

When I arrived at the hospital, my mother met me at the door. "He's in intensive care. We need to go in and see him right away.

He's on the edge of a coma!" Mom said with tears in her eyes as we headed for the elevator.

As we entered his room, Dad tossed upon the bed, mumbling incoherently. Mom and I sat with Dad for a few moments. Suddenly, Dad's voice rose and became much clearer.

"Oh, Jimmy! Oh, Frank!" Dad cried deliriously. "I'm so sorry, boys! If I had been there, I'd have gotten those fighters that shot you down. I was the best – I let you down! I'm so sorry!" Exhausted, Dad fell back on the bed. Sometime thereafter, Mom and I left the room.

"What was that all about?" I questioned Mom.

"Your father was trained as a waist gunner on a B-17 bomber during World War II," Mom said. "You know he's always loved to hunt; he basically grew up with a gun in his hands. Well, he was a great gunner in the Army Air Force, too. He won several medals for excellence as a machine-gunner."

"Your dad got sick during training – he developed lesions on his lungs," Mom continued. "He washed out of flight school during training and spent his World War II days stateside working on radios in training planes. Dad's B-17 was sent to England. One day, it didn't come back - it had been shot down by German fighter planes. Dad must have carried the guilt about his mates' deaths around with him all these years!" Mom sobbed dejectedly.

My mind flew back to the medals I'd discovered in the attic all those years ago. The abruptness of manner and far-away look in Dad's eyes all made sense now.

Dad recovered and lived another twenty-three years. But he was never the same in my eyes. Dad taught me that it was OK to be a man and still be supremely loyal and caring to those that you loved, and that you didn't wear your virtues on your sleeve. No longer was he a dad like everybody else's dad. From that point on, I saw him as a great human being: a member in good standing of The Greatest Generation.

Yesterday's Titan

1977

Written in 2002

By

John Eric Vining

In March of 1977, I had the chance to meet a remarkable man. I was ready to graduate from college, and had a job interview with a corporation in Decatur, Indiana. I met with the CEO of the corporation, and he suggested that the man who potentially would be my immediate supervisor join us. In strode a very large man, probably 6'4" tall and 240 pounds. Rex moved with massive grace, yet with a light, confident gait. He sat in the chair beside me, both of us facing the CEO across the desk from us. Rex sat in a rather Buddha-like pose, leaning forward at the waist ever so slightly, elbows resting on the arms of the chair, hands folded lightly in his lap, and feet crossed at the ankles. I got the distinct impression that he was able to take in everything about me, yet Rex never seemed to look at me as we both conversed with the CEO.

As we discussed my potential position with the firm, I got the chance to glance at Rex and take in details. My first impression was of his piercing brown-black eyes behind steel-rimmed glasses. "Those eyes don't miss much," I decided. He had distinguished-looking salt-and-pepper hair, neatly parted on the left side, of a fashionable length for the period. He was large-featured, with a dark, though not necessarily tanned, coloring. "He probably spends too much time in the office to get much of a tan," I thought. Once more, I was impressed with his large, athletic build, though he was out of shape in a middle-aged sort of way. Rex was dressed casually, yet formally enough to not be out-of-character for the office setting we were in. I decided here was a man perfectly suited for his station in life – a life in command and control of the financial well-being of a vibrant corporation – a titan of business.

Twenty-five years have passed since that warm spring of 1977, and I am now able to evaluate my relationship with Rex in a different light. Far from being "the old man," Rex was only thirty-five at the time. He was basically a mid-manager with an imposing title in a small, closely-held corporation – subject to the whims of a petty martinet who was essentially the sole-proprietor of the business. Rex had kids, a mortgage, monthly bills, a schedule to juggle, cars that broke down at inopportune times, a house he was remodeling himself to save a buck...in a sense, he was "Everyman."

Rex became more than a hero and mentor to me; he became the pattern for my life. For I find, as the years pass, I have become what in reality he was; just a guy doing his best to make his way through life and not hurt anybody in the process...not a bad legacy for Rex to have created, I hope.

Setting the Stage for "The Kids Who Saved a City"

Funny thing about brothers...probably because they share the same genes, upbringing, and experiences growing up, no matter how many years apart in age they are, they tend to think and act alike long after they have both left their common home.

Take the following story, *"The Kids Who Saved a City,"* a tale (the true background story made the national bylines and merited an article in *Readers Digest*) of the near-miraculous survival of Fort Wayne, Indiana from deadly flooding in March, 1982.

The winter of 1981-'82 was a rough one in Northwest Ohio. A six-inch overnight snowfall was pretty much standard all winter long – 82 inches of snow fell on our part of the Midwest that year. I can remember getting up nearly every morning at 5:30 AM to shovel the driveway so I could get out to the road and go to work.

As spring broke, the early warm weather created a rapid snowmelt, and brought early spring rains as well. I was living on our small farm, on a tributary of the St. Mary's River, well upstream of where the St. Mary's united with other rivers in the heart of Ft. Wayne. I remember the impassioned pleas over the television for volunteers to help sandbag the dikes in Ft. Wayne, to enable that city to survive potentially disastrous flooding. I clearly remember thinking that this was my water which was contributing to this flooding, and that I should go there and help. So I called in for a vacation day at work, strapped on boots and a jacket, and went the 35 miles downriver to Ft. Wayne, to fill sandbags and build dikes; to attempt to save the city.

I never knew that my brother Bob was thinking and doing nearly exactly the same thing at nearly exactly the same time! In fact, we must have been working within a few blocks of each other on Spy Run Avenue, near the St. Joseph River in Ft. Wayne, as the account in this story unfolded. He never said anything about it, and neither did I. I only found out about all this after he passed away in the fall of 2006, and I was left in possession of some of his short-story manuscripts. Among those manuscripts was this account of Bob's activities in the drama that is now popularly remembered as *The Great Fort Wayne Flood of 1982*.

Funny thing about brothers…

THE KIDS WHO SAVED A CITY

1982

By

Robert E. Vining

I steered my one-ton, blue GMC truck into the left-hand turn lane and stopped for a red light. Morning was breaking. I looked to my left, and through the light fog, I could see the outline of the Fort Wayne Memorial Coliseum. The light turned green; I turned into the drive of the Coliseum parking lot.

This is crazy! I thought. *It will never work. What am I doing here?* I parked my truck along edge of the lot where it would be out of the way, and peered toward the Coliseum. Hundreds of busses, cars, vans, and pickups unloaded thousands of high school students. They filled the Coliseum.

The deep winter snow had melted fast. Then came heavy rains, and the three rivers in Fort Wayne, Indiana flooded. By Sunday, March 14, 1982, evacuations began. By Tuesday afternoon it was clear this was no ordinary flood. Fort Wayne faced disaster. The mayor, Winfield Moses, pleaded on the radio and television for volunteers to sandbag the levies. I was a farmer and couldn't do much work on the farm anyway, so I answered the call.

I stepped out of my truck, stuffed my blond hair under my green Army cap, and threw on my old Army jacket. On my feet I wore knee-high gum boots to slog through the mud and standing water. I looked like an authority figure and was ready for a hard day of work. I strolled around a while, checking the place out; it was mass confusion. I noticed a huge pile of sand. Nearby kids filled sandbags and threw them onto trucks. Several trucks full of sandbags were parked nearby. These were a reserve, ready to rush to critical areas along the rivers. I moved on; eventually, I spotted what appeared to be the headquarters for the operation. I approached a short, thin, gray-haired man who jotted notes on a pad. "Hi, I'm Bob."

The man looked up. "I'm David." Introductions were made.

"You're in the Army?" asked David.

"Was," I replied.

"I'm very busy. I need you to be in charge of a group of twenty-five kids. Will you do it?"

"Sure, but I also brought a one-ton truck."

David scribbled on his pad. "I'll note that in case we need it, but right now we have enough trucks and enough drivers have volunteered. What we need are strong people who won't quit on us. Go inside and get the kids as fast as you can, then wait over there." He pointed to a nearby roped off area where several groups of kids waited.

"Okay!" I turned and hustled toward the main entrance to the Coliseum. When I reached the door, I hesitated, going over the routine I had used many times before. I put a frown on my face and curled my lips down at the corners. *Don't smile!* No smiling was one of the first things I learned in basic training. Military life is not supposed to be fun. If a soldier smiles, the officers commanding him think something must be wrong and go out of their way to make life more miserable for him.

Thus prepared, I entered the building and saw hundreds of high school students milling about, waiting to be told what to do. Straightening up to my full 6'4", I stomped forward and towered over a group of them. Feet spread, I put my hands on my sides, elbows out, and barked: "I need twenty-five tough kids who don't know the meaning of the word 'quit;' come with me now!" I whirled and marched toward the exit, doing my best not to laugh about my acting job. *I hope those kids don't find out I'm really a wimp!*

At the door I spun around. Boys and girls had followed me. I held the door as they marched by. *Amazing! If I dress like an authority, act like an authority, and talk like an authority, people think I am an authority and obey me instantly. Thirty minutes ago, I was a total stranger; now I'm in charge.*

My group headed to the assembly area. I counted the students: fourteen boys – ten girls. All were dressed in work clothes; all looked out of shape. I shook my head. *They'll never last the day. Never!*

The kids strolled along, heads down, shoulders drooping. *I've got to break the ice between us.* So I picked up the step and chanted cadence, "Ain't no use in looking down!"

The kids looked up and smiled

I grinned. "There ain't no discharge on the ground!" A small redheaded boy marched beside me.

"We're in for a long day," I said.

The boy nodded. "We'll work hard. This city is our home. We don't want to see it wiped out."

I studied the boy. With a freckled face, a pointed nose, and buck teeth, he reminded me of Woody Woodpecker. "What's your name?"

"Ed."

"You really believe you kids can save this city?"

Ed shrugged. "Maybe; maybe not, but we won't give up. What part of town do you come from?"

"I don't. I'm from Mercer County, Ohio," I answered proudly.

"Then what are you doing here?"

I hesitated, rubbing the side of my head with my hand. "I don't know, to tell you the truth. It's that…sometimes a person has to do what he thinks is right regardless of how crazy it seems."

The group had reached the assembly area. David hustled over to me as two vans screeched to a halt. "Pile your kids into those vans," he ordered.

I opened the side door and frowned. No seats. "Pile in!" Somehow the kids squeezed in and the vans sped off – "canned kids on wheels" - you might say.

"Where are we going?" one of the girls asked the driver.

"Spy Run"

Spy Run, I thought. *The St. Joseph River.* That river flows south into the city where it meets the northwest-flowing St. Mary's to form the third river, the Maumee, in mid-city. The Maumee then flows northeast into Lake Erie.

The two vans zipped through the traffic and came to a halt at a strip mall. The driver pointed out the window. "Your sandbags are over there."

I saw a jumbled pile of sandbags dumped by the pavement. The river ran behind the mall. "Let's go!"

The kids and I tumbled out of the vans and quickly formed a line to the river. Sandbag after sandbag after sandbag zipped down this human conveyor belt. The routine was arm-to-arm, then catch, twirl, and toss. I stood at the end of the line on the levee to the build the wall that hopefully would contain the rising waters. The normally lazy, placid St. Joe was now a brown, swirling monster, a juggernaut ripping right through the heart of the city. It would be a race against time to contain this monster.

The first bag reached me. I grabbed it and "PLOP!" threw it down. Then another next to it. Then another, another, another. A sandbag wall formed as I worked my way south to where another team built their stretch of the wall. We linked up. Then I turned back north, bag after bag. Everyone huffed and puffed; the sweat rolled.

While working my way north, I kept looking for another team to link up with, but no other team was in sight. My team reached its limit, with kids stretched as far as they could. *What do we do now?*

I headed south again. Soon, another team arrived to extend the wall further north. And so it went, hour after hour, both the wall and the water rising in unison. To pass the time, the kids sang:

> "Oh when the saints…go marching in…
>   Oh when the saints go marching in!
> Lord, I want to be in that number,
>   When the saints go marching in!"

Trucks stopped by and dumped more sandbags. The Red Cross handed out cheeseburgers, fries, and soft drinks donated by

McDonalds. The kids took a quick break, gobbled down the food, and went back to work.

Into the afternoon the sandbagging continued at a frantic pace. I pondered the madness of the undertaking I was involved in – the raging rivers, the endless toil, the race against time – then thought of the military general this place was named for: *Mad Anthony Wayne.*

"Bob! Bob!" I looked around and saw Ed pointing. David stood at the road waving his arms. Everyone rushed to him. "Quick! Hop into these two vans!"

The kids squeezed in and soon it was again "canned kids on wheels" cruising down Spy Run. The vans jerked to another sudden stop. I hopped out. Other vans and pick-up trucks full of kids converged on the area. Other trucks full of sandbags rumbled in. "What's up?"

"Hole in the dike!" screamed a girl. "Water is pouring in!"

David waved his arms again. "Form lines! Form lines!"

The kids complied. Trucks backed up as close as they could. The human conveyor belts were at it again, wall-to-wall kids tossing sandbag after sandbag toward the hole in the dike. The PLOP! PLOP! PLOP! soon was more like the RAT-TAT-TAT of a machine gun as one hundred sandbags per minute hit the dike. Fifteen minutes passed; the water still flowed through the wall. Thirty minutes; the frenzied pace continued. Forty-five minutes; an hour.

"It stopped!" someone yelled. "The water has stopped!"

The jubilant kids breathed a sigh of relief and collapsed wherever they could. But not for long: the St. Joe River continued to rise. Soon the "canned kids on wheels" sped back to their original assignment.

The sun set. I wiped the sweat from my brow. "When is the river supposed to crest? I don't think…"

"Not until sometime tonight," interrupted Ed, shaking his head.

I sighed. "I don't think we can hold up that long."

"We have to! Somehow we have to!"

There was no letup. The St. Joe continued to rise at an alarming rate. The kids and I were dirty, sweaty, and exhausted. With glazed eyes and drawn, taut faces, we toiled on like drones. Would the PLOP! PLOP! PLOP! ever end?

Midnight approached. Then someone yelled, "It's going down! The river is going down!"

"Yeah!" the kids shouted in unison, a mighty roar of joy that echoed up and down the St. Joe. The score: Fort Wayne Kids – One; Monster Rivers – Zero. But the battle was far from over. One victory by the Rivers would be the knock-out punch.

We returned to the Coliseum after midnight and crawled out of the vans. We looked into each others' eyes for a moment. Something special was ending – a miracle we would remember for the rest of our lives. We had been a David against a Goliath and had won. With hugs and handshakes, we said our goodbyes.

I returned to my truck. The steel mule sensed my weariness and carried me home. I stumbled into my house. My wife, Martha, had waited up for me.

"I've been so worried," she exclaimed. "I though something went wrong, that you'd been hurt or something, and I…"

"I've put in an exhausting day," I cut in. "But I'll be okay. What's happening along the rivers?"

"There's good news and bad news," said Martha. "First the good news. Both the St. Mary's and the St. Joe are going down."

I grinned. "That's great news!" The score: Fort Wayne Kids – Two; Monster Rivers – Zero.

"But the Pemberton Dam along the Maumee River is going to break. An evacuation has been ordered."

"Oh, no!" I cried. "All my work today is for nothing." I wrapped my arms around Martha.

"No, it's not," she replied. "You and the kids and the truck drivers did what you believed you had to do. I'm very proud of you."

Every muscle in my body ached; I was dirt and sweat from head to toe. I took a bath, went to bed, and fell asleep immediately.

I woke up early the next morning and hurried to the living room. Martha was watching the news on television.

"What's happened?" I asked.

"You won't believe it! The kids ignored the evacuation order; they worked all night; the Pemberton Dam still stands."

My eyes widened while I stared at the television. The scene reminded me of the hole at Spy Run but on a much bigger scale. It was wall-to-wall kids and bumper-to-bumper trucks, with hundreds of sandbags hitting the dam. Then a commercial came on.

"Wow!" I yelled. "We've still go a chance to beat the rivers. I've go to get with it and get going." I dashed to the kitchen and poured myself a cup of coffee.

When I returned, Mayor Winfield Moses was concluding his news conference. "It has come down to this," said the mayor. "We will win or lose at Pemberton."

"I need to get back there," I said, stretching my arms and yawning. "But I'm so tired."

"I don't think you should go," said Martha. "You'll just be in the way. They have enough kids."

"I can still drive truck! I'm not too tired for that."

Martha shook her head. "Plenty of truck drivers have volunteered. The best thing you can do is stay here and pray the Pemberton Dam doesn't break."

I threw my arms into the air. "I suppose you're right. I'm really too tired to be of any good."

We spent the rest of the day glued to the television. The Maumee River and the dikes along it rose in unison. Late in the evening, the river crested. All Friday the vigil continued; by late Friday evening, the battle was over. Final score: Fort Wayne Kids – Three; Monster Rivers – Zero. Against all odds, the kids had won.

Still mentally and physically exhausted, I went to bed early that night, but I couldn't sleep. I went over and over again the unbelievable events of the past few days. And I wasn't the only one that held such views. After inspecting the Pemberton Dam, a general from the Army Corps of Engineers declared, "This dam is an engineering miracle. The kids did the impossible! They did what could not be done."

I pondered my role in the amazing drama. I had dressed up to look like an authority when in fact I was only one of over 50,000 volunteers. I walked into the Coliseum and asked for twenty-five kids who didn't know the meaning of the word "quit," believing I would not find any. How wrong I was. In the winter of 1982, Fort Wayne, Indiana, had thousands of kids who didn't know the meaning of that word. What was it that made them struggle on when every aching bone and muscle in their worn-out bodies screamed for them to stop? I don't know, but while an admiring nation watched on television, the kids of Fort Wayne proved to everyone how tough they were. The third week of March, 1982, will forever be their moment; their finest moment in time.

Setting the Stage for "Religion"

John Eric Vining

For most kids in our area of the rural Midwest, going to church was a major part of the "growing up" process. Every two or three square miles in the country, there was a little church sitting on a crossroad corner. The evangelical movement of the Third Great Awakening had heavily affected our part of the Midwest. There was a strengthening of the older evangelical religions such as Methodism and the Wesleyans. These were mixed with such newer conservative denominations of the mid-to-late 1800s as the United Brethrens and the Nazarenes, to form a very conservative base for the eastern section of the Midwest. Even rural Catholics and Lutherans in our area were more conservative then their big-city counterparts.

Sunday morning, Sunday night, and Wednesday night; we all piled in the family car and went to church. While it seemed to me (and I would imagine all the adults in our congregation as well) that I was basically just filling a pew most of the time, a lot of what I was hearing in all those services took hold. I became interested in what the Bible had to say, and I must admit that when I was young I was most interested in the seeming contradictions the Bible seemed to hold. This led me to explore the scriptures, and in some cases write about subjects that fascinated me.

Thus, the next section of this collection contains short stories about subjects that drew my attention. Again, I must admit that in my youth I enjoyed writing on subjects about which I could assume the position of "devil's advocate," to more or less stir up the staid, ultra-conservative "oldsters" in the congregation! I'm sure they shook their heads and wondered where I was headed with my life. Well, guess what? Now I am one of those old conservatives that shake their heads at the youngsters in the congregation!

I hope you enjoy some of the "controversial" religious writings of my younger days.

Amos, the Peasant Prophet

1975

By

John Eric Vining

The subject of this essay is the Biblical prophet Amos. The first pages will be a review of the book of Amos in the Old Testament. The last pages will be an evaluation of Amos' impact on Israel's society.

Book Review

Amos was born in the village of Tekoa.[1] He was a herdsman who one day had a vision from God. This vision occurred during the reigns of Uzziah of Judah and Jeroboam II of Israel, in approximately 760 to 750 B.C.

In this vision, the Lord roared and the pastures of Mount Carmel withered. Initially, the Lord indicted seven nations and stated their punishments:

- *Damascus* had killed many people in Gilead, so her people would be carried way as slaves.
- *Gaza* had sold God's people as slaves; therefore, all the Philistines would be killed.
- *Tyre* had broken a treaty with Israel; therefore, she would be burned to the ground.
- *Edom* had defeated Israel in battle; therefore, she would also be burned.
- *Ammon* had committed many war crimes, so she would be left leaderless and be a helpless victim to a cruel enemy.

- *Moab* had defiled the tombs of the kings of Edom; therefore, she would be completely destroyed.
- *Judah* had rejected the laws of God, so He was going to destroy their beautiful temple in Jerusalem.

God allotted His most scathing indictment and punishment for Israel:

-*Israel* had been filled with sin, so God saved his greatest punishment for them, his chosen people. They were to be scattered like dust, never to be brought together again in one nation.

In the third chapter, Amos berates the nation of Israel for turning a deaf ear to him. In verses one through six, the Lord, through Amos, tries in vain to get Israel's attention. In one place[2] He says, "Would I be roaring like a lion unless I had a reason?"

Later in the same chapter[3] He speaks in a parable. The Lord said, "A shepherd tried to rescue his sheep from a lion, but it was too late; he snatched from the lion two legs and a piece of ear." This is a very interesting piece of writing which will be more fully discussed in the evaluation which follows.

In chapter four, Amos cuts down the high society of Israel, both men and women. He mockingly tells them to go ahead and keep sinning, sacrificing to false gods, and tithing improperly. The day is coming when He would put hooks in their noses and lead them away like animals.

Next the Lord[4] told of all the troubles He had sent to Israel. He had made them hungry, sent rain to one city while withholding it from another, sent blight, locust, and plagues, and still the people would not return to Him. Therefore He told Israel to prepare to meet its doom.

In chapter five the Lord tells of what the people will be saying about Israel once she is destroyed. "Beautiful Israel lies broken and crushed upon the ground and cannot rise. No one will help her. She is left alone to die."[5] This chapter is simply a call, made over and over again, to repent and come back to Him. Examples of this are found in Amos 5: 4, 6, 8, 14, and 24.

When Amos sees that men have become so sinful that appealing to their good points does no good, he once more attacks their evil ways. God, through Amos, says, in effect, "Okay, that is it; there is no way out now. I will destroy you completely."

In chapter seven, Amos has a vision in which the Lord is contemplating ways of destroying Israel. First, the Lord wants to send a swarm of locusts and destroy all the crops. The people would starve. Amos asks the Lord not to do it and the Lord relents. Next, the Lord thinks about sending a great fire to burn Israel. But Amos again asks the Lord not to do this and the Lord relents. Finally, the Lord is standing by a wall with a plumbline. He said He would measure His people with the plumbline and if they didn't measure up, He would not turn away from destroying them. Amos was quiet.

A priest heard that Amos was receiving visions and told the king of Israel. The king became angry and tried to have Amos deported, using the premise that Amos was a false prophet. But Amos said, "I am not really a prophet, the Lord is just using me."

In chapter eight, Amos sees a vision of a basket of ripe fruit. He likens it unto Israel, which was ripe for punishment. Chapters eight and nine are much alike except for two versus: Amos 9: 8 and 9. There the Lord promises that the rooting up of Israel would not be permanent. She would be sifted and thrown about but not one kernel would be lost. The final few verses state that some day the kernels would be firmly planted and not be pulled up again.

Analysis

Amos was a rural man, not from a family of prophets. Yet, we cannot consider him a stupid man; he was a man of some reputation and substance.[6] Also, the city which Amos came from, Tekoa, was not just a peasant village, but an armed garrison in the time of Uzziah. Therefore Amos was not just some country hick who had been drinking too much and saw things. He was a well-known man who should have been taken seriously.

Another interesting thing about the early writings of Amos, dealing with God's prophecy, was God's frequent referral to himself as a lion. The lion's habits were well known to the people of Israel. The lion was the king of all the animals. He was complacent when unprovoked or well-nourished. However, when provoked, the lion was shifty, powerful, and deadly. God's referral to himself as a lion is symbolic. As long as the people of Israel kept Him well nourished with praise and thanksgiving, He was peaceful and loving. However, when provoked repeatedly, He was quick to strike with a vengeance at the people of Israel.

The Lord gave a hint to the punishment of Israel in Amos, Chapter 3:12. This is the story of the shepherd who tried to save a sheep from the jaws of a lion, but all he saved was two legs and a piece of an ear. This, in a way, is what happened to Israel. The best of its people were carried away and scattered, and all that was left were the poor and sick, who were almost helpless.

The Lord tries one last time to get the people to return to Him. Over and over again he says, "See the Lord and live." But there are no takers. The mood of the book of Amos changes perceptibly in the middle of the fifth chapter. Up until that point, the mood seemed to be, "Look, I'm going to sit judgment on you people if you don't come back to me." In verse fifteen of the fifth chapter he comes right out and says, "Perhaps even yet the Lord God of hosts will have mercy on his people who remain."

After verse fifteen, the judgment time was passed. The mood now is, "Okay, I've tried and tried. It is just a matter of how and when now, not if." In chapter seven we see the Lord thinking about ways of destroying the nation of Israel. Only the pleas of his servant Amos save the people of Israel from a terrible death. Finally even Amos cannot stand up for the people of Israel, for in his heart he knows that the Lord is right and the people must be punished.

Even the punishment that God metes out to Israel shows His deep love for them. He could have utterly destroyed every one of them, yet He let them live, although in bondage. He also promises that this rooting out would not be permanent; that eventually, no one would be lost. God gave them hope that one day they would be firmly planted, never to be pulled up again.

FOOTNOTES

[1] This outline is based on the Living Bible Translation, Book of Amos, Pages 748 to 754.

[2] Amos 3: 4, page 750.

[3] Amos 3: 12, page 750

[4] I use the Lord and Amos interchangeably since the Lord was speaking through Amos at the time.

[5] Amos 5: 2, page 750.

[6] Gerhard Von Rod, _The Message of the Prophets_, page 102.

Bibliography

The Living Bible. (Wheaton, IL Tyndale House Publishers; London: Cloverdale House Publishers, July, 1973.)

Von Rod, Gerhard, *The Message of the Prophets* (Evanston, IL, New York, San Francisco, and London: Harper and Row, Publishers; 1967.)

THE HEROD DYNASTY

1975

By

John Eric Vining

For a period of roughly 140 years, the Holy Land and surrounding areas were controlled by a group of men collectively known as the Herod Dynasty. Although related with blood ties, the Herods were different politically, but all had an impact on the life of Jesus and the history of Israel.

The first member of the Herods was Antipater.[1] Through shrewd political practices, he gained control of Hyrcanus, high priest of the Jews. After the fall of Pompey, Antipater cleverly switched allegiance to Julius Ceasar. For his support, Antipater was awarded the rule of Palestine. He split his rule, with his son Phasael ruling Judea and his other son Herod controlling Galilee.

At Antipater's death in 43 B.C., the last of the Hasmoneans, Antigonus, tried to rule Palestine. Herod prevented him from becoming outright king of Palestine, but Antigonus still ruled as king and high priest of the Jews in other areas. Herod gained support and marched against Antigonus, destroying him and becoming well established as king of all the Jews, not just the ones in Judea and Galilee.

The Herod that we are talking about was to become known as Herod the Great. A clever politician and able ruler, his rule was one of the best in Palestine's history. Three years after becoming king, he married Miriamme, who was descended from both the Hasmoneans and a leading Jewish family. He therefore strengthened his Jewish ties, for as an Edomite, he was really a foreign king of the Jews. Herod was the king at the time of Jesus' birth.[2]

One thing must be made clear at this point. Although Herod ruled the Jews from an interior standpoint, he was not really supreme ruler of Palestine. He held his title with approval from Rome; his was a client kingdom of the Roman Empire. The Roman Empire had conquered this area, and now all they wanted was tribute, so they allowed native rulers to control in their respective areas.

Herod was a capable ruler, but he tended at times to be too rash. He was a ruthless politician, even to the point of slaying his own family members for political subversion. However, politics was still his strong point. In 31 B.C., Antony and Cleopatra were defeated at Actium by Octavian, and Octavian was now ruler of the Roman Empire. Herod, who had supported Antony, was faced with a severe problem. He met with Octavian and convinced him that he was loyal. Herod became one of the few vassal kings to survive the general purge in the East in 27 B.C. and retained his crown.

Herod was a capable ruler from other standpoints. He approved the building of temples and public houses at Rhodes, Nicopolis in Greece, Antioch in Syria, Tyre, Sidon, Damascus, and a complete facelift for the city of Samaria. Herod constructed the great port city of Caesarea and dredged its harbor.

At Herod the Great's death in 4 B.C., his domain was split between his three sons, Herod Antipas, Herod Archelaus, and Herod Philip. Herod Antipas ruled the longest, with his rule extending from 4 B.C. to 39 A.D. He controlled Galilee and Perea. He built and refurbished several cities, including Tiberias, the capital of Galilee. He was a man of considerable abilities and was mentioned in Luke 13:32 as "that fox." However, Herod Agrippa I, who took over Philip's realm, accused Antipas of revolt, and he was exiled to Gaul.

Herod Archelaus was the least capable of the Herod kings. Archelaus, who was a cruel, stupid person, slew 3,000 Jews at the Passover because they raised a clamor against his inept handling of internal matters. At least three revolts occurred during his reign, and finally, the Roman Emperor Augustus had him exiled, and his land came under direct control of the Roman governors.

Herod Philip ruled several small areas, including Trachonitis, Auranitis, Paneas, Ituraea, Batanaea, and Gaulanitis. Philip's rule was characterized by building activities. He built Caesarea Philippi and Bethsaida. Philip was calm and moderate, but died without heir, and Herod Agrippa I took over his domain after a few years of Roman rule.

Herod Agrippa I was the most able of the Herods after Herod the Great. Agrippa I was appointed by Caligula and was a grandson of Herod the Great. Agrippa I convinced the insane Caligula to abstain from placing a statue of himself in the Temple of Jerusalem, thereby preventing a riot in Palestine. Later in his reign, Judea and Samaria were added to his domain, thus making his kingdom as large as the one belonging to his grandfather Herod the Great. Herod and the new Roman emperor, Claudius, joined forces and set forth to persecute the Jews. Agrippa persecuted James and Peter, killing the former and imprisoning the latter. Claudius expelled the Jews from Rome and also expelled all Jewish and Gentile Christians from Rome.

Agrippa I died unexpectedly in 44 A.D., and his only son, Agrippa II, was too young to rule at this time. So Roman governors ruled Palestine from 44 A.D. to 50 A.D. Herod Agrippa II ruled in coalition with the Roman governors from 50 A.D. to 66 A.D. In 66 A.D., Agrippa II was forced from power and the Jewish Revolt began. It was forcefully crushed by the Romans, and by 73 A.D., the nation of Israel ceased to exist, never to arise again until 1948.

In conclusion, the Herod Dynasty was partly good and partly bad. The Herods, being great politicians, were able to secure Roman technology and do many great works for the people of Palestine, such as the building of the new port cities of Caesarea on the Mediterranean Sea and Bethsaida on the Sea of Galilee. The general refurbishing of the Temple of Jerusalem was also one of Herod the Great's big projects. However, as always, there were political motives behind even this. Herod, being an Edomite, became king of the Jews through appointment rather than through the logical succession of Jewish kings. The Jews were angry over being ruled by a foreign king instead of a Jew. To appease the Jews and keep them from revolting, he planned a general rebuilding of all holy places and was even "converted" to Judaism, although in name only. The Herods were first in allegiance to Caesar. This was bad for the general citizenry, because as rulers, they were always ready to stab the people in the back in order to please the Roman emperors. In fact, it was their general nature to be ruthless. Although the Herods were "Jews," they were not above persecuting their Jewish subjects. All in all, the period of the Herod Dynasty was a time of chaos and forward movement toward the time of the end of the Jewish State.

FOOTNOTES

1   *Oxford Bible Atlas*, by May, Hamilton, and Hunt, pages 37-42.

2   Matthew 2: 1, 7, 19: Mark 1: 14.

Bibliography

Ben Gurion, David. *The Jews in Their Land*. (Garden City, NY: Doubleday & Company, 1966).

May, Herbert G., R.W. Hamilton, and G.N.S. Hunt. *Oxford Bible Atlas*. (London, New   York, Toronto: Oxford University Press, 1962).

The Living Bible. (London, Wheaton, IL: Tyndale House Publishers, 1973.)

ARE WE GAMBLING WITH OUR LIFE? (AND AFTERLIFE?)

1976

By

John Eric Vining

"Gamble...To expose, risk or hazard something of value in the hope of advantage or gain."[1]

As a general rule our society considers gambling, especially for high stakes, a vice. Yet it may be possible for us as common people and Christians to be gambling the highest stakes of all – our lives and afterlives.

Let me explain the basic position I am asserting at the beginning of this essay. As Christians we are expected to live a life which will prepare us for an afterlife with our Lord. Yet what if the basic assertion of an afterlife is false? What if Christ indeed was not resurrected and was not what He said He was? Therefore, we as Christians are gambling on what some would say are unproven facts and are missing some of the things this world has to offer.

Let's consider some points. First, there were no human eyewitnesses to the physical resurrection of Christ. The soldiers on guard had apparently been put to sleep or had fallen asleep if we are to believe the Biblical account of the Resurrection. Mary Magdalene apparently came after the fact and could not conclusively admit to seeing Christ resurrected. As far as justifying the fact with our senses, then, we cannot be absolutely sure that Christ did indeed rise from the dead.

The second point, and the one that I feel is the most valid, can best be illustrated by an analogy. As a person crosses a street, a car approaches. Now that person can choose to cross the street, believing in all faith that the car will not hit him. Yet reason tells him that, regardless of the amount of faith he possesses, if he does walk in front of that car, he will be struck, seriously injured, or killed. It is like a gamble. Thus, in a parallel thought process, very few of us are likely to take the gamble of believing by faith that we will be resurrected and live in some sort of "life" with our Lord; logic tells us that it is impossible for life to continue after death. Not one of us has seen a person who lives after death. To think otherwise is "to believe in the unbelievable."

Yet these arguments can be counterbalanced by certain facts. First, there is considerable historical evidence that Christ did in fact arise from the dead. "Within the gospel narrative there are several detailed testimonies to support"[2] the fact that Christ indeed died. The first witness was the centurion in charge of the execution squad. Due to his many years of battlefield experience, he would have known if Christ had died or merely had fainted. His comment, "Truly this man was the Son of God" (Mark 15:39) shows by its past tense that Christ was truly dead.[3]

Also, there are several positive evidences of a resurrection, 1) the material facts concerning the displaced stone, the empty tomb, and the grave clothes, 2) the physical appearances of Christ described by numerous witnesses[4] and 3) the rise and growth of the Christian church.[5] Consider these assertions: if grave robbers had chosen to rob the grave of Christ, first, could they have moved the huge stone, and second, would they have taken time to unwrap the grave clothes? To both I say, "No, it is highly unlikely." As for number two above, I find it highly unlikely that good moral people such as the disciples would go around spreading the lie that Christ had arisen if they had not seen him. Finally, no institution in the history of mankind has grown large or lasted long while being built on a lie. The mere fact that the church is almost 2,000 years old and known in some form virtually the world over is proof of its validity.

The second argument about the apparent disparity between faith and logic is a somewhat more difficult nut to crack, However, I think the first major fault of the contention that Christ was not resurrected is that it is based on induction. Philosophers from time immemorial have debated whether induction is a valid basis for assertion. For instance, just because the sun has never burned itself out, is it logical to assume that it will never burn out? Not necessarily.

Another point against this argument can be stated as follows: How many of us have ever seen a person hit by a car? Probably none of us. Yet we believe with no doubts that if we step in front of a speeding car, we will be killed. Why can't we then believe that Christ was indeed resurrected and lives and we, too, will live after death?

I choose by faith "to believe in the unbelievable." I believe that there is a life after death and that Christ was indeed resurrected. I can explain my position best by another analogy: A farmer lives in Iowa. Only once in the past 20 years has there been a drought. In that one drought year the farmer almost lost everything he owned. Now as a prudent man, what should he do? Should he save a portion of the money from his crops each year and live below the standard of life he could attain and have money in case another drought occurs, or should he gamble that he can struggle through if a drought occurs? Naturally, most of us would say, "Save now and prepare for later." That is exactly what we should do in our personal lives. It is a gamble but not so great of a gamble as it appears. It is a momentous forced option. Either we live as we wish now and gamble that there is no afterlife and, therefore, no reason to live prudently by faith. Or we can believe in the plan of salvation set up in the Bible, and gamble that Christ indeed died as a blood sacrifice to save us from our sins, arose, and now sits at the right hand of the Father to intercede in our behalf before Him. There is no middle road. I feel that the only logical road to take is to prepare now for the life later. How many of the things that we would be giving up would actually improve us? Not very many, I suspect. Sure we could cheat in business and claw our way to the top, but would we really be gaining happiness?

I feel the gamble of living to prepare for an afterlife with Christ is well worth taking. If all of us would do this, society, and life as a whole, would be much more worth living.

FOOTNOTES

[1] *Webster's Third International Dictionary* (Springfield, MA: G. & C. Merriam Company, 1961), p. 932.

[2] Merrill C. Tenney, *The Reality of the Resurrection* (New York, Evanston, and London: Harper & Row, 1963), p. 106.

[3] Ibid.

[4] Thomas S. Kepler, *The Meaning and Mystery of the Resurrection* (New York: Associated Press, 1963), pp. 96-5.

[5] Richard R. Niebuhr, *Resurrection and Historical Reason* (New York: Charles Scribner's Sons, 1957), pp. 129-33.

BIBLIOGRAPHY

Kepler, Thomas S. *The Meaning and Mystery of the Resurrection*. New York: Associated Press, 1963.

Nicholls, William. *Conflicting Images of Man*. New York: The Seabury Press, 1966.

Niebuhr, Richard R. *Resurrection and Historical Reason*. New York: Charles Scribner's Sons, 1657.

Tenney, Merrill C. *The Reality of the Resurrection*. New York:, Evanston, and London: Harper & Row, 1963.

Other Source:

Webster's Third New International Dictionary. Springfield, MA: G. & C. Merriam Company, 1961.

THE NATURE OF THE GHOSTS: FIVE WAYS TO CATEGORIZE THEM

A Critique of Henry James' _"The Turn of the Screw"_

1975

By

John Eric Vining

The nature of the ghosts in Henry James' _"The Turn of the Screw"_ has been a perplexing problem ever since the book was first published. Were the ghosts real beings, present in solid flesh and bones, or were they merely the governess's wild imaginings? Were they the result of the governess's repressed sex drive for her employer, as Freudian theorists would have us believe? Or was there something deeper? Could it be that evil emerged in the form of Quint and Miss Jessel, or was it Satan himself in the form of two dead souls, hoping to capture two more (the children) for his eternal home? We shall survey the evidence and draw a conclusion.

There is ample evidence to support the theory that the ghosts were quite literally real, visible apparitions. Allen Tate, in a review on radio of James's works states: "It is perfectly evident that nobody sees them as physical existences but the governess. I don't say that destroys their reality,"[1] Tate feels that to take the governess's sightings of the ghosts as illusions and hallucinations would shrink the power and significance of the story and render it useless.[2] In a completely different review of the book, Robert Heilman states that he is "convinced that, at the level of action, the story means exactly what it says: that at Bly there are apparitions which the governess sees, which Mrs. Grose does not see but comes to believe in because they are consistent with her own independent experience, and of which the children have a knowledge which they endeavor to conceal."[3] The flat statement of the feelings of the theorists is revealed in the radio symposium: "The statement the governess sees the ghosts is a true statement."[4]

There are several fine critics who feel that the ghosts were all a part of the governess's imagination. Katherine Anne Porter, a third member of the symposium, has this to say about the book: "When I first read the story, I accepted the governess's visions as real..."[5] Later on in the same passage, she continues: "But as I went on reading the story...I decided that the ghosts were a projection of the governess's imagination and were a part of her plot."[6] This plot may have been a plot by a lonely or imbalanced woman to keep the children closer to her both physically and psychologically.

The Freudian viewpoint has received much support but has slipped in popularity in recent years do to increased study. This theory states that the ghosts are figments of the governess's imagination due to the fact that she is unable to handle her suppressed sex drive. "The theory is, then, that the governess who is made to tell the story is a neurotic case of sex repression, and that the ghosts are not real ghosts but hallucinations by the governess."[7] The governess definitely had a strong feeling for her master, as is established in the context of the work. Yet, "when we look back, we find that the master's appearance has never been described at all...it is impossible for us to know how much the phantom resembles the master--the governess, certainly, would never tell."[8] Could it be that the governess was making up the ghost to take the place of the master, who was far away and unreachable?

Also, one has to take into consideration the odd psychological make-up of governesses. As Wilson states: "By reason of their isolated position between the family and the servants, [governesses] are likely to become ingrown and morbid."[9] Therefore, it would be perfectly natural for a lonely woman, who lacks a meaningful relationship with a man, to conjure an image to hold onto and think about in place of a true relationship. Another view, also, in support of the Freudian theory is *"Another Reading of*

'The Turn of the Screw.'" The author feels that "Quint...'has been ambiguously confused'--in the governess's mind--'with the master and the master's interest in her.'"[10] A summary of this theory is the statement, "it is...a story of man's bewilderment in comprehending the opposite sex."[11]

The appearances of the ghosts have prompted some critics to speculate that the ghosts are evil in human form. Fagin says that "the apparitions are the personification of evil."[12] Miles appeared to be frightened to death but "more likely too corrupted to live without evil."[13] Mark Van Doren supports this belief with the statement that "all James was able to do was ask us to believe in the return--somehow--of two very evil individuals. They are not devils...they simply are evil..."[14] Heilman also appears to believe that the ghosts represent evil. He said, "The ghosts are evil, evil which comes subtly, conquering before it is wholly seen..."[15] Mr. Heilman feels that the real shock of the story comes not from the sudden appearing of the ghosts, but the shock of discovering evil for the first time after it has made such deep inroads into the soul.[16]

Finally, there is the theory that Satan himself has possessed the souls of Quint and Miss Jessel and has returned to overcome the children. The main evidence of this is Quint's appearance. His physique has been likened to that of the Devil. "Quint...has red hair and red whiskers, [which is] the conventional guise of the Devil."[17] These physical features were also noted in the radio symposium alluded to previously: "...She notes that he has red hair, and strange pointed eyebrows...all the physical attributes of the legendary devil."[18] Robert Heilman goes into detail: "His eyes are sharp-- awfully; ...rather small and very fixed. These are unmistakably the characteristics of a snake."[19] He also points to "the coming of Quint...[which is likened to] the coming of the serpent into the little Eden that is Bly..."[20]

From a personal viewpoint, I would consider the theory that Satan has possessed the souls of Quint and Miss Jessel and has returned to Bly for the children. I have several reasons. Most of the other commentaries on *The Turn of the Screw* also mentioned the fact that Quint has the physical attributes of the devil. Surely Mr. James did not pick these characteristics, out of the tens of thousands he could have used, for no particular reason at all. Also, if Quint and Miss Jessel were Satan reincarnated, evil would radiate from them, thus giving them the appearance of evil, as some critics have offered. Another angle is that Miles speaking to Satan in the form of Quint would "poison" him, just as Eve speaking with the devil in the form of the serpent "poisoned" her. Quint always appears in weird situations, never when the governess is on the lookout for him. This is similar to Satan, who always strikes in inopportune moments, never when one is prepared for him. I believe the above facts substantiate my claim that the ghosts in *The Turn of the Screw* are indeed Satan in human form.

Footnotes

1   Katherine Ann Porter, Allen Tate, and Mark Van Doren, "James: *The Turn of the Screw.*" A Radio Symposium. *"The New Invitation to Learning."* Mark Van Doren, ed. (New York: Random House, 1942), p. 223, rpt. in Gerald Willen, ed., *A Casebook on Henry James's "The Turn of the Screw."* (New York: Thomas Y. Crowell Company, 1969), p. 161.

2   Radio Symposium, p. 162.

3   Robert P. Heilman, *"The Turn of the Screw"* as Poem," <u>The University of Kansas Review,</u> 14 (Summer, 1948), p. 277, rpt. in Gerald Willen, ed., *A Casebook on Henry James's "The Turn of the Screw."* (New York: Thomas Y. Crowell Company, 1969), p. 175.

4   Radio Symposium, p. 162.

5   Ibid., p. 160

6   Ibid.

7   Edmund Wilson, "The Ambiguity of Henry James," <u>Hound and Horn</u> 7 (New York: Oxford University Press, 1948), p. 88, rpt. in Gerald Willen, ed., *A Casebook on Henry James's "The Turn of the Screw."* (New York: Thomas Y. Crowell Company, 1969), p. 115.

8   Ibid., p. 118.

9   Wilson, p. 121.

10 Nathan Bryllion Fagin, "Another Reading of *The Turn of the Screw*," <u>Modern Language Notes</u> 56 (March, 1941), p. 197, rpt. in Gerald Willen, ed., *A Casebook on Henry James's "The Turn of the Screw."* (New York: Thomas Y. Crowell Company, 1969), p. 155.

11   Leon Edel, "Dream of Fair Women," <u>Henry James: The Untried Years</u> (Philadelphia: J.B. Lippincott Company, 1953), p. 258.

12   Fagin, p. 158.

13   Ibid.

14   Radio Symposium, p. 163.

15   Heilman, p. 175.

16   Heilman, p. 175.

17   Fagin, p. 157.

18   Radio Symposium, p.163.

19   Heilman, p. 181.

20   Ibid.

A Selected Bibliography

Edel, Leon. <u>Henry James: The Untried Years 1843-1870</u>. Philadelphia: J.B. Lippincott Company, 1953.

Fagin, Nathan Bryllion. "Another Reading of *The Turn of the Screw*." <u>Modern Language Notes</u>, 56 (March, 1941), 196-202. Rpt. in Gerald Willen, ed. <u>A Casebook on Henry James' "The Turn of the Screw."</u> New York: Thomas Y. Crowell Company, 1969.

Heilman, Robert P. "*The Turn of the Screw* as Poem." <u>The University of Kansas Review</u>, 14 (Summer, 1948), 272-289. Rpt. in Gerald Willen, ed. <u>A Casebook on Henry James' "The Turn of the Screw."</u> New York: Thomas Y. Crowell Company, 1969.

Porter, Katherine Anne, Allen Tate, and Mark Van Doren. "James: *The Turn of the Screw.*" A Radio Symposium. <u>The New Invitation to Learning</u>. Mark Van Doren, ed. New York: Random House, 1942. Pp 223-235. Rpt. in Gerald Willen, ed. <u>A Casebook on Henry James' "The Turn of the Screw."</u> New York: Thomas Y. Crowell Company, 1969.

Wilson, Edmund. "The Ambiguity of Henry James." <u>Hound and Horn</u>, 7 (April-June, 1934, 385-406. Revised for the first (1938) edition of <u>The Triple Thinkers</u>. Further revised for <u>The Triple Thinkers</u>, rev, and enl. ed. New York: Oxford University Press, 1948. Pp. 88-132. Rpt. in Gerald Willen, ed. <u>A Casebook on Henry James' "The Turn of the Screw."</u> New York: Thomas Y. Crowell Company, 1969.

PART II

Growing Up in the Rural Midwest:

"At 40, you don't care what *anybody* thinks about you."

Setting the Stage for "The Capstone Projects"

Like most high school seniors in Bob and John's day, students at our high school were required to complete a writing project before graduating. In those days, it was called the Senior Term Paper, but for later students it would be known as "The Capstone Project." Bob's project was for Senior Social Studies, would be completed in late-April, 1964, and would be entitled, *"The Russian Revolution: Its Causes and Results."* It is a very good piece of research (particularly for a seventeen-year-old), and does a great job of outlining the revolution and how the modern Soviet state evolved.

John's paper was written in May, 1973, as the Watergate Scandal was gaining a great consciousness among the American public. It was completed in conjunction with John's Senior Government class, and emphasized the government's suppression of information associated with the Vietnam War. Straightforwardly enough, it was entitled *"Is the Government Covering Up Too Much Information?"* Though much less sophisticated and detailed than *"The Russian Revolution,"* it introduced a topic that would come up in Bob's stream of social consciousness much later: <u>The thought</u> (or perhaps the fear) <u>that issues in government, and in the affairs of the wider world, had grown too complex for the "ordinary people"</u> (as represented by a Congress "by the people," and by extension, the administration that served the executive branch) <u>to handle.</u> Bob would also explore this topic (independent of John's knowledge of Bob's doing so) in his essay entitled *"Nuclear Common Sense,"* from the 1984-'85 time period (contained later in this book).

That this line of thought was a valid premise for debate was validated by none other than Robert McNamara with his *"11 Lessons from Vietnam,"* contained in his 1995 book, *"In Retrospect: The Tragedy and Lessons of Vietnam."* Lesson 11 from this book states: "Underlying many of [the] errors lay our failure to organize the top echelons of the executive branch to deal effectively with the extraordinarily complex range of political and military issues."

With this introduction, I hope you enjoy the brothers' capstone projects and the beginning of the brothers' writings in their "social consciousness" periods.

THE RUSSIAN REVOLUTION: ITS CAUSES AND RESULTS

1964

By

Robert E. Vining

The immediate cause of the Russian Revolution which happened in 1917 was the hardship brought on by the First World War. However, by studying the geography of the land and the history and culture of the Russian people, one can find many steps that led to the revolution. Present day Russia is a vast land with a great mixture of different races. The races range from Slavic in the west to Oriental in the east. There are 150 national groups in Russia and many different languages. Russia is a very cold land because almost all of Russia's 8,650,140 square miles lie north of the 40th parallel.[1] One thing the reader should remember throughout this research paper is that the Russian people have never had freedom, and because of this, it is as hard for Russians to understand American customs as it is for us to understand Russian ways.

About the time of the birth of Christ, Slavs began to settle in central Russia which is now called the Ukraine. These tribes fought among themselves, and in the ninth century Vikings led by Rurik went into Russia to protect some northern tribes. The Vikings later united all of Russia into one state. Kiev became the capital, and the ruler was called Czar. The name Czar comes from Caesar, which the Russians learned from the Byzantine Empire.[2] Through trade, the Slavs had come into contact with the Byzantine Empire. Because the ruler in Constantinople was called Caesar, the ruler of Russia became known as Czar. Another important lasting result from the contact with the Byzantine Empire was the acceptance of the Eastern Orthodox religion by Czar Vladimir in 988. This was important because it was another factor which kept Russia separated from the West.

In the thirteenth century, a Mongolian army led by Batu conquered Russia. Their rule lasted for three centuries until Ivan the Terrible drove the Mongolians out. Ivan easily established an absolute monarchy without any trouble because the people were afraid that unless there was a strong central government other nations would conquer them. Ivan formed a new government with his capital at Moscow. He introduced the Western characteristic of serfdom with an absolute monarchy. However, it is important to note that serfdom came to Russia at a time when it was starting to crumble as a political structure in Europe. In other words, Russia was about five hundred years behind the rest of Europe.

During Ivan's time, the expansion of the empire into Siberia was started by the Cossacks, a nomadic group of people who lived just north of the Black Sea. This eastern exploration continued until 1637, when the Cossacks reached the Pacific Ocean. The Russians did not follow up these explorations with an attempt to settle the area and Siberia has remained sparsely settled even into our own times.

After Ivan died, Russia entered a "Time of Troubles." The people objected to becoming slaves and rebelled. Autocracy triumphed in the struggle for many years until it ended in 1613. In 1613, Michael Romanov became Czar of Russia. He established a dynasty that lasted for three hundred years.[3]

From the time of Michael Romanov until the nineteenth century, little happened in Russia. Russia remained a backward agricultural country, although there was a vigorous but vain attempt by Peter the Great to westernize the country. He might have succeeded if he would have lived longer and if the rulers following him would have continued his domestic policies. The foreign policy during this time was one of expansion and an attempt to acquire a "window" to the sea. This foreign policy was started by Peter and reached its climax during the reign of Catherine the Great, who extended the Russian Empire into Poland and northern Turkey.[4]

In 1812, Napoleon, the adventurous French emperor, invaded Russia. His soldiers spread the ideas of liberty, equality, and fraternity which they had learned during the French Revolution. Although the invasion marked the beginning of the end for Napoleon, it was the spark that started a series of revolutions which ended with the Bolshevik victory in 1917. After the defeat of Napoleon at Waterloo in 1815, Czar Alexander I of Russia emerged as the strongest ruler in Europe. At first he favored reform, but he soon came under the influence of Metternich, the Austrian statesman who wanted to keep Europe under the control of monarchs.[5] During Alexander's rule, Russia began to settle Siberia. All of Siberia would be under the control of the Russian Empire by the end of the century. It was also under Alexander's reign that there was the first of the series of revolutions which would eventually overthrow the monarchy. This revolution, called the December Conspiracy, occurred in 1825. It failed in a disaster, but it was the first appearance of a revolutionary force in Russia.[6]

Reform movements began to appear in Russia after 1825. Russian writers began to mature, and some of the Russian people began to westernize. There was political unrest throughout Russia, but it was effectively suppressed by Nicholas I, Alexander I's successor. After Nicholas' death in 1855, his son Alexander II began to reform Russia. In 1861, he freed the serfs and established legislatures on a local level. A few years later he revised the legal system. If Alexander had lived longer, he might have completely reformed Russia, but he was murdered in St. Petersburg (now Leningrad) in 1881. His death was a turning point in Russian history because the last two rulers, Alexander III and Nicholas II, were reactionaries. The people, who had a taste of freedom, were not going to slip back into slavery. A revolution and the fall of the Romanovs became inevitable.[7]

While Russia was going through many changes during the nineteenth century, Karl Marx was setting down some of his theories about government in a book, the Communist Manifesto. His theories provided the intellectual spark that ignited the Russian Revolution in 1917. Marx's theory states that all things should be held in common. He wanted the workers of the world to unite and throw off the yoke of capitalism by revolution. His theories became very popular in Western Europe. However, there were no revolutions because of the fallacies in Marxism. The fallacies are as follows:

1) Communist revolutions take place in countries where capitalism is in an early stage instead of at a high degree as Marx said.
2) The heart of Marxism – that poverty would become more widespread in capitalist countries – is not true.
3) Marx didn't take into account that some men have more ambition than others.
4) Marx didn't realize what the advancement of scientific invention and technology could do.[8]

The first party in Russia based on the theories of Marxism was the Russian Social Democratic party, which was formed in 1898. During its second meeting in Brussels, it split between the Bolsheviks, meaning majority, and the Mensheviks, meaning minority. Actually the Mensheviks had the majority, but the Bolsheviks had the better leaders in Nikolai Lenin and Leon Trotsky.[9]

In 1904 and 1905, Russia was engaged in a disastrous war with Japan. This war brought on many hardships to the people of Russia. On January 22, 1905, a large group of workers, led by a priest, went to Nicholas II at his Winter Palace at St. Petersburg to protest the hardships. On their way soldiers fired on them, killing more than 500 people. The result of this "Bloody Sunday" was a revolution. The Czar was able to curb the revolt by promising a constitution and a legislature, call the Duma. The soviet, or council, the revolutionaries had set up in St. Petersburg was dissolved after an uprising by the Bolsheviks failed. However, after the war with Japan was over and the Russian soldiers returned home, Nicholas II asserted his power, and constitution and Duma came to nothing.[10]

The Revolt in 1905 was, as Lenin once said, just a dress rehearsal for the Revolution of 1917.[11]

The Romanovs brought about their own end when they entered Russia into World War I. Conditions in Russia had been growing worse. The government had come under the influence of a notorious monk named Rasputin. The war clearly revealed the inefficiency and corruption in the Czar's government. Russia's army was ill-equipped, ill-supplied, and defeated. Food was scarce, and there were many bread riots. When some noblemen killed Rasputin, the Czar dismissed all liberals from the government and appointed tyrannical men to run the government. The conditions for a revolution had gathered in Russia just as clouds gather before a storm.[12] Starting in February, the storm broke and it ended with the Bolshevik victory in October of the same year.

By the beginning of 1917, the condition of Russia was in a terrible state of affairs. The strikes increased, and bread riots were very frequent. The Russian armies were being beaten badly by the Germans, and the soldiers were deserting in great numbers. The Duma telegraphed the Czar, who was at the front, to do something immediately, or he would loose his throne. The Czar sent word that troops were to fire on all riots.[13] On March 12, 1917, (February 27 by the Old Russian Calendar)[14] riots broke out in Petrograd (St. Petersburg), and the garrison, when ordered to shoot people, refused to do so. Thus what seemed to be an ordinary riot turned into a full scale rebellion. The Czar gave up his right to the throne, and the Duma set up a Provisional Government headed by Prince George Lvov. The Czar was imprisoned, and on July 16, 1918, he and his family were executed, thus ending the long rule of the Romanovs. Soon the government controlled all of Russia. Many reform laws were passed, and many prisoners were released. The Provisional Government prepared to set up a permanent government, but because it had no dependable army, it lacked the power to carry out its policies.[15]

The Russian leaders had set up a liberal government which would have probably become a democracy. However, this new government made the mistake of continuing the war with the

Germans. Because of this, the hardships and miseries of the people continued. The radical Bolsheviks, who opposed the Provisional Government, began to gain power in the soviets in the big cities. When Prince Lvov resigned in May, 1917, the new leader, Kerensky, drove the Bolsheviks underground. In August, General Kornilov, the leader of the army, tried to overthrow the government, but his attempt failed. His followers then switched their support to the Bolsheviks. By mid-September the powerful Petrograd Soviet had a Bolshevik majority. Lenin, who was in hiding in Switzerland, urged revolution. The Germans eventually provided him with transportation back to Russia because Lenin was in favor of ending the war with the Central Powers.[16]

Friction increased between the Petrograd Soviet and Kerensky's government. Kerensky planned to destroy the Bolsheviks, but he didn't have enough support. Lenin, who realized the weakness of the Provisional Government, urged an immediate revolt. On the night of November 6-7, 1917, (October 24-25 by Old Russian Calendar) the Bolsheviks stormed the Winter Palace where the government officials were and arrested most of them. Kerensky escaped and went to the front to rally his troops. However, the soldiers wouldn't support him, so he fled to America. On November 8, the All Russian Congress opened with the Bolsheviks in control. Lenin was elected chairman, and he immediately began his program to control all of the industry in Russia. Lenin also asked the Germans for a peace conference which was held at Brest-Litovsk in Poland. This Brest-Litovsk treaty gave the Germans much of western Russia.[17]

The significant part about this revolution is that the huge country of Russia was taken over by Marxist revolutionaries who were a minority group. The reason the Bolsheviks were able to gain control of Russia is that they were highly organized and had very able leaders in Lenin, Trotsky, and Joseph Stalin. Although Lenin was the leader of the revolution, Trotsky and Stalin were the two main men in the Military Revolution Committee of the Petrograd Soviet. These men should be given most of the credit for the success of the revolution because on the night of the revolution, their soldiers were so well organized that they were able to take over the whole city of Petrograd without firing a single shot except when they stormed the Winter Palace. The soviets in the other cities were also well organized. Within a short time most of Russia was under control of the Bolsheviks.[18]

Lenin's plan to control all industry and land was met with great resistance and finally resulted in a civil war between the White and Red Russians. The Reds controlled central Russia while the Whites were strong in southern Russia. The Allies sent aid to the White Russians, but because the Russians were out of World War I, the German forces on the eastern front were rushed to the western front in a last desperate drive to take Paris. This kept the Allied forces concentrated in France. The civil war raged throughout southern Russia with the White armies being very successful at first. In 1919, General Anton Denikin's White army drove to Orel, a town less than two hundred miles from Moscow. It looked as if the Whites might win. However, Denikin's lines were so thin that the Red armies crushed his southern flank, cut him off from supplies, and forced him to surrender. By the end of 1920, the White resistance in Russia was at an end, but Russia was involved in a war with Poland. This war turned into a stalemate and was finally ended by the Riga treaty which was signed on March 18, 1921.[19]

During the same time wars and revolutions were raging through Russia, a system called war communism was being established in Russia. The plan was to have distribution and production of goods to be controlled by the government. The result of this new experiment was disastrous. Production of goods dropped off, and when the peasants found that there were few consumer goods, they cut down on farm production. Soon there was a shortage of food, and as a result, many people starved. Government money became worthless through inflation, and the government stopped interest payments on bonds and stocks. After the uprising at the Kronstadt Naval Base, Lenin realized that communism according to Marx's theories was a failure. He would have to make drastic changes if he was to remain in office.[20]

Late in 1921, Lenin introduced the New Economic Policy (NEP) which gave the peasants an incentive to produce. No longer would the peasant have to give all his produce to the government. Instead he would have to give a definite amount to the government. This plan would have worked if famine hadn't struck in 1921 and 1922. Millions of people died, and many more would have if it hadn't been for the food sent by the American Relief Administration which was headed by Herbert Hoover. Slowly the Russian economy revived itself. A new currency was issued which was backed by the government. When foreign capitalists were invited to invest in Russian industry, it appeared as if the Russians were going toward capitalism. However, the government remained in full control of the big industries in Russia.[21] (Russia is now called the Union of Soviet Socialist Republics because the Russian government changed its name in 1922.)[22]

When Lenin's health began to decline in 1922, political leaders began to wonder who would take over after Lenin died. Most of them thought Trotsky, who was second only to Lenin, would. However, immediately after Lenin's death on January 21, 1924, Joseph Stalin formed an alliance with two powerful men in the left wing of the party. This triumvirate proved too powerful for Trotsky, and it finally drove him from his post of War Commissar. Stalin proved himself the master of the double-cross when he turned against his former allies and forced them from their posts in the government. By 1928, Stalin had driven all of the powerful members of the government from office. He consolidated their power so he would be in full control. After Trotsky was exiled from Russia, Stalin become absolute ruler of the Soviet Union and of the world-wide communist movement.[23]

Stalin's rise to power in 1928 marked a turning point in communism. The revolution which had happened eleven years before had brought an end to the rule of the Romanovs. It had brought men into office who had high ideals, and who wanted to help the Russian people. These eleven years proved that true communism could not work. Russia again had fallen into the hands of a tyrant ruler, who would exploit the Russian people for his own personal gain and power. Joseph Stalin ruled Russia from 1928 to 1953. During his time there was the expansion of industry under the Five-Year Plans, the converting of small farms into collective farms, and the purges, which resulted in many prominent men being executed or exiled to Siberia. Also there was the expansion of Russia in Eastern Europe before and after World War II.[24] In 1947, a "Cold War" began between Russia and her satellites and the Western Powers because of Russia's desire for expansion. When Stalin died on March 5, 1953, a scramble for the head of the government began between Malenkov, Beria, and Khrushchev, the last finally gaining power in 1958.[25] The goal of world domination still remained the chief goal for the Soviet Union, but life for the Russian people became somewhat easier than what it had been under Stalin. Thus the Revolution of 1917 changed Russia into an armed camp which could destroy modern civilization at the order of a single man.

Footnotes

1. "Russia", <u>The World Book Encyclopedia</u>, Vol. XV, 1962, p. 486.

2. <u>Ibid</u>., p. 498.

3. <u>Ibid</u>.

4. C.J.H. Hayes, P.T. Moon, and J.W. Wayland, <u>World History</u>, pp. 360-374.

5. E.P. Smith, D.S. Muzzey, D. M. Lloyd, <u>World History</u>, pp. 332-334.

6. <u>Ibid</u>., pp. 415-416.

7. "Russia", <u>World Book</u>, p. 500.

8. R.F. Wilson, J. Willcox, <u>What You Should Know About Communism and Why</u>,   pp. 22-26.

9. "Russia", op. cit., p. 501.

10. Wilson and Willcox, pp. 29-30.

11. A.E. Adams, <u>The Russian Revolution and Bolshevik Victory</u>, p. 7.

12. Smith, Muzzey, and Lloyd, pp. 534-535.

13. <u>Ibid</u>., p. 537.

14. "Russia", <u>World Book</u>, p. 501.

15. Smith, Muzzey, and Lloyd, p. 536.

16. <u>Ibid</u>., pp. 535-536.

17. "Russia", <u>World Book</u>, p. 501.

18. Adams, pp. 97-102.

19. "Russia", <u>World Book</u>, pp. 502-503.

20. Wilson and Willcox, pp. 39-40.

21. <u>Ibid</u>., pp. 40-41.

22. "Russia", <u>World Book</u>, p. 503.

23. Wilson and Willcox, pp. 42-43.

24. "Russia", <u>World Book</u>, pp. 504-505.

25. Smith, Muzzey, and Lloyd, pp. 735-740.

BIBLIOGRAPHY

Adams, A.E., <u>The Russian Revolution and Bolshevik Victory</u>, Boston, D.C. Heath and Company, 1960.

Hayes, C.J.H., Moon, P.T., and Wayland, J.W., <u>World History</u>, New York, MacMillian Company, 1936.

"Russia", <u>The World Book Encyclopedia</u>, 1962, Vol. XV, pp. 490- 506.

Smith, E.P., Muzzey, D.S., and Lloyd, D.M., <u>World History</u>, New York, Ginn and Company, 1955.

Wilson, R.F., and Willcox, J., <u>What You Should Know About Communism and Why</u>, New York, Scholastic Book Services, 1962.

IS THE GOVERNMENT COVERING UP TOO MUCH INFORMATION?

1973

By

John Eric Vining

I feel the government has too much power to hold information from the public. The most famous case of government cover-up was the beginning of the United States' heavy involvement in the Vietnam War circa 1964-'65. The so-called "Pentagon Papers," leaked from the Pentagon in mid-1971, reveal that Lyndon Johnson and Robert McNamara planned to escalate the war in mid-1964. They evidently did not deem it "necessary" to inform the American public until March and April of 1965 that the war was now costing thousands of lives and millions of dollars.

Johnson heavily and successfully downplayed information about the escalation of the Vietnam War until the elections of 1964 were over (in that election, Johnson ran as the "dove" candidate and Barry Goldwater as a "hawk"). The justification to escalate the War was the "Gulf of Tonkin Incident," occurring August 2nd, 1964. In the "Gulf of Tonkin Incident," North Vietnamese planes and boats "reportedly" attacked U.S. ships in the Gulf of Tonkin, adjacent to North Vietnam. The *Tonkin Gulf Resolution* arose over this "attack." The *Resolution* (in so many words) said that the Executive Branch had unlimited power to wage an undeclared war. This resolution was in flagrant violation of the U.S. Constitution.

The C.I.A. had stated that the "domino theory of Southeast Asia" (which stated, among other things, that if Vietnam fell, the rest of Southeast Asia would fall) was incorrect and that the war was little more than a civil war. They advised that we keep a close watch on things but stay out of it. However, the government took the war as a chance to show American might to the Communists in case they had any ideas of further aggression. The Pentagon Papers tell the story of the course that America followed during the mid-'60s.

The study's first entries are from July, 1964. It plainly states that Lyndon Johnson and Robert McNamara tried to cover up the bombing of Laos. According to the Pentagon study, Laos was being bombed in July and August. Yet the government insisted that they were simply armed reconnaissance raids. Whenever a fighter plane was shot down in Laos, the government insisted that plane had been shot down escorting reconnaissance planes in Laos.

Late in 1964, Johnson and McNamara realized that North Vietnam would have to be bombed. All through August and in early September, Johnson studied and thought in seclusion. According to the report, the final decisions to bomb were made as early as September 7, 1964.

After starting the bombing, Johnson once more concealed an important aspect of the war. Up until this time the South Vietnamese had been running their own war and were losing. Johnson moved troops into the Da Nang airbase to protect American interests there. Unknown to the public of the United States, these troops were soon sent into offensive battle with South Vietnamese troops supporting them, instead of the other way around. Yet on the day of the American entry into large scale ground fighting in South Vietnam, the President told a press conference that he knew of "no far reaching strategy change" while all the time his men were engaged in "search and destroy" missions.

The bombing was handled in a rather shady manner after April of 1965 also. After small and scattered raids in the early part of 1965, the President stopped it to see if the North Vietnamese had had enough. When it was apparent that they had not, the bombing was started again on a larger scale. It was started and stopped many times, each time increasing in intensity. This so-called "ratchet theory" was invented by Johnson and McNamara long before it was put into effect. It provided a smooth way of escalating the war and flexing America's muscles.

Finally, in 1967, when the formerly arrogant and robust McNamara began to have doubts about the real purpose of the war and began to feel the burden of almost 200,000 casualties, he order the Pentagon study as a historical record. He hoped the lesson told by the study would be well-learned by future generations. Even though he and President Johnson, among others, were splattered with mud by the report, he was willing to have it written. Fate had one last trick to play on him, though. The study was not published, as he had hoped, but labeled top secret by war strategists and was not allowed to be published. Thus nothing was known of the report until Daniel Ellsberg, a superhawk turned superdove, leaked it to the New York *Times* in the celebrated Pentagon Papers case.

Even here the government tried to cover up its own tracks by getting an injunction preventing the newspapers from printing the so-called "top secret" paper. The Supreme Court saw otherwise, however, and allowed the newspapers to continue printing the papers they had.

In 1968 the butchering of 124 civilians in My Lai was covered up for 2 years until a guilt-ridden member of the squad which shot up My Lai confessed. It shocked the nation and the world.

By 1968 American was bogged down in a war which nobody thought would last this long and of which everybody was tired. In the beginning it was a God-given chance for America to flex her muscles before the Communist world. By 1968 it was a man-made Hades. Orders were or were not given to "teach the people of My Lai a lesson." The Tet Offensive by the North had just killed many Americans. Fuses in men's minds were short. At any rate, indiscriminate murdering of men, women, and children took place.

Nobody knows whether the order was or was not given. Nobody knows just how many high ranking government officials were involved. Why? Because the government (mainly, the Pentagon) wanted it this way. A victim had been found; a scapegoat for the officials. Lieutenant William Calley was saddled with murdering 102 villagers and ordering another 22 killed. Why was the inquest indecisive? Because the Pentagon succeeded in so miring it down with red tape that its final results were clouded.

Mr. Johnson's administration is not the only one to be blamed for hiding facts, however. It is now clear that Mr. Nixon escalated the war in Laos early in 1969 and hid it from the public until late 1969. Early in 1969 Mr. Nixon declared flatly, "There are no combat troops in Laos." However, reconnaissance missions prove that American troops were operating in Laos. It has also been proved that bombing missions have been made in Laos as long as we have been bombing North Vietnam. Mr. Nixon has conceded that there are reconnaissance flights over Laos, but there is little doubt that the Ho Chi Minh Trail in Laos is being bombed almost daily by American bombers. And as for Mr. Nixon's statement that there were "no combat forces" in Laos, either he was terribly misinformed or he lied. A Laotian offensive in mid-1969 would have been impossible without American support. It has been proven that a 12,600-man army, a highly trained group of soldiers, has been operating in Laos since 1969.

I could go into detail on several incidents such as the recent Watergate break-in, the old Teapot Dome scandals, and the Grant Administration scandals, which would prove that the government has the means to pull the wool over the public's eyes. In fact, the Mexican-American War (1846-1848) was started by deceit, when President Polk sent an American Army into disputed territory and provoked an incident. He then told the public that Mexican troops had attacked American soldiers on American soil. If a whole war can be started by lying to the public, then what is to keep the government from lying to the people on small, everyday things?

What I am trying to say is that the government has made laws to protect us from cheating and deceiving each other, but we have no way of seeing if the government is cheating us. If fraud is discovered between two people, the court system will quickly try and convict the appropriate party. Who is to check to see if the government is using the American tax dollar, or worse, American lives, incorrectly?

I think that there should be a board of qualified citizens, or better yet, several boards of qualified citizens, who could check not only military activities, but all workings of the government. This board should have complete access to all government buildings and documents. The reason I call for this is that when I started checking into this, I found that nobody even questioned most of the things that the government did for *two years!* Why, in two years the world could be destroyed and we would never know the reasons why.

The next question that will be raised is, "How are we going to pay for these civilian boards?" With tax money. "Oh, sure," the critics will say, "Look at how much money we pay already." The critics don't realize the money that is squandered by the government. If the government knew that somebody was going to be checking on them every time they appropriated money, they would be more careful how they spent it.

What's more important, if the Pentagon knew that every time they made a major change in tactics, they would have to answer to a board of inquiry, they would be more careful how they spent American lives. The useless slaughter of half a million Americans and countless civilians in places like Vietnam might never be repeated.

Setting the Stage for "Social Consciousness"

By the early 1980s, both Bob and John had reached a point of concern about the turn of world events. As products of the Cold War, they were concerned about East versus West confrontations in Europe, and also about the prospects of the Earth's resources sustaining human life for the long term.

Bob was a deep thinker. As such, he concerned himself with large scale issues such as the proliferation of nuclear arms both within the superpower sphere of influence and by unstable Third World elements. Bob was obviously concerned that the failure to control the knowledge and use of these weapons would lead to nuclear holocaust. He drew up a set of strategies to control these situations in his essay *Nuclear Common Sense*.

John was also fearful of nuclear holocaust, but from a different perspective. He feared the imbalance of military weaponry (particularly in terms of airpower) in the East versus West confrontation in Europe would lead a Western local theater commander, in danger of being overwhelmed by superior numbers, to fall back on the use of tactical nuclear weapons to retrieve the situation. From there the situation could uncontrollably and fatally escalate into the use of strategic nuclear weapons. John provided ideas on how this conventional imbalance in airpower could be corrected in his essay *Tactical Aircraft for the 1990s.*

As an agri-businessman, Bob was aware of the various 50-year economic cycles of the past two centuries. He was also concerned about the destruction of the Earth's fragile ecological base. Bob outlined the history of the cycles and the nature of the threat to the ecosystem in his essay, *The Years of Jubilee.*

John also was aware of the (apparently) growing shortness in supplies of natural resources as the 1980s continued. He was a freshman in college at the time of the first oil shock in late-1973. This shock originally arose as an Arab economic weapon in the Yom Kippur War of 1973, but soon took on a life of its own. John was concerned about the continuing use of this "resource weapon," its affect on the United States' well-being, and its ability to destabilize the world in various ways. He outlined the nature and history of Middle Eastern oil in *The Rise and Fall (and Rise Again) of OPEC*.

Please share with Bob and John as they look into the arena of 1980s world issues.

Nuclear Common Sense

1984

By

Robert E. Vining

It has been over two hundred years since Thomas Paine wrote *Common Sense*, an article so instrumental in bringing forth the new nation of the United States, which for the first time put into practice the ideals of the Enlightenment. Today, as this nation created in the fire of the Revolutionary War is threatened to be destroyed in the fire of nuclear explosions, I feel compelled to write this article in a sense of responsibility, not only to my country, but also to my fellow man, and to whatever it is that we call God. I hope that whoever takes the time to read this will think seriously about what is written and improve upon it.

It has been nearly forty years since the secrets of the atom were revealed, producing a bomb of staggering power. In those intervening years, we have moved from zero megatons capacity to over thirteen thousand megatons capacity and climbing every day. Many scientists believe that after the world passed three hundred megatons, how much more we added was academic. But the other part of the problem, and perhaps the most important in my opinion, is the spreading knowledge of nuclear technology from a few men in Chicago in 1943 to thousands of men and women all over the world. These two factors will make any further control of these weapons difficult and unlikely, although we must continue to try.

What, then, is the solution? Are we doomed to a never-ending arms race and eventual destruction? We have avoided doomsday for forty years. But will our luck hold forever? As things stand now, it may be only a matter of time. Fortunately, however, we have several options for increasing mankind's odds of survival. The rest of this article is composed of five policy proposals that can be adopted to increase our chances of avoiding nuclear war.

I

The policy of nuclear deterrence or "nuclear umbrella" no longer has relevance as a credible response to a conventional Soviet attack. Strategic nuclear war (the use of intercontinental ballistic missiles) is suicide and should be viewed that way. Tactical nuclear war (the use of nuclear weapons on the battlefield) could lead to strategic war and therefore must also be viewed as suicide. Any massive use of nuclear weapons by either side would also surely upset the delicate fabric of ecological balance, making further life on this planet only problematical at best. After all, it is ecological collapse that brings great civilizations down. Look, for example, at the Maya in Guatemala and the Yucatan, or North Africa, the granary of the Roman Empire, or the Fertile Crescent of the ancient Near East. All of these centers of great civilizations fell as a result in great part to the failure of their agriculture. After nuclear war there would be so much smoke and dust in the atmosphere that agriculture would collapse in the ensuing "nuclear winter." Therefore we, as well as all other countries that possess nuclear weapons, must adopt a "no first use" policy. That is, nuclear weapons would only be used in retaliation of a nuclear attack.

If the United States adopted a "no first use" policy, what then should we do with all those atomic weapons that we have? Can we unilaterally disarm in the hope that the Soviets will follow? Should we strive for a verifiable "freeze" at levels we now have? Can we "build down" the number of weapons that both we and the Soviets hold? Or can we turn in the plutonium "triggers" to be destroyed, as some propose?

Unfortunately, I fear none of the above will prove workable. All would require U.S./Soviet negotiations which in the past have not proven very productive. Furthermore, agreements would require elaborate verification procedures which, because technology will likely produce a moving target, will have to be continuously updated or the agreements could simply fall apart. Also, plutonium "triggers" which are turned in could always be rebuilt. One wonders how many secret "triggers" already exist from the two tons of plutonium that have come up missing since that element was first produced. Also, an elaborate "Star Wars"-type defense will not prove effective because the Soviets will likely follow us into space with satellite "mines." The Soviets have demonstrated both a determination and ability to not allow the United States any "superiority." They could even build a "doomsday" nuclear weapon system to be exploded in Siberia, and let the smoke, dust, and fallout do us in. What then can we do?

II

The best choice both the United States and the Soviet Union have in the immediate future is to build many small, mobile, and widely dispersed atomic weapon systems. We have been especially good at this, and hopefully in the future we will do away with all fixed missiles in silos and become complete mobile. The Soviets still have approximately seventy percent of their warheads on missiles in silos, but their new generation of missiles, now in development, is to be of the mobile type. Hopefully as these new systems are deployed the old will be eliminated and we should encourage them to do this. Then as both sides face each other with completely mobile systems, if one side were to launch a surprise attack on the other, few if any of the missiles needed for a counterattack would be destroyed. Some people argue that no national leader would order a counter-attack after his country had been destroyed, but then a leader contemplating a surprise attack in the first place will never know for certain how the other leader will react.

These mobile systems will also remove the greatest threat to strategic nuclear war, and that is war by accident. A few years ago the nuclear fuse was about thirty minutes long, but the introduction of new fixed weapons systems could shorten this fuse to as short as seven minutes. That is, future leaders may have as short as seven minutes to decide whether or not to push the doomsday button, and this makes the chance for war by accident or miscalculation greater. But with completely mobile systems a leader would have plenty of time to decide how to react to an attack because few, if any, of his systems would be destroyed in any first strike.

III

If nuclear weapons no longer provide a useable defense for the western democracies, what then should be our defense policy? We must now return totally to thinking in terms of conventional "balance of power," which has been part of the western world in modern times. Ever since the sixteenth century when the French, in their newly created modern state, got ambitions to expand into Italy, peace or the lack of it has been dependent on the "power balance" in Europe. This system has now been spread world-wide.

There is really no point in arguing the fact that this system is bad, immoral, and inadequate. It is the system we have and will have for the foreseeable future. The Soviet Union is just the latest in a long line of expansionist European powers, but ever since the defeat of the Spanish Armada by the English in 1588, Great Britain and now the Anglo-American alliance have been quite successful in checking expansionist powers through sea power and various geo-political alliances. There is no reason why this system cannot continue to be successful, provided that we are committed to do whatever is necessary to maintain the power balance.

First, we must determine at what military level the Western alliance balances the forces of the Soviet Union and the Warsaw Pact, and then we must spend the money necessary to do the job. If it means a return to the military draft, then we must do it. Also, our isolationist tendencies must be put aside, because the nations of the world simply have become too interdependent for us to turn our back on our responsibilities. Hopefully, if the Soviets realize that we are committed to power balance and not superiority, eventually force levels could be maintained at relatively low levels of balance, the goal for which we should be striving.

IV

A study of modern times in the western world is full of disputes, conflicts, and wars. One can easily draw the conclusion that of all the ways to settle disputes, war is by far the poorest. The purpose of having military forces is not wanting to commit them to combat, but that they will be committed only if all other means of solving a dispute fail. Therefore, in order to have a more peaceful and stable world, we must have a sincere commitment to negotiate not only on the issue of nuclear arms, but on all disputes that arise between us and another country.

In the American tradition, we view war in total terms. This comes from our three hundred year frontier experience during which we fought a series of total wars with the American Indian plus the first of the modern wars in our American Civil War. Now, however, since World War II (also a total war) we are engaging in eighteenth century-style limited wars, in which the point is not to destroy our enemies but to persuade them to negotiate settlements with us. This is difficult for the American people to understand, and causes a weakening of the link between the people and the U.S. military establishment, which is after all a peoples' army. It is necessary though, that we are involved around the world, because power balance is maintained not only through military force but also by means of strategic geographical locations and political-military alliances with other countries. In the opinion of many well-informed people, this geo-political power balance is, unfortunately, likely to shift against us as revolutionary upheavals in developing countries bring governments unfriendly to ours. Hopefully in the future, though, we will be able to use the ability to project our power as well as have a sincere willingness to solve disputes peacefully, by negotiating agreements that will make the world a safer place for everyone.

V

Up to this point I have been drawing conclusions from many different sources and condensing them for the sake of brevity. It is my desire that many people read what is written here; to think, criticize, and expand upon it. But in this last proposal, I hope to inspire the greatest thought because I have thought this through the least.

When the Founding Fathers were writing the Constitution in 1787, they could in no way envision how the government of the United States would evolve. In the beginning the government was small, the problems facing it were not so technical or complex, and the times were slow. Today government is big, the problems facing it are very technical and complex, and the national and international scene is fast moving. At times it seems as if the government limps along and then lurches from crises to crises. How, then, can our government be made to function and respond better in the time of great and deadly danger?

Perhaps the process of governing and policy formation could be greatly improved through what Plato called "Philosopher Kings" (which today would include "Philosopher Queens"). The majority of the people who run our government are products of universities, and with a modern telecommunications network the most brilliant of these people could be linked together to serve in an advisory capacity.

Many people believe that we all ready have too much government, so why should we have more? The reason is that we have always thought of governing in strictly a political sense. Other organizations have in the past risen to form governments but not in the way we are used to thinking about governments. The medieval church is a good example. A much more recent example is the rise of corporate America. When the economy started through a structural shift in the 1870s, it transformed America from an agricultural to an industrial economy, and also brought into power a class of corporate managers. These people, though unelected, today exercise a powerful control over millions of Americans. The current economic structural shift we are going through will make possible the rise of these new "Philosopher Rulers," whose ability to rule will be in direct relation to their ability to affect public opinion.

We have already seen the emergence of the type of system that I envision but in a disorganized form. Examples include Lyndon

Johnson's meeting with the "Wise Old Men" in March of 1968, the formation of the Greenspan Commission on Social Security, the Scowcroft Commission on the MX missile, the Kissinger Commission on Central America, former President Ford's gathering of former leaders of the Western democracies in Colorado, and a Walter Cronkite-sponsored debate on the deployment of new missiles in Europe, to name a few.

The "Philosopher Kings and Queens" would gain access to this new communication net through election by their peers from the university system, somewhat like Nobel Prize winners are selected with participation out of a sense of duty. Perhaps two groups could be selected: one for domestic and economic policy and the other for foreign policy. Maybe the rest of America would be able to tune in and be able to listen and watch right from their living rooms.

Hopefully this new system would facilitate several changes that are needed now. One would be to aid in the formation of a bi-partisan foreign policy that most of the American people can support. Another would be to provide an escape for politicians who often must choose between political suicide and voting for what is best for the country. In other words, the "Kings and Queens" could take the blame. Still another use would be as a ready pool of brilliant people would could study a complex problem and offer bi-partisan solutions that could be passed by Congress. Still another use could be to keep former people in earlier administrations still participating in determining what the best policies of our government should be.

This new system would also hopefully correct one of the problems of our educational system. Of necessity, we educated people to be a specialist in one field in order to function most effectively in our highly complex economic system. People go to school mostly to enhance their career opportunities and quite often become peaks of genius surrounded by valleys of ignorance. This new system could build bridges of knowledge between many peaks and thus make the educational process a lifelong experience.

One can think much about power – nuclear power, military power, economic power, voting power, geo-political power. But I have concluded that for the survival of mankind and his ability to respond to the challenges that face him, the most important power is the power of knowledge. I used to pessimistic, almost fatalistic about mankind's future. Now, however, while not optimistic, I see hope. The "Kings and Queens" are already doing their job, and slowly but steadily the knowledge of and respect for the delicate ecological balance that all life on this planet depends upon is being spread. What many farmers have known by instinct for centuries, modern science has now confirmed: the threshold of agricultural collapse is quite low. As the communication revolution that we are going through will allow knowledge to be disbursed even wider, perhaps the day will come when all people realize that any attack upon our biological system is suicide and must be avoided.

In the last forty years the power of knowledge has taken mankind's fate from nature and put it in the hands of man himself. Nothing we can do can turn our fate back to nature because the power to destroy ourselves will exist in our minds forever. But it is this same power of knowledge that can make it possible for us to preserve not only this generation for human beings, but all future generations that hopefully will inhabit this beautiful Earth of ours.

AFTERWARD

(Written shortly after the completion of *"Nuclear Common Sense."*)

By

Robert E. Vining

This article is the result of over a year of research that I completed at IPFW, Fort Wayne, Indiana. I farm for a living, but have always been a student of history. As most historians do, I sense the great danger we face in the next twenty years, as we search for solutions to protect ourselves from self-destruction. This article is about nuclear weapons, but could also be applied to chemical and biological weapons as well. The responsibility I feel to defend our society is great, to me an inherent obligation of the social contract.

What I hope to accomplish by this article is to bring consensus to our foreign policy that will have stability and continuity which will not be affected much by changes in administrations. I also hope it will result in bringing a margin of safety in our nuclear weapons systems.

The part of this article that concerns me most is the likely shift of the geo-political power balance against us. The Middle East with its Islamic religious fanatics bent on waging "holy" wars and now gaining nuclear capabilities scares me the most. But this will also be combined with the peace movements gaining strength in Europe, and as the political pendulum swings, the NATO alliance will likely weaken. Perhaps someone will send this article to Petra Kelly, because it applies equally to Europe. We also run a great risk of becoming involved in a type of "economy of force" operation in Latin America that would adversely affect our ability to project power at a time with the need to project power is the greatest.

THE YEARS OF JUBILEE

1985

By

Robert E. Vining

*"And you shall hallow the fiftieth year, and proclaim
liberty throughout the land to all inhabitants; it shall be
a jubilee for you, when each of you shall return to his
property and each of you shall return to his family."* –
Leviticus 25:10

A study of history reveals that at least since the dawn of
agricultural civilization some eight thousand years ago, at fifty
year intervals the affairs of mankind become so chaotic that a
restructuring must take place. There is evidence of this not only
in Old World civilizations but also for ancient civilizations of the
New World, who were on a fifty-two year cycle. In the conquest
of Mexico, a part of the success of the Spaniards led by Cortez
was that they arrived in 1519, the end of a fifty-two year cycle
and considered an evil time by the Indians. So apparently these
economic restructuring periods have been around for a long time.
But with the dawn of the industrial civilization in the middle of the
eighteenth century, these periods have taken on a new dimension,
as economies shift from one stage of technology to a higher stage of
technology. They have also brought serious social problems because
these periods usually last around a decade and are characterized by
low profits, bankruptcies, high unemployment, and low commodity
prices. The world is currently going through one of these periods,
and we, as products of the past, should study the past in order to get
a clearer picture of what the future will be like.

The industrial age was born in an economic shift, and in the current fifth subsequent restructuring shift, it will die. The civilization based upon fossil fuels, iron, and factory labor will be replaced by a civilization based on silicon, renewable fuels, and robots. People in this country fear this change but they should not do so. Every shift that Western man has gone through in modern times eventually has resulted in a higher standard of living, but it is the pain associated with the shift that distresses so many people. Unfortunately, nothing can be done to shorten the time significantly. We will eventually come through this period and arrive in this new civilization with a potential for greatness that we cannot fully envision now. Perhaps this would be a good time to review the industrial age and what its effects have been on this country, as well as the three shifts (to date, not counting the one we are currently embarking upon) after this.

The industrial age began with a shift in England in the middle of the eighteenth century. As America primarily had an agricultural economy at this time, the usual collapse in commodity prices (particularly tobacco) had a great effect on the course of American history. In the one hundred years preceding the American Revolution, Great Britain fought four major wars, primarily against France, to see who would be "the top of the heap" in Europe. Although eventually the British would win the second "hundred years war" with the defeat of Napoleon in 1815, they "bled themselves white" in doing so. Meanwhile, the New England Yankees would get incredibly rich supplying the British, their enemies the French, and the pirates – the enemies of everyone. (It seems that worshiping on the alter of the "almighty dollar" has been with us a long time.) When the terrible "German George" the Third decided it was time that *all* British subjects start to pay, the Yanks were ready to rebel. But how do they get those good Anglican Virginians to go along?

Well, it just so happens that between 1760 and 1763, the price of tobacco fell eighty percent. The Virginia planters fell deeply into debt to finance their subsequent losses. Who financed these losses? The beneficent British financiers! Thus, at the eve of the Revolution, for all practical purposes British bankers owned Virginia. As Everett Dirksen said many years ago, "There are many factors that are important in politics, but come Election Day the most important factor is the price of hogs in East St. Louis." This statement also applied to the price of tobacco in Virginia as a major factor in bringing about the Revolution. The Americans eventually won the right of "home rule" in 1783. (As a continuing revolution, we now have an expensive spectacle every four years to see who will rule at home.) But because all these old debts to the British bankers were not repaid, the British refused to give up their hold on the Ohio country; thus the Revolution continued in that area continued until Anthony Wayne's Legion won the Battle of Fallen Timbers and Wayne negotiated the Treaty of Greeneville in 1795. During this period, in the Ohio country, many historians believe western civilization reached the low ebb of its long history.

The second shift was to bring the beginning of the classic economic struggle that characterizes American politics – which boiled down, amounts to hard money versus soft money. In Europe, it gave birth to the socialist response, as Karl Marx viewed with dismay the exploitation and oppression of the working people of Manchester, England. Although the Soviets were later to betray the ideals of the movement, one cannot deny the success of the western socialists to peacefully create a more humane (although somewhat more inefficient) society. In America, Andrew Jackson's struggle with Nicholas Biddle and the Second Bank of the United States, and the severe depression this created throughout most of Martin Van Buren's administration, are all characteristics of an economy in change.

The third shift was to be of great importance to America because the economy shifted from primarily an agricultural one to an industrial one, eventually making the United States the world's industrial giant. In Europe it was characterized by the collapse of the London and Vienna stock exchanges and prolonged depression. In this country, high unemployment and low commodity prices brought the cheap money/hard money struggle to a new level of intensity as populism spread.

The origins of this struggle go back to the beginnings of our monetary system, which was based on bimetallism – gold and silver. We still have something similar today in that with our instantaneous communication system and free market, dollars are priced in gold and silver, and gold and silver are priced in dollars, depending on how one looks at it. We still have economists developing new theories about man's age old relationship to the precious metals, a relationship that will probably always lie deep within man's psyche.

The early relationship had to work without the benefit of rapid communication, and therefore the government tried to fix the price. But the market is hard to fool, and as Mr. Gersham pointed out to Queen Elizabeth four hundred years ago, "bad" money always drives "good" money out of circulation. In America, "bad" gold drove "good silver" out of circulation and we went on a de facto gold standard. After the Civil War the frontier literally leaped across the West, and huge new deposits of silver were discovered. This made silver "bad," and the cry of the populist was for the free coinage of silver at the old fixed rate. The populists' high water mark came in 1896 when the Democratic candidate for president, William Jennings Bryan, ran on a campaign of, *"You shall not crucify mankind on a cross of gold."*

The Populists lost the election but were not destroyed. Instead they waited and with the coming of the next shift (the "Great Depression" of so many still-living Americans) they triumphed with the election of Franklin D. Roosevelt in 1932. Taking us off the gold standard and fighting the depression with Keynesian economics, the new populists were not very successful because the world economy was drowning in an ocean of protectionism. With the coming of the Second World War, protectionism ended and the war "primed the pump" that led to recovery. Regardless of the faults of our current administration, it resisted protectionism when the rest of the western world was sliding towards it, and for this we all should be grateful.

This gives us a unique opportunity to study how these shifts operate from the eyewitness accounts of people who lived through one in Mercer County, Ohio. In 1929 Mercer County was (as it is today) primarily an agricultural community but farming was done with horses. By 1940 all the horses were gone, and the farmers were using tractors. Why the change? I happened to talk one day with a retired farmer who owned an early model Fordson tractor. With a long string of profane four-letter words which could never be written here, the farmer vividly explained that they were both unreliable and uneconomical. Throughout the 1930s, though, technology improved, so right through the most severe depression on record, the horse went to market and agriculture was mechanized. Today, something similar is occurring, only this time in the field of electronics. Computers and robots that a few years ago cost hundreds of thousands of dollars and were unreliable now cost only a few thousand dollars, are extraordinarily reliable, and are making their appearance everywhere. This leads to the whole point of this paper: *What are we going to do with today's "horses," who are* **people**, *and because we are humane we can never send to the "market?"*

The answer lies in developing all people to be able to function effectively in this new civilization that dawns before us. It will be a process of education and training but not entirely in the ways we have thought before. In the past, schools were a type of "parts factory" for the industrial machine - stressing punctuality, rote memorization, and generally suppressing the creativity inherent in every human being - through mass education. But the communications revolution now taking place will allow the educational process to be a lifelong experience. The basic skills needed are those in math, writing, reading, comprehension, and above all the burning desire to learn, achieve, and create.

Something similar to this already exists in Mercer County. I live in the most productive agricultural area in the world, with some of the greatest farmers mankind has ever known as neighbors. How can we be so good at farming when other equally rich agricultural areas aren't good at all? In high technology farming, *learning can never stop.* Our farmers learn their basic skills in formal school, and now still go to school every day in an informal way. I know farmers that, to look at them, one wouldn't think they were smart enough to "walk and chew gum at the same time," but in reality are peaks of genius. They are better at farming than I ever will be because they concentrate all the time on farming. However, I don't need to concentrate that way. Next spring, I will take a "course" from the "professors" in their "classrooms." (I.e.: I will *shoot the bull* with these smart farmers in their farm shops.) The high tech age we are entering now will <u>require</u> a somewhat similar *creative lifelong learning experience.*

As a conclusion to this paper, I want to try to explain what we do have to fear from the future. It isn't the new era we are entering, but the fragility of the ecological base that we exist upon. People who study in the social sciences have only belatedly begun to recognize that the main social problem mankind faces is his tendency to destroy his environment. Modern technology provides man with many more powerful tools with which to destroy it. Why has this been so overlooked in the past? Perhaps it is because, as the end product of our educational system, we want to produce a specialist who can compete well in our highly complex economic system; but as a consequence has great difficulty "seeing the forest because of all the trees." Those people who study a wide range of subjects relating to human existence realize the danger that we are in. Eons ago "matter" (more correctly the four basic forces of nature manifested in matter and also in anti-matter) was raised to consciousness and later (at least in human beings) to intelligence. The combined intelligence of the human mind knows no limit to what it can do. But all of this potential greatness is supported by a rather delicate biological system that could be so easily destroyed by the intelligence that it supports. Thus, the great test of the new civilization will not be in economics, but in the social problem of how to organize the four-and-one-half billion people now living, plus the billions more in the future, in such a way that they protect rather than destroy our life support system.

2013 POSTSCRIPTS: "NUCLEAR COMMON SENSE" AND "THE YEARS OF JUBILEE"

Both essays written circa 1984/1985 by Robert E. Vining

2013 postscripts by

John Eric Vining

It is interesting to look back on the essays of a contemporary writer that one esteems from a vantage point of nearly 30 years later. However, the key points of those essays should be considered in reviewing just how valuable and prescient those writings were - in light of 30 years of subsequent history. Here is my view on the above two essays.

Part One: "Nuclear Common Sense"

Bob Vining was a product of the Cold War, being born in the War's very initial stages (1946) and dying approximately 15 years (in 2006) after the War's end (1991). As such he was very concerned with the specter of "The Bomb" hanging over the world's collective heads, and also with the extremely short reaction times available to a potential leader in any mid-War crisis. Bob had lived through the Cuban Missile Crisis and was quite sensitive to the effect of any miscalculation that might occur during the super-pressurized elements of a nuclear crisis. Bob made five recommendations with which he hoped to sooth his own social conscience, and more importantly, help the world through some of its most dangerous times.

I

No First Use. Bob was spot-on that any first use of nuclear weapons in either a tactical or strategic crisis would be catastrophic. Bob wrote his essay from the vantage point of 1984-'85 when the Soviet Union was still a viable enemy. In the 5 to 7 years the Soviet Union had to exist at that point, no crisis arose where "first use" would be contemplated or needed.

"Star Wars." Bob thought that a "Star Wars" defense would not be successful due to the technological obstacles of targeting and destroying *every* incoming enemy missile. Also, Bob thought the Russians had demonstrated a propensity to follow every Western strategic initiative with a defensive initiative of its own. He did not realize that the true value of "Star Wars" was that it was a political, and most importantly an economic, weapon. Political, in that for its own well-being (and to follow its own stated objectives), the USSR was virtually duty-bound to follow a "Star Wars" initiative into space, although confounded by the technical complexities this might entail. The Americans had pulled off many technological wonders in the 20th Century, so the Russians could *not quite be sure* the USA could not pull this off as well.

But it was as an economic weapon that (unknown to the U.S.) the "Star Wars" defense initiative was most effective. The West could not know that the Soviet Bloc was a veritable economic "house of cards," and that an initiative of this magnitude (which again, the Soviets *must* match) was enough to drive it over the financial cliff. Thus "Star Wars" was successful, even though not one anti-missile defensive weapon under this program ever made it into space.

II

Small, mobile, widely dispersed nuclear missiles. The missile silos in the Dakotas, Wyoming, Montana, and other parts of the Midwest are empty in 2013. The *"MX"* (potentially) mobile missile was a reality from 1986 to 2005. United States Air Force *Pershing* mobile missiles and mobile *cruise missiles* were deployed in Europe, as were the Soviet's *SS-20* mobile missiles. None were ever fired in anger at the other superpower bloc, and at least the *MX* was credited with helping to win the Cold War. Bob hit the bulls-eye on this factor.

III

Balance of Power. This was an area with which both Bob and John were concerned during the Cold War. John's concerns were with the conventional balance of tactical power in Europe. He felt the growing imbalance of air and armored power (in favor of the Warsaw Pact) might tempt a Western local area commander to use tactical nuclear weapons to save a deteriorating battlefield situation, thus unwittingly setting off nuclear escalation. He addressed this factor with his mid-1980s essay *Tactical Aircraft for the 1990s* (contained later in this collection).

Typically, Bob took a big picture view of the situation and concentrated on macro-political issues. He applauded the success of the Anglo-American (and larger *North Atlantic Treaty Organization* [*NATO*]) geo-political alliance in maintaining a general balance of power that the Warsaw Pact dare not cross too blatantly. He silently applauded Nixon's effort to befriend Communist China as a counterweight to the Soviet Union. And he also perhaps silently applauded Western political efforts to keep the Middle East powder keg in fragile balance. However, he rightly feared that geo-political balance would tilt against the West in the near future as southern/eastern birthrates outstripped northern/western birthrates. Bob correctly foresaw the rise of Islamic Fundamentalism as an upcoming challenge to Western stabilization efforts.

IV

Total War versus Political War. Bob realized the uselessness of pursuing the Western (particularly the United States) concept of "Total War" in the nuclear age. He recognized the political and contemporary dissatisfaction with the "political wars" waged from Korea to Iraq (with the exception of the 1990-'91 *Gulf War*, which sent petty tyrant Saddam Hussein reeling back into the Iraq boundaries). However, Bob saw the political wars' necessity in the age of potential total nuclear war annihilation; yet he still found any war a distasteful way to settle political disputes. Sadly, in the nearly 30 years since this essay was written, mankind has still not found a totally nonviolent way to settle the affairs of state.

V

Philosopher Kings and Queens. Interestingly enough, Bob independently picked up on a theme that John broached as early as his 1973 Capstone Project with the following statement:

"I think that there should be a board of qualified citizens, or better yet, several boards of qualified citizens, who could check not only military activities, but all workings of the government. This board should have complete access to all government buildings and documents."

This early stream of consciousness statement really encapsulated a thought that was slowly evolving in both men's minds: *"The thought* (or perhaps the fear*) that issues in government, and in the affairs of the wider world, had grown too complex for the 'ordinary people'"* (as represented by a Congress "by the people," and by extension, the administration that served the executive branch) *"to handle."*

As usual, Bob was a much deeper thinker and thought through the duties of the proposed "philosopher kings and queens" more thoroughly than John could ever do. The last part of his essay was filled with ideas of the roles these groups could fill.

Is the concept of elite teams of intellectuals, banded together to solve problems, coming to pass? Bob himself outlined some of the ways that these types of groups were beginning to function in the United States as early as 1968:

"We have already seen the emergence of the type of system that I envision but in a disorganized form. Examples include Lyndon Johnson's meeting with the "Wise Old Men" in March of 1968, the formation of the Greenspan Commission on Social Security, the Scowcroft Commission on

the MX missile, the Kissinger Commission on Central America, former President Ford's gathering of former leaders of the Western democracies in Colorado, and a Walter Cronkite-sponsored debate on the deployment of new missiles in Europe, to name a few."

Is this "Philosopher King/Queen" concept being adopted in other parts of the West? Let's take the experiences of our closest ally, Great Britain, as an example. As Andrew Roberts writes in his iconic *"A History of the English-Speaking Peoples Since 1900,"* in discussing military alliance protocols in the event of war in 1906:

"The decision to authorize these secret Anglo-French Staff talks was taken by a tiny group of Cabinet ministers. Other than [British Foreign Secretary Sir Edward] Gray himself, only the Prime Minister Sir Henry Campbell-Bannerman, the Chancellor of the Exchequer Herbert Asquith and the Secretary for War Richard Haldane knew about them; the rest of the Cabinet was kept in the dark. The absolute necessity to shroud issues of this importance in utter secrecy made it impractical to tell something as notoriously leaky as a Cabinet of over a dozen people. This decision to keep the decision on a ministerial "need to know" basis predated that of the six members of the Atlee Government in 1946 who decided to build the hydrogen bomb, the equally small number in the Wilson Government who in 1967 decided to buy the Chevaline nuclear deterrent, and the half-dozen members of the Blair government in 2003 who were permitted to see the Attorney-General's report on the legality of the Iraq War.

"When vital national interests are at stake, the English-speaking peoples have rightly tended to put security and operational efficiency before collective Cabinet responsibility."[1]

But is this right? Isn't this heresy for a democracy such as the United States to take some of the decision-making power "from the people" and invest it in an "intellectual elite?" Didn't we fight a war from 1775 to 1781, and again from 1812 to 1815, to get away from this and keep it from ever happening again "over here?" Pierre Berton, in his classic *"The American Invasion of Canada: The War of*

1812's First Year" sums up the position – and the dilemma – quite satisfactorily:

"Thus the key words in Upper Canada were "loyalty" and "patriotism" – loyalty to the British way of life as opposed to American "radical" democracy and republicanism. Brock – the man who wanted to establish martial law and abandon habeas corpus – represented these virtues. Canonized by the same cast that organized the Loyal and Patriotic Society, he came to represent Canadian order as opposed to American anarchy – 'peace, order, and good government' rather than the more hedonistic 'life, liberty, and the pursuit of happiness.' Had not Upper Canada been saved from the invader by appointed leaders who ruled autocratically?

"This attitude – that the British way is preferable to the American; that certain sensitive positions are better filled by appointment than by election; that order imposed from above has advantages over grassroots democracy (for which read 'license' or 'anarchy'); that a ruling elite often knows better than the body politic – flourished..."[2]

The answer? I leave that for the reader to decide. Part of the stimulation of intellectual review is reading differing modes of thought, then accepting or rejecting them in whole or in part. You decide.

Part Two: "The Years of Jubilee"

The first several pages of Robert Vining's 1985 essay involved the definition of the theory that Western economic cycles are dominated by fifty year spans, at the conclusion of which dramatic changes and corrections take place. Bob then did what he does best: explain difficult subjects thoroughly and succinctly. Bob explained the four latest American economic adjustments, not including the shift we were just entering in the early to mid-1980s as this essay was written. The first was the beginning of the Industrial Revolution in America, starting roughly in 1776-1780 and characterized America's independence, shipbuilding, and mechanization of the textile industry (the "Baltimore Clipper"-type merchant ship was becoming famous in Chesapeake Bay and the cotton gin was invented in 1793). This was followed approximately fifty years later by the 1830s "Second Bank of the United States" struggle between Andrew Jackson and Nicolas Biddle, and the Panic of 1837. The third restructuring was the "Gilded Age" of the "robber barons," the controversy of free coinage of silver versus "hard" gold, and was characterized by the various financial panics between 1873 and 1893. The fourth restructuring was the infamous "Great Depression" of the 1930s, during which a curious event occurred. America accelerated its mechanization and manufacturing base and became both "Breadbasket of the World" and the "Arsenal of Democracy" during the greatest depression the country had known. The point was that America always restructured and advanced, and the various fifty-year cycles always resulted in a higher standard of living in the end.

Bob then moved on to the meat of the essay:

"The industrial age was born in an economic shift, and in the current fifth subsequent restructuring shift, it will die. The civilization based upon fossil fuels, iron, and factory labor will be replaced by a civilization based on silicon, renewable fuels, and robots."

Bob could not have been more spot-on had he been looking through a time portal into the future! One look at Youngstown, Ohio, and the adjacent Mahoning Valley will show that the industrial age truly did die in the early to mid-1980s. This area is now known as *The Rustbelt*. Silicon for computer chips is everywhere and in everything. Ethanol renewable fuel plants dot the Midwest. Robots build the industrial output America does produce: factories that once employed thousands now employ tens and hundreds: robots do the work.

"This leads to the whole point of this paper: What are we going to do with today's 'horses,' [the powerplant of yesterday, now overtaken by mechanization and robotics] *who are **people**... The answer lies in developing all people to be able to function effectively in this new civilization that dawns before us. It will be a process of education and*

training ... the communications revolution now taking place will allow the educational process to be a lifelong experience."

Bob might or might not have grasped the power of the internet to educate. The internet certainly was in its very early stages when this report was written in 1985. When watching television today, nearly every station break is dominated by advertisements for on-line universities. Every computer comes with instructions on how to master the basics of getting the computer up and running. Virtually all corporations have in-house classes on how to operate both basic computer functions (e-mail, word processing, and spreadsheets) and company-specific functions. Almost all knowledge-based disciplines have computer-based degree/designation programs which provide broad-based knowledge of the discipline in question, and at very low cost. The death of the industrial age and the birth of the information age truly fostered an explosion in the availability of lifetime learning.

Finally,

"I want to try to explain what we do have to fear from the future. It isn't the new era we are entering, but the fragility of the ecological base that we exist upon."

Bob and John were both concerned with the havoc that the destruction or dissolution of natural resources might play upon the economic well-being of the United States during the mid-1980s. John's concerns revolved around oil, as was natural since the first oil crisis occurred during his freshman year in college and he had plenty of time then to contemplate it. This eventually resulted in his report, *The Rise and Fall (and Rise Again) of OPEC* (contained later in this compendium).

Bob, being both a farmer and historian, was concerned with the continued destruction of the agricultural ecology of the Midwest. I remember talking with him about the destruction of the ancient Fertile Crescent, and also discussing that the Midwest agricultural belt of the United States had lost between a third to a half of its topsoil between the beginning heavy agricultural production (roughly 1870) and 1980.

Bob may or may not have envisioned or noted the vast changes in grain farming in the time period between 1985, when we gave up farming, and his death in 2006. Autumn moldboard plowing, one of the chief culprits of topsoil erosion, is virtually no more. One can pass farm after farm and see perfectly good moldboard plows rusting in the weeds. Modern combines eject finely chopped corn, bean, and wheat stubbles, which wash into the soil during the fall rains to provide binding material which holds soil in place through the windy Midwest winters. Fall ground preparation, if it does take place, now involves "chisel-plowing," utilizing machines which are designed to mix earth and stalk residual output from grain harvest, once again to hold soil in place.

It is rare to pass an open drainage ditch or natural creek in the eastern Midwest that is not bounded by approximately 20 yards of natural grassland. The intent of this practice is that the grass will serve as a filter to prevent agricultural effluent or chemical runoff from polluting the topical water table.

Agricultural spills that were once passed off as part of the farming process are now treated as major ecological events. I witnessed an example of this a couple of years ago. A semi-trailer/tanker loaded with agricultural chemicals overturned adjacent to a small stream near my home. In the 1970s this would have passed as the "wastage" that was a normal part of farming, and life would have gone on the next day as if nothing had happened. Instead, in 2010, a federal government ecological team descended on rural "Podunk, Ohio," the area was roped off with yellow "do not enter" tape, the road was closed, the creek was dammed down-stream to contain the spill, and the entire spill site was treated as if nuclear contamination had occurred (complete with yellow rubberized haz-mat suits for the workers).

What a change (for the better) 40 years had wrought! I don't know if Bob's paper had any bearing, or whether enough like-minded ecologists were in the proper positions to render a difference, but our agricultural ecosystem is now being protected as never before. I think Bob would have been happy to be even a small part of this change.

FOOTNOTES

[1] Andrew Roberts, *A History of the English-Speaking Peoples Since 1900* (New York: HarperCollins Publishers, 2007), p. 84.

[2] Pierre Berton, *The American Invasion of Canada: The War of 1812's First Year* (New York: Skyhorse Publishing, 1980, 2012), pp. 313-314.

Bibliography

Berton, Pierre. *The American Invasion of Canada: The War of 1812's First Year*. New York: Skyhorse Publishing, 1980, 2012.

Roberts, Andrew. *A History of the English-Speaking Peoples Since 1900*. New York: HarperCollins Publishers, 2007.

Setting the Stage for *"Tactical Aircraft for the 1990s"*

John Vining wrote *"Tactical Aircraft for the 1990s"* in the 1984-1986 time period. At that time, Ronald Reagan, as Commander in Chief of the U.S. Armed Forces, was overseeing one of the (if not "the") largest peacetime military buildups in U.S. history. Many analysts were concerned with how much money was being spent and upon what it was being spent. During the refinement of the report, John was confirmed in his thought processes by such *Wall Street Journal* articles as *"Will Canadian Waters Become the Next Maginot Line?"* by Eric Margolis (*WSJ*, Friday, February 21, 1986, p. 19), *"After INF: Getting Our Planes Off the Ground,"* by John Train (*WSJ*, Tuesday, May 17, 1988, p. 26), and *"Hitler Used Arms Control to Advantage,"* by Robin Ranger (*WSJ*).

Also influential was the conservative magazine *Insight*, published by the *Washington Times*, with such articles as *"The Other Side of the SDI Debate,"* by Woody West (*Insight*, May 25, 1987, p. 64) and *"Imagining the Next War in Europe,"* by Philip Gold (*Insight*, February 22, 1988, p. 17.). *Insight* dedicated two cover stories in its March 9, 1987 issue to the subject *"Reagan's Military: Billions and Billions Everywhere, But Not That Much to Show."* Perhaps the piece which influenced John the most in this period was the book *"The New Maginot Line,"* by Jon Connell (New York: Arbor House, 1986.) The following quote from the back cover of this book seemed to summarize (in John's mind) all that was wrong with the 1980s military buildup:

"The greatest fallacy in modern military thinking is the notion that somehow high tech can do it all, that endless refinements in military hardware can be a substitute for the more traditional military arts. We may fondly imagine that scientists can take all the effort out of defense, that microchips and pieces of metal are all we need. But history suggests it is a delusion. Defense is not a video game. You do not win wars by pushing buttons."

These, plus other information, were the influences that caused John such anxiety and caused him to examine the situation. Without further ado, here is *"Tactical Aircraft for the 1990s."*

TACTICAL AIRCRAFT FOR THE 1990S

1985

By

John Eric Vining

With the recent Pentagon decisions to develop the F-20 *Tigershark* and the *Enforcer* only for the United States' allies and the incredible foot-dragging by the Air Force in adopting V/STOL aircraft such as the Hawker-Siddley *Harrier* as standard equipment, I felt I could no longer delay the production of this essay. This report serves to emphasize certain fallacies in military procurements taking place in the West today.

I am an amateur historian in addition to being an accountant by profession. I find the more modern periods for roughly 1846 to the present to be among the most fascinating of all eras of history. Naturally, with the technical nature of my education, I find the technical aspects of the modern, mechanized wars to be of great interest.

I feel the U.S. as a military power is forgetting some of the lessons of the past. An ironic note is that a plaque in the United States Air Force Museum at Wright-Patterson Air Force Base in Dayton, Ohio, states, *"Those who cannot remember the past are condemned to repeat it."* – George Santayana, 1863-1952.

Let me begin this essay with a brief review of the war in the air in World War I. Twice during that air war, the Germans wrested air superiority from the Allies through the introduction of technologically superior weapons – once through the introduction of the Fokker *Eindekker* with the first truly effective synchronized machine gun and once again through the introduction of the

Albatros fighters, with high performance, maneuverability, and superior firepower. Twice the Allies gradually wrested control back again. How? Through the introduction of very good, but not completely outstanding aircraft produced in vast numbers (an estimated 3 to 1 numerical superiority from mid-1917 onward[1]). The French Nieuport *11* and *17* ended the "Fokker Scourge" in mid-1916, and the French SPAD *XIII*, British Bristol *F2B*, RAF *SE-5a*, and Sopwith *Camel* appeared shortly after "Bloody April," 1917, to reestablish Allied dominance. In the late-1930s and early-1940s, Germany and Japan built the finest air forces in the world. Yet, by 1944, both were essentially destroyed as air powers. Author Martin Caiden, quoting Asher Lee, RAF, has stated the Germans, especially, could claim their single engine fighters were the technological equal of any plane in the world right up to the last year of the war[2] (the date is assumed to be around May 7, 1944). Indeed, the finest pistoned-engined planes operational in the European Theater during World War II in terms of pure speed, maximum altitude, and climb performance were the German Me109 K-4 and Focke Wulf Ta152 C-1, produced from October, 1944 onward.[3]

How could this startling contrast exist? First, both powers had put their faith in relatively small numbers of highly trained pilots, with few facilities for training large quantities of replacements. Second, neither power appreciated the value of true numerical superiority over its opponent. Only 10,449 Mitsubishi *Zero* (A6M series) and only 5,919 Nakajima *Oscar* (Ki-43 series) fighters were produced in total, and these were Japan's most numerous fighters.[4] A substantial majority of all *Zeros* produced were of the subtype "A6M5," produced from October, 1943 onward,[5] long after the critical year 1942 had passed and Japanese air superiority had been irretrievably lost. It is probable that only 1,634 of the truly devastating A6M2 series[6] were produced and available for the critical "1941-fall 1942" period, when this variant was by far the most dominant fighter in the Pacific Theater.

Similarly, although the Messerschmitt ME 109-series fighter was the most produced fighter of all time, with between 33,000 and 35,000 examples built,[7] nearly seventy percent[8] were of the "Me 109G" variant, produced from mid-1942 to late-1944. This was long after the critical 1940-1941 period. Adolf Galland, referring to this 1940-'41 period, states, "The Me 109 was at that time the best fighter plane in the world. It was not only superior to all enemy types between 1935 and 1940, but was also a pioneer and prototype for international construction. The Me 109 did not result from demands made by aerial warfare. On the contrary, it was a gift from the ingenious designer Messerschmitt, which was at first looked upon with great distrust and was nearly turned down altogether. It was put into mass production far too late. Had this stage been reached during the first two years of the war, it would have given the Germans absolute supremacy in the air."[9] Approximately 6,418 Me 109s were produced in 1943, 14,212 in 1944, and 2,969 in 1945.[10] The Me 109 was the only single-engined fighter in service between 1939 and late-1941 when the FW 190 was introduced. Therefore, it is probable that only 9,401 Me 109s were available in the period 1939 to 1942. This number includes Me 109Bs, Cs, and Ds, produced between 1936 and 1938, and either not used or used only sparingly in the very initial stages of World War II. Thus, the Germans were numerically inferior in fighters in 1940-'41 when their fighters were technologically dominant.

On the Eastern Front, the Germans were locally outnumbered 30 to 1 at various times from mid-1942 onward.[11] This is even more remarkable when it is noted that the Russian Air Force's front-line strength was virtually destroyed by the first week of July, 1941.[12] By mid-1942, the Russians had reached roughly numerical parity with the Germans by the introduction of the MiG-*1* and -*3* fighters, the introduction of the LaGG-*3* fighter, and accelerated production of the obsolete *I-15* and *I-16* fighters in late-1941/early-1942. By 1943 they had reached numerical superiority and technical parity through the introduction of the Yak-*1*, -*9*, and -*3* fighters, and the La-*5* fighter. How was this possible? The Mikoyen, Lavochkin, and Yakolev fighters were simple, tough aircraft, but more importantly, were easily mass-produced (2,100 MiG-*1s*,[13] 3,322 Mig-*3s*, 6,528 LAGG-*3s*, and 8,700 Yak-*1s*[14] were delivered by mid-1942) and were extremely well-suited for the climate and conditions in which they were to operate.[15] In contrast, much German effort was expended merely in just maintaining their generally superior aircraft, which were completely unsuited for the Russian climate and airfield conditions.

In late-1943 and early-1944, during their peak deployment in the West after the start of the two-front war, the Germans had as few as six hundred day fighters[16] to oppose the vast armadas of the Americans. After the early stages of Guadalcanal, the Japanese *never* operated in a position of numerical superiority in a major battle. Under these circumstances, even the elite of the world could not survive.

The United Nations forces in Korea found themselves equipped with the wrong aircraft for the conditions encountered. At this point, I am going to quote extensively from the publication *War Planes, 1945-1976*, by Bill Gunston, John Davis, and Richard Humble, all respected aviation authorities.

Regarding air operations in Korea...

"...the new types of aircraft were often ill-suited to the vitally urgent task of providing close-support firepower to the hard-pressed ground troops in South Korea. The new breed of jet fighters were fine and impressive aircraft, and such machines as the F-80 *Shooting Star*, F-84 *Thunderjet*, and F-86 *Sabre* of the U.S. Air Force and the F9F *Panther* and F2H *Banshee* of the Navy and Marine Corps appeared to be better than the scattered array of old machines deployed by the North Koreans..."

"But all of these aircraft were designed to operate either from aircraft carriers or from good paved runways of at least 6,000 feet long...on the Korean mainland there were no good permanent airfields at all, except for the airport at Seoul captured by the North..." (Aircraft carriers) "could not come nearer than about 70 miles, which is long enough when you are struggling back with battle damage...

"Moreover, the jet fighters were designed for air combat. Although some could carry offensive stores...they suffered from long takeoff and landing runs, rather sluggish performance when laden with offensive stores, and generally deficient range or endurance...

"This left only the piston-engined machines, of which by far the best were the F-51 *Mustang* and the F4U *Corsair* and the AD *Skyraider*. These could operate more safely from the short Korean airstrips, and carry good loads, and also had better flight performance, but they were also more vulnerable, and, when operated extensively, their pilots became exhausted...

"During the first months of the war a motley assortment of Allied aircraft operated much as had been done in Northern Europe in 1944-'45, except those in Korea were based on extremely poor makeshift airfields. The typical runway was pierced-steel planking (PSP) less than 5,000 feet long, with uneven surfaces, occasional bad bumps, and rough patches that often caused burst tyres (sp). Trying to operate the new jets from such strips was fraught with danger. Their laden weights were greater than for the pistoned fighters, say, 18,000 lbs., compared with 11,000 lbs. and their tyre (sp) pressures were higher, making them highly unsuited to PSP laid on uneven ground. Their take-off speeds were higher – say, 160 m.p.h. compared with 120 m.p.h."...(There were) "cost and logistic problems. Like all jets, the basic problem remained that fuel consumption was very high at low altitudes. The jet fighters had been expected to do dogfighting at heights over 30,000 feet, but over Korea they were crawling over the battlefields at 1,000 or less to try to help the Allied troops...the best answer was later found by Ed Heineman, designer of the Douglas *Skyraider*, who quickly conceived a small and simple jet, the A-4 *Skyhawk* – but Korea was over before it flew.

"Once battle was joined, speed seldom rose much above 450 m.p.h. unless one fighter tried to escape. Victory invariable went to the better pilot. The point should also be made that the American pilots enjoyed better and more lavish equipment than the Communists; but this was not always judged an advantage.

"The APG-30 gunfight was a case in point. It was far more costly than the simple optical gunfight fitted to the MIG-*15*, and might be supposed to have conferred a great feeling of superiority to the man using it. Yet to a considerable degree, the reverse happened. Korea was a rough, tough place, and the American pilots often began to wish for rough, tough aircraft. The feeling grew that the hundreds of items of equipment carried by the American fighters often did little more than increase cost, burden the aircraft with excess weight so that it could not outfly the MiG, keep the aircraft on the ground through being continually unserviceable, and general cause more problems than they were worth...during the remainder of the Korean campaign, American pilots were almost unanimous in thinking that the fighting capability of the aircraft would be improved if many components – even such useful ones as ejection seats and some of the guns – could be left off.

"Allied airfields were ill-guarded against air attacks, and a handful of Communist pilots were able to obtain disproportionately good results in individual night attacks...it was an uphill struggle to such aircraft serviceable.

"Korea is not a good place to deploy advanced combat aircraft. Its terrain is a mixture of abrasive sand and dust, waterlogged rice paddies, and rugged mountains. Its climate is highly variable... When this was added to the need to operate from rudimentary airstrips, which broke landing gears and lacerated multiply tyres (sp), the problem can be seen to be considerable. On top of all these problems was the fact that the industry supporting it was on the other side of the world.

"Korea was an unexpected and stern test with caught the technically superior allied nations off-balance. They never did produce the kind of aircraft for supporting a land war in difficult virgin territory. The capitalists did try to build aircraft incorporating Korean lessons, notably Heineman's Douglas A-4 *Skyhawk* and Johnson's F-104 *Starfighter*, but most defense money was lavished on nuclear strategic weapons tailored to a totally different kind of conflict."[17]

During America's involvement in Vietnam, two highly significant conflicts (from an aerial war standpoint) erupted between India and Pakistan. The first occurred in 1965 and the second occurred in 1971. Once again, I will quote extensively from *War Planes, 1945-1976*:

"Both countries used supersonic aircraft. The Indian Air Force used the subsonic *Gnat*, built in India, and the supersonic *Marut* and the MiG-*21* (both built in India). The Pakistani Air Force had a mixed bag of MiG-*19s* (bought from China where they were made), second-hand F-104 *Starfighters* and new *Mirage IIIEP* all-weather fighter-bombers.

"Many lessons were learned in the fierce fighting. One was that supersonic mattered very little, because hardly any pilot ever exceeded Mach I. In low-level ground–attack missions, few aircraft can exceed Mach I, and then only marginally. In dogfighting it is impossible to pull violent maneuvers except at modest speeds below 500 m.p.h., thus the extra speed of the MiG-*21*, F-104, and *Mirage* was not used. On the other hand, the older MiG-*19* scored heavily, with its robust structure, good maneuverability, and hard-hitting large calibre guns, with very much greater propellant charge than the ammunition for the equal calibre (30 mm) guns of the *Mirage*. This war also served to demonstrate, if any proof was needed, that the supposedly dangerous F-104 can be operated safely under difficult conditions. It has a higher wing-loading than any other production aircraft ever built, yet in the first ten years Pakistan lost only three: one flew though the debris of its Indian victim and the pilot had to eject, the second did not pull out in time when strafing a surface target, and the third was landing in a violent duststorm.

"Whereas Mach 2 suddenly seemed to be of no great advantage, the ability to turn tightly without losing speed became all important. Supersonic aircraft need great engine thrust to overcome drag at full speed, so it follows that at lower speeds they have plenty of excess thrust. This can be used to help push them around sustained turns, or other maneuvers, without the speed falling off. The little *Gnat* also did surprisingly well. Though it had a small engine, with no afterburner, it could maneuver very well, and was so small it was very difficult to shoot down. Thus the first real warfare between supersonic fighters showed that the 1950-53 vision of fighters streaking through the sky at 1,500 m.p.h. was not coming to pass. Instead, aircraft needed the traditional qualities of outstanding maneuverability, good resistance to battle damage, and by no means least, the ability to operate from short, rough, primitive forward bases and still remain serviceable."[18]

In Vietnam, with its aircraft not greatly opposed by hostile aircraft, the Air Force and Navy found the "fast movers" *(F-4 Phantom II,* F-100 *Super Sabre,* and F-105 *Thunderchief)* were ill-suited for low-level, close support activities. Once again, World War II-era aircraft were utilized. In fact, in nearly every major conflict since 1945, the West has reverted to World War II piston-engined aircraft in the absence of good, low cost, close-support tactical aircraft. Examples are the F-51 *Mustang,* the B-26 *Invader,* and the AD *Skyraider* in Korea and Vietnam, the British *Spitfire* used against insurgents in Malaya in he late '40s,[19] and the venerable *DC-3* as AC-47 *Puff the Magic Dragon* in the later stages of Vietnam.

The United States now finds itself in similar situations to each of these cases. We possess relatively few, highly technological, heavy aircraft, with a proportionally small reserve of spare parts. Some estimates place the West at a potential 4 to 1 numerical disadvantage to the Eastern Bloc nations. All this means the West will be outnumbered, its aircraft generally unserviceable, and it will be unable to maintain air operations if its long, hard air bases are destroyed or captured by enemy attack. As tanks are highly dependent on air cover, and because the West is also outnumbered 2.5 to 1 in tanks, this means its ground forces also face serious difficulties. For historical verification, note the German armor's difficulties with rocket-carrying *Typhoons* and *Thunderbolts* during the Battle of France, specifically in the Falaise Gap. Also note the German decision to start the tank-spearheaded Battle of the Bulge during bad flying weather, after air superiority had been lost by the German Luftwaffe in 1944 in Northern Europe.

In reflection of the history of aerial warfare, battle testing has proven that air forces which ultimately maintain air superiority are typified by the following characteristics. They possess:

1. Large numbers of individual aircraft
2. Large numbers of superiorly trained personnel
3. Ruggedly built aircraft, able to
   a. Resist severe battle damage
   b. Operate from short, rough forward bases
   c. Remain serviceable through relative simplicity of design, backed by a multitude of spare parts
4. Aircraft with excellent maneuverability and adequate, but not necessarily devastating firepower, coupled with adequate, but not necessarily extreme speed.
5. Facilities for the rapid training of replacement pilots and service personnel for those lost in combat

I think you will agree that the U.S. air forces are deficient in nearly all of these categories, except for the training of the personnel we now possess.

Other nations are recognizing these points and are designing aircraft accordingly: "Europe's first advanced combat aircraft is the *MRCA*, the multi-role combat aircraft" {known as the *Tornado*} "being developed by the U.K., Germany, and Italy working together in a tri-national company called Panavia. *MRCA* is the most refined and versatile military aircraft of its day, being designed for short rough-field performance, tremendous load-carrying ability, and outstanding performance at all flight levels. The two Turbo-Union R.B. 99 three-spool reheat fan engines are a vital factor in this remarkable flexibility, and the swing-wings, electrical signal flight controls, and advanced equipment also play their part. It can perform most of the mission of the F-111, though much smaller and under half as heavy."[20]

Another collaborative effort in Europe is the SEPECAT *Jaguar*. It "has great range and load and is simple and cheap. Though small, it carries as much load as a Phantom or a Lancaster over extremely long ranges."[21]

The U.S. has steadfastly refused to adopt simple, light fighters and fighter-bombers, with the exception of the A-4 *Skyhawk*. Small numbers of the initial versions of the Lockheed F-104 were adopted

(208 retained by the U.S., according to one source[22]). However the F-104G *Super Starfighter* was not adopted, despite the fact that the F-104 became the first aircraft ever to hold both the speed record (1,404.2 m.p.h., set May 5, 1958) and the altitude record (91,360 ft., set on May 7, 1958 and subsequently bettered to 103,389 ft. on December 14, 1959) at the same time.[23] Other nations quickly realized the potential of the F-104, with roughly 2,205 produced on license oversees.[24]

Likewise, the lightweight Northrup F-5 *Tiger* and the F-5E *Tiger II* essentially were not produced for the U.S. military, but for friendly allies. Nearly 1,475 F-5s and F-5Es had been produced as of 1976 overseas, with 675 more ordered. Yet the U.S. has only purchased a relative few F-5s (used mostly in war games because of its similar profile to the MiG-*21*) and two-seat T-38 *Talon* trainer version. This is so even though in war games the F-5s often outfly the F-4 *Phantom II*, bulwark of the West in the '60s and '70s, frontline equipment in many Western air forces, and the main second-line fighter in the U.S. yet today. In similar fashion, the improved lightweight Northrup F-20 *Tigershark* has not been adopted because of the presence of the General Dynamics F-16 *Fighting Falcon* in the U.S. arsenal. This is not to deprecate the F-16, which is in itself a step in the right direction. However, the F-20, with similar performance, is approximately $4-5 million dollars less per unit than the F-16. The U.S. would do well to include both in its arsenal.

This all sounds very grim, but there are some straightforward answers to the problems. Various officials have agreed with the President's efforts to build up our defense capabilities and restore military balance, while not necessarily supporting the President's defense budget "down the line." I ask consideration be given to supporting the following weapons and concepts at the expense of exotic technologies:

1) Continue to support research into new technologies, with relatively small production of the F-15 and F-18, with relatively larger production of the F-16 and F-20. There are two reasons for this:

a) We cannot allow ourselves to be outclassed completely in "leading edge" technology. Much good for other weapons systems comes from research into new weapons. A parallel can be drawn between the above statement and the research for space flight in the 1960s, which provided technology for many consumer goods of the 1970s and 1980s. Examples are microwave and computer technologies now in widespread use in consumer products.

b) We need relatively smaller numbers of "high tech," high performance planes to assure the survival of the relatively larger numbers of the "low tech" aircraft aircraft outlined below. These "high tech" aircraft are needed to battle the enemy's "high tech" weapons until both sides have destroyed each others' bases, and "high tech" aircraft on both sides are grounded for lack of facilities and serviceability.

There is historical precedence for this approach. The newer, higher performance *Spitfires* were sent to tangle with the German escort fighters during the Battle of Britain so the older, more numerous *Hurricanes* could win the battle by destroying the German bomber force. Later in that same war, a similar scenario occurred. In 1943-'44, the smaller, faster, high-altitude Messerschmitt *Me-109s* were stripped down to take on the American escort fighters while the more heavily-armed Focke-Wulf *FW-190s*, whose performance fell off drastically over 21,000 feet, could attack the bombers during the Battle over Germany.[25] The concept was valid, but do to the shortage of veteran German pilots by this point in the war, it was not successful. Caiden has pointed out that two pilots of equal ability, one in the *Mustang* and one in the *Me-109*, would have found themselves extraordinarily well-matched.[26]

2) Start or accelerate production of the following combat aircraft:

a) The Hawker-Siddeley AV-8A *Harrier*. Although derided as impractical, the V/STOL concept had been proven by the *Harrier*, which is operational in Spain, with the U.S. Marines, and is combat-proven with the British Navy in the Falklands War. At least one authority has stated the Western powers have made a serious error in overlooking the unique capabilities of the *Harrier*. Less than 300 have been manufactured in total at this point. The *Harrier* combines the flight characteristics of an air superiority fighter in matters of maneuverability, climb, and dogfight performance, with near zero field length, varied weapons capability, multimode (air/air or air/surface) radar, and general compatibility with small surface vessels equipped with small, flat operating plarforms.[27] The *Harrier* can be armed with two 30mm cannons, two *Sidewinder* air-to-air missiles, and various general purpose missiles all totaling between 5,600 to 8,000 lbs. It is capable of a top speed of 737 m.p.h. The *Harrier* can be hidden in dense woods and can take off from any reasonably hard surface only slightly larger than itself.

b) The *Enforcer*. This is a low-cost, close support prop-jet which could be available in numbers, very quickly. The *Enforcer* can employ modern missiles and with the proper engine, fly faster than the U.S. Air Force's present A-10 close support twin jet. It's much smaller, more heavily armed, and resists detection by heat seeking missiles by mixing cold air with hot exhaust and emitting it over a wing. It can be produced for $2 to $3 million dollars (in 1984 dollars), an unheard of figure in the field of heavily-armored close support weapons. The Air Force has rejected it and the Army is barred from using it by a roles and missions agreement.[28] Tests have proven the *Enforcer's* potential, and its bloodlines are exceptional, as it is derived from the P-51.

The *Enforcer* evolved from another company in the U.S. which produced a derivative of the P-51. "Trans-Florida Aviation" in Sarasota, Florida, was licensed by the Federal Aviation Administration to begin its remanufacture of *Mustangs* in February of 1959. Eventually the company adopted the name of Cavalier Aircraft and continued to turn out reconditioned *Mustangs* not only for sports use but later as counter-insurgency aircraft for Central American countries. These later modifications incorporated full armaments systems and updated communications systems. The aircraft were furnished to Bolivia, the Dominican Republic, Guatemala, and Salvador under the Military Assistance Program.

A further modification of the Mustang has been the Cavalier *Mustang III* which utilizes the Rolls-Royce Dart turbo-prop engine. Using this engine, the aircraft has a dash speed of some 470 knots. Standard armament is six .50 calibre machines guns and provision is made to carry 100-gallon drop tanks for increased loiter time.[29]

c) The successor to the Folland *Gnat*, the BAe *Hawk*. Although the RAF originally rejected the *Gnat*, developed by the renown H. P. Folland, the concept of the light combat aircraft of no great sophistication which might be able to achieve the same results at less cost was proven valid in the Indo-Pakistani Wars, as noted earlier, and the Nigerian Civil War of 1968-69. The *Gnat* was developed privately as was the Bristol *Beaufighter*, the DeHavilland *Mosquito*, and the P-51. The BAe *Hawk* is the natural successor to the *Gnat*, currently being produced in the U.S. and Great Britain. The following is a comparison of the battle-proven *Gnat* with the newer, more capable *Hawk*:

	Gnat	*Hawk*
ENGINE	4,320 lb. thrust	5,340 lb. thrust
WINGSPAN	24'0"	30'10"
LENGTH	31'9"	39'2.5"
HEIGHT	10'6"	13'5"
WEIGHT (loaded)	8,560 lb.	16,260 lb.
MAX. SPEED	636 mph @ 31,000	645 mph
CEILING	48,000 ft.	50,000 ft.
RANGE	1,180 mi.	750 mi.
ARMAMENT	1,000 lbs. plus	5,600 lbs. including
	2 aerial cannons	1 30mm cannon

These weapons systems possess all the prerequisites for survivability and operational viability in an all-out conventional war. First, they would be able to use any network of available roads as landing strips, with woods for cover. Again, there is historical precedence for this approach. The Germans used the tree-line Autobahn as an airbase after their permanent bases were under nearly constant attack by allied tactical strike forces in 1944-'45.[31]

Second, it has been proven that light aircraft can wreak considerable damage on a technologically superior enemy in low-level ground attack. In 1968-'69, the province of Biafra attempted to secede from the African nation of Nigeria. The stronger Nigerians rained death down on the Biafrans in a series of devastating bombing attacks. Carl Gustav von Rosen, a Swedish humanitarian, sought a means to neutralize the death-dealing Nigerian Air Force. He chose the MFI 9B, a light sport plane with a 100 horsepower engine, a 19-foot length from nose to tail, and a top speed of only 145 m.p.h. However, the plane had been designed in a ground attack version, with specially strengthened wings. Modified with an extra fuel tank and rocket pods for twelve 76mm rockets, the now-lethal MFI 9B had a range of 600 miles. In a series of hedgehopping raids, von Rosen rocketed military airfields, inflicting severe damage on the radar-equipped Nigerians.[32]

Finally, and most importantly, large numbers of these cost-effective aircraft can be produced relatively inexpensively, and pilots can be rapidly trained to operate them. This will go far to help assure air superiority, which the Russians used to defeat the Germans in the air in World War II.

3) Support the production of spare parts and an efficient distribution system. This is absolutely essential for success in winning an air war. Aircraft cannot support ground troops or shoot down other aircraft while sitting on the ground, and also become targets for enemy aircraft while remaining there.

4) Support expanded training facilities for replacement pilots and ground crew. This includes making wages and benefits for trained, veteran pilots and crew competitive with the private sector. Inexperienced aircrew has little chance against veterans. In World War I, novice pilots had an average life expectancy of three weeks after beginning combat operations.[33] In Korea, F-86 *Sabres* "could fight the MiG on roughly level terms. Flight performance was similar, though the Communist fighter was much lighter and thus was superior in climb and maneuverability. True figures will never be known, but the Allied claims suggest a kill ratio of 12.5 to 1 in favor of the F-86 *Sabre*. The U.S. Air Force's superiority over the MiG-*15* rested on pilot skill and experience."[34] It is essential the U.S. assures a well-trained force to operate its aircraft.

The above report is a mere outline of the many facts and figures which support my theories. These theories were developed over a twelve year period of study, and I am firmly convinced these concepts are valid and workable. Please consider this work very carefully, as the stakes in this particular game are extraordinarily high.

"Let none say, it cannot happen here." – Sophocles

FOOTNOTES

1. Lou Cameron, *Iron Men with Wooden Wings* (New York: Belmont Productions, Inc., 1967), p. 121.

2. Martin Caiden, *Me 109: Willy Messerschmitt's Peerless Fighter* (New York: Ballantine Books, a subsidiary Random House, Inc., 1968; Fourth Printing, April, 1977), p. 9.

3. Ibid., p. 130, and Enzo Angellucci and Paolo Matricardi, *World War II Airplanes, Volume 1* Milano, Italy: Europa Verlag, 1976. Published in the U.S.A.: Chicago: Rand McNally and Company, 1978), p.128, 176-77. Also, Bill Gunston, *An Illustrated Guide to German, Italian, and Japanese Fighters of World War II* (New York: Arco Publishing, 1968, pp.24-28, 58-63.

4. Enzo Angellucci and Paolo Matricardi, *World War II Airplanes, Volume II* (Milano, Italy: Europa Verlag, 1976. Published in the U.S.A.: Chicago: Rand McNally and Company, 1978), p.282.

5. Hedley Paul Willmott, *Zero A6M* (Secaucus, New Jersey: Bison Books Ltd./Chartwell Books, Inc., 1980), p. 63.

6. Ibid., p. 62.

7. Caiden., p. 13.

8. Ibid. p. 111.

9. Adolf Galland, *The First and the Last – The Rise and Fall of the German Fighter Forces, 1938- 1945* (New York: Ballantine Books, a subsidiary of Random House, Inc., 1965; Eleventh Printing, March, 1971) p. 10.

10. Caiden, p. 128.

11. Richard Humble, *War in the Air, 1939-1945* (London: Salamander Books, Ltd., 1975) p. 36.

12. Ibid., p. 36.

13. Bill Gunston, *An Illustrated Guide to Allied Fighters of World War II* (New York: Arco Publishing, Inc., 1981), pp. 75-76.

14. Russell Miller, *The Soviet Air Force at War* (Alexandria, VA: Time-Life Books, Inc., Third Printing, 1985), pp. 88-89.

15. Angelucci and Marticardi, *Volume II*, p. 237.

16. Edward Jablonski, *America in the Air War* (Alexandria, VA: Time-Life Books, Inc., 1982) p.90.

17. Bill Gunston, John F. Davis, and Richard Humble, *War Planes, 1945-1976* (London: Salamander Books, Ltd., 1976), pp. 10-14.

18. Ibid., p.36.

19. John Vader, *Spitfire* (New York: Ballantine Books, a division of Random House, Inc., 1969, Fifth printing, November, 1978), p. 158.

20. Gunston, Davis, and Humble, p. 61.

21. Ibid., p. 63

22. Enzo Angelucci and Paolo Marticardi, *World Aircraft – Military, 1945-1960* (Milano, Italy" Europa Verlag, 1978. Published in the U.S.A. Chicago: Rand McNally and Company, 1980), p. 98.

23. Angelucci and Marticardi, *1945-1960*, p. 99.

24. Ibid., pp. 98-99.

25. Caidin, p. 122-123; also p. 112-113; also p. 12.

26. Ibid., p. 9

27. Gunston, Davis, and Humble, p. 62.

28. Edward H. Sims, in the syndicated column "Looking at Washington," *The Enforcer Tests* (Willshire, OH: *The Photo Star*, Volume 88, Wednesday, September 5, 1984, p.1; col. 1.)

29. William Hess, *P-51- Bomber Escort* (New York: Ballantine Books, a division of Random House, Inc., 1971; Third Printing, 1977), p. 157.

30. Angelucci and Marticardi, *1945-1960*, pp. 192-193.

31. Heinz Nowarra, Edward Maloney, and the Aeronautical Staff of Aero Publishers., Inc. *Junkers Ju- 87* (Fallbrook, CA: Aero Publishers., Inc., 1966), p. 29.

32. Sterling Seagrave, *Soldiers of Fortune* (Alexandria, VA: Time Life Books, Inc., 1981), pp. 109- 143.

33. Karl Schneide, "The Great War" *Wings*, 13, No. 6, December, 1983), p. 48.

34. Gunston, Davis, and Humble, pp. 12-13.

BIBLIOGRAPHY

Angellucci, Enzo and Paolo Matricardi. *World War II Airplanes, Volume 1*. Milano, Italy: Europa Verlag, 1976. Published in the U.S.A.: Chicago: Rand McNally and Company, 1978.

Angellucci, Enzo and Paolo Matricardi. *World War II Airplanes, Volume I1*. Milano, Italy: Europa Verlag, 1976. Published in the U.S.A.: Chicago: Rand McNally and Company, 1978.

Angellucci, Enzo and Paolo Matricardi.. *World Aircraft – Military, 1945-1960*. Milano, Italy: Europa Verlag,1978. Published in the U.S.A.: Chicago: Rand McNally and Company, 1980.

Cameron, Lou., *Iron Men with Wooden Wings*. New York: Belmont Productions, Inc., 1967.

Caiden, Martin. *Me 109: Willy Messerschmitt's Peerless Fighter*. New York: Ballantine Books, a subsidiary Random House, Inc., 1968; Fourth Printing, April, 1977.

Galland, Adolf. *The First and the Last – The Rise and Fall of the German Fighter Forces, 1938-1945*. New York: Ballantine Books, a subsidiary of Random House, Inc., 1965; Eleventh Printing, March, 1971.

Gunston, Bill. *An Illustrated Guide to Allied Fighters of World War II*. New York: Arco Publishing, Inc., 1981.

Gunston, Bill. *An Illustrated Guide to German, Italian, and Japanese Fighters of World War II*. New York: Arco Publishing, 1968.

Gunston, Bill, John F. Davis, and Richard Humble. *War Planes, 1945-1976*. London: Salamander Books, Ltd., 1976.

Hess, William. *P-51- Bomber Escort.* New York: Ballantine Books, a division of Random House, Inc., 1971; Third Printing, 1977.

Humble, Richard. *War in the Air, 1939-1945*. London: Salamander Books, Ltd., 1975.

Jablonski, Edward. *America in the Air War.* Alexandria, VA: Time-Life Books, Inc., 1982.

Miller, Russell. *The Soviet Air Force at War.* Alexandria, VA: Time-Life Books, Inc., Third Printing, 1985.

Nowarra, Heinz, Edward Maloney, and the Aeronautical Staff of Aero Publishers., Inc. *Junkers Ju- 87* . Fallbrook, CA: Aero Publishers., Inc., 1966.

Schneide, Karl. "The Great War" *Wings*, 13, No. 6, December, 1983.

Seagrave, Stirling. *Soldiers of Fortune*. Alexandria, VA: Time Life Books, Inc., 1981

Sims, Edward H., in the syndicated column "Looking at Washington," *The Enforcer Tests* (Willshire, OH: *The Photo Star*, Volume 88, Wednesday, September 5, 1984).

Vader, John. *Spitfire*. New York: Ballantine Books, a division of Random House, Inc., 1969, Fifth printing, November, 1978.

Willmott, Hedley Paul. *Zero A6M*. Secaucus, New Jersey: Bison Books Ltd./Chartwell Books, Inc., 1980.

Postscript: Why Didn't Events Occur in the 1990s as John Projected?

Shortly after John completed the foregoing essay, two major events happened. First, in 1989 the Soviet Union and the Eastern Bloc fell, and VERY suddenly the U.S. didn't have a conventional European adversary anymore. Second, Saddam Hussein invaded Kuwait with the world's 4th largest army: The 1990-'91 Gulf War was upon us. And to many military analysts' surprise, there were the United States' high tech weapons, decimating Saddam's war machine. There for all to see were videos of America's laser-guided bombs (dropped by the high tech, stealthy F-117) unerringly hitting their targets, with the F-117 missions destroying Iraqi targets all out of proportion to their number of sorties completed. The F-15s and F-16s ruled the skies; the F-20 was not needed. There were the maligned M-1 "Abrams" tanks and the more-maligned "Bradley Fighting Vehicles" decimating the Iraqi's latest-generation Soviet-built tanks. The A-10 destroyed vast numbers of Iraqi soft armor and convoys; the *"Enforcer"* was not needed. The U.S. high-tech logistical system functioned spectacularly, moving a quantity of military supplies comparable to a city the size of Oklahoma City from the U.S. to the Middle East in a matter of a few months.

A veteran of the 1991 Gulf War noted on an internet forum:

"I do know that it was a massive shock to everyone when "stealth" aircraft, precision guided munitions, GPS navigation and weapon guidance, and US night fight capabilities were revealed in '91. The absolutely dumb-founded articles in the Russian Academy journals were nothing less than comical."

John (as well as many other military analysts) had fallen in the trap of "planning for the last war." Had the Soviet Union stayed together, and had the U.S. been compelled to fight them, perhaps the suggestions contained in *"Tactical Aircraft for the 1990s"* might have been useful! As it turned out, the suggestions contained in this report were prescriptions for fighting a war of an earlier era.

THE RISE AND FALL (AND RISE AGAIN) OF OPEC

1988

By

John Eric Vining

Introduction

Although one would not find the following definition of the "energy crisis" in Webster's Dictionary, this definition could easily be applicable to just about any time in the past fifteen years:

ENERGY CRISIS: A multiple-choice crisis (pick one answer in each category) caused by the current shortage (glut) of world oil supplies which has led to a sharp rise (fall) in the price of oil and threatens to exhaust the world's oil supplies (oil suppliers). Creates obscenely high (low) profits for the oil cartels, and strengthens (weakens) our enemies (friends) in the Middle East.

Barbara W. Tuchman wrote the Pulitzer Prize winning non-fiction work, _The Guns of August_, in 1962. In chapter three, she wrote the following characterization of Turkey in 1914 on the eve of World War I. Substituting the term "OPEC" for "Turkey" (or the "Ottoman Empire") and shortening the time frame references down to approximately five to seven years, she could just as easily be speaking about OPEC as viewed from the West today:

"Turkey at the time of Sarajevo had many enemies and no friends because nobody considered her worth an alliance. For a hundred years, the Ottoman Empire, called the "Sick Man" of Europe, had been considered moribund by the hovering European powers who were waiting to fall upon the carcass. But year after year the fabulous invalid refused to die, still grasping in decrepit hands the keys to immense possessions."

What is the Organization of Petroleum Exporting Countries (OPEC)? What economic factors affected its formation and organization? How could it rise to the pinnacle of power, then fall to the depths of near helplessness in less than 30 years? Most importantly, what is its future? We will explore all these questions in the next few pages.

What is OPEC?

Before we can truly understand OPEC, we must define some market structures which control the competitive positions to which OPEC aspires. Three terms are central to understanding OPEC:

MONOPOLY: A market structure characterized by a single seller of a well-defined product for which there are no good substitutes and by high barriers to the entry of any other firms in the market for that product.

OLIGOPOLY: A market situation in which a small number of sellers comprise the entire industry. Its characteristics include interdependence among firms, substantial economies of scale, significant barriers to entry, and products which may be either homogeneous or differentiated.

CARTEL: An organization of sellers designed to coordinate supply decisions so that the joint profits of the members will be maximized. It may also be defined as a combination of political groups for common action.

With the above in mind, we can now begin a definition of OPEC. The Organization of Petroleum Exporting Countries is a cartel consisting of thirteen nations that depend largely on oil exports for their income and foreign trade. It provides a common oil policy for its member nations. These members are:

1. Algeria	7. Kuwait	13. Venezuela
2. Ecuador	8. Libya	
3. Gabon	9. Nigeria	
4. Indonesia	10. Qatar	
5. Iran	11. Saudi Arabia	
6. Iraq	12. The United Arab Emirates	

At the height of its power, OPEC produced more than half of the oil used in the world. It supplied 85% of the oil imported by nonmember nations. Referring to the definitions above, OPEC operates in an economic climate of oligopoly.

Considerations in OPEC's Organization and Growth

The 1950s and 1960s

In 1956, several major oil companies ventured into the Middle East in search of new oil pools in that region. A record number of oil wells (58,160) had been drilled in the United States in 1956, but the time of easy, low-cost drilling in the continental United States was past. Since the huge gusher at Spindletop, near Beaumont, Texas, had ushered in the tremendous Texas, Louisiana, and Oklahoma oil pools on January 1, 1901, the U.S. had steadily depleted its reserves of easy, low-cost oil. The foray into the Middle East was successful, and huge oil pools were found in the region, especially in Saudi Arabia. The major oil companies, in conjunction with the Saudi Arabian government, formed the Arabian-American Oil Company (ARAMCO), with U.S. interests holding 60% of the stock and the Saudi government holding the remaining 40%. Other countries entered into similar agreements.

These new wells were very cost effective. The costs to construct wells, pump and store the oil, and ship it to markets were well below any other producer outside the Middle East. The Middle East states found themselves to be in a position of **comparative advantage** to every other oil producer in the world. With this comparative advantage, the Arabs found it would be to their advantage to specialize in the production and exporting of crude oil, since these countries could produce oil at the lowest **opportunity cost** of any producer in the world (they had virtually no other exportable products). As both absolute cost and marginal cost leaders as well, this advantage was magnified.

Further, the Arab states realized the oil industry was an **oligopoly**, in which a relatively small number of sellers comprised essentially the entire industry. An oligopoly is characterized by:

1.) interdependence among firms
2.) substantial economies of scale
3.) significant barriers to entry
4.) products of the industry which are either homogeneous or differentiated

In comparing the attributes of the oil sheikdoms to the characteristics of the oligopoly model, it can be seen that there are obvious similarities. There was great political interdependence between the individual states and great economic interdependence between the state oil companies and the huge multinational oil companies. Economies of scale are synonymous with large oil operations, because the large fixed costs of drilling and oil equipment become lower per unit costs with greater and greater production. Cost can be seen as a significant barrier to entry, as the fixed costs necessary to build a large-scale oil operation are substantial. Also, the United States government gave the Arab nations a great boost by enacting price ceilings on domestically produced oil. This discouraged oil exploration and exploitation in the U.S., and virtually assured that eventually, the Arab nations would control "swing production" of this essential resource. Finally, the crude oil industry is selling a basically homogeneous product. However, it was possible to introduce some product differentiation. For example, it was possible to differentiate "Arab Light" (the eventual OPEC benchmark crude oil) from such heavier oils as

"Venezuelan Crude," By and large, however, crude oil is crude oil, and there was little opportunity for non-price competition.

The Arab leaders recognized an effective way to coordinate their interdependent political and economic agendas would be to form a cartel, and to collude in setting price and production schedules. **Collusion** is an agreement among firms (or in this case, economic-political entities) to avoid competitive practices, particularly price reductions. The Sherman Act prohibits collusion in the U.S.; however, it is perfectly legal in other parts of the world, as evidenced by the formation of the Organization of Petroleum Exporting Countries in 1960.

OPEC's early history was one of dependence on the Western oil companies for technology, capital, and managerial abilities. OPEC quickly tried to flex its muscles in 1962 by pushing for a price increase, but was forced to back down by the powerful major oil companies. For the remainder of the decade, such leaders as Sheik Ahmed Zaki Yemani, Saudi Arabia's Harvard-educated Oil Minister and coordinator of the cartel, quietly monitored world events and maintained prices (see Exhibit 1). They watched price regulation in the U.S. drive the number of new wells drilled from 58,160 in 1956 to 42,600 in 1963 to 34,000 in 1968, thus limiting the amount of proven U.S. reserves. They noted the lack of funding, and thus, the slow pace of development, for such products as shale oil recovery in the American mountain areas and coal gasification technology.

OPEC also was increasing its managerial and strategic forecasting abilities through the efforts of such people as Yemani. They were well versed in economic principles. For example, they could visualize the West's **demand** curve was shifting to the right and how this affected the demand for oil. The following determinates of shifts in demand were analyzed:

1.) **Changes in the income of consumers influence the demand for a product.** As the West's income was expanding, its consumers were spending more on consumption. This meant demand would increase for oil to fuel the production of these consumer products.

2.) Changes in the distribution of income influence the demand for specific products. In the 1960s, substantial income was being allocated to capital formation. It was logical that the demand for oil would rise to fuel these expanding capital products.

3.) The prices of closely related goods influence the demand for a product. As there was no commercially viable fuel closely related to oil and gas, the low-cost producer would have a stranglehold on the market.

4.) Changes in consumer preferences influence demand. While consumer preferences were difficult to gauge, it seemed the preference of the West was for consumption and debt (note the rise of credit cards in the '60s). Thus, oil would be in greater and greater demand.

5.) Changes in population and its composition influence the demand for a product. The West, and particularly the U.S., was in the midst of the greatest "baby boom" in history. This would seem to ensure long-term demand for oil.

6.) Expectations influence demand. The West, and again, in particular, the U.S., was in the midst of the longest postwar economic boom then recorded. This too had a stimulating effect on the demand for oil.

OPEC further analyzed the **price elasticity of demand** for oil and found it to be **relatively inelastic**. This meant a percent increase in price results in a smaller percent reduction in sales (see Exhibit 2). OPEC analyzed the determinants of elasticity as follows:

1.) The availability of substitutes. As mentioned previously, there were no good substitutes for oil and gas in the 1960s and funding for technology to create breakthroughs was being held back.

2.) The share of total budget expended on the product. If the expenditures on a product are quite small relative to the consumer's budget, demand tends to be more inelastic. The U.S. had come to rely on OPEC for just 6% of its oil needs by 1973, but it was a larger share of home heating oil and was not replaceable elsewhere.

3.) Time and adjustment to a price change. OPEC could see that the West was complacent regarding oil supplies, and that most countries had neither a national energy policy nor the ability to switch rapidly to alternate, less ecologically acceptable fuels.

Political events caused the cartel to grow more militant. Israel's defeat of the combined Arab powers in the 1967 "Six Day War," substantially brought about by great amounts of U.S. economic and military aid, caused the Arab nations to cast about for an effective counter to the "Washington-Tel Aviv" axis. The continuing Arab support for the Palestinian factions, and the social and economic drag this entailed, meant increased revenues and a short-term solution to the problem were necessary. Finally, increased Islamic fundamentalism and unrest meant that increased revenues were necessary to placate the masses and let such rulers and the Saudi Royal Family and the Shah of Iran remain in power.

With all these factors in place, the OPEC cartel watched and waited, biding its time until the proper moment arrived. That moment was to present itself in late 1973.

OPEC Unleashes Its Power

The 1970s

On October 6, 1973, the combined armies of Egypt, Syria, Iraq, and Jordan struck Israel simultaneously on two fronts in a surprise attack. Armed with Soviet-made weapons, the combined Arab forces sent Israel reeling into retreat. Massive Western aid, including direct shipments of supplies, weapons, and intelligence from the U.S. and the Netherlands, tipped the balance back in favor of Israel. The so-called "Yom Kipper War" ended some three weeks after it began, with the Arabs winning in the early going and Israel pushing the Arab forces back to the original frontiers in the later battles. The war, for all intents and purposes, was a tactical draw. However, from a strategic standpoint, it was a decided Israeli victory, as the Arab nations had failed once more to push the Israelis into the sea and extinguish the nation of Israel.

Nearly overshadowing the Yom Kippur War was the decision by OPEC to unleash its "oil weapon" in support of the Arab cause. In the later stages of the war, OPEC cut off all shipments of oil to the U.S. and the Netherlands, and severely curtailed shipments of oil to Western Europe. Further, the individual OPEC member nations speeded "nationalization" of foreign oil producing assets and OPEC collectively nearly quadrupled the price of oil from roughly $3.00 per barrel in October, 1973, to $11.65 per barrel on December 31, 1973 (see Exhibit 3).

OPEC's timing was excellent, and their analysis of the economics of oil production was stunning. For several years in the early 1970s, the United States had been incurring a slowly increasing shortfall between domestic production and domestic consumption. Because of price ceilings on domestically produced crude oil which made it unprofitable to explore and develop oil fields in the lower 48 states, the U.S. had turned increasingly to OPEC. Europe and Japan had also turned to OPEC to fill their own shortfalls, making OPEC "swing producer of the world" in oil. This gave OPEC tremendous power, which the West blithely chose to overlook at the time.

Further, as has already been stated, OPEC operated in an economic climate of oligopoly. Again reviewing Exhibit 2, the conventional wisdom at the time was that the demand for oil was **relatively inelastic**. It was felt that the demand for oil, given the great necessity of use and limited direct substitutes, would not change greatly with price changes. That is, the customer would pay whatever it took to get whatever was needed. A weapon of tremendous economic and political power had been forged.

The impact on the U.S. economy was immediate and extensive. The result of the trade embargo and price hike was a massive transfer of wealth from the oil importing nations to the oil exporting nations. The resource base of the importing nations was severely contracted, as cheap oil was no longer available. Aggregate supply fell, but there was no decrease in aggregate demand. This generated a rise in inflation to 11% in 1974 compared to 6.2% in 1973, and the steepest recession (up to that time) of the postwar era from late 1973 to mid 1975. This "oil shock," combined with a fiscal policy of high tax rates and a planned budget deficit, served to make this a time of both economic stagnation and inflation.

The mid-1970s were a time of reflection on the significance of the '73-'74 "oil shock." The Arabs, particularly the Saudi Arabians, were astounded by the magnitude of the effect they had brought about. Sheik Yemani many times stated words to the effect that OPEC simply could not afford to severely damage the U.S. economy. After all, the oil purchases were denominated in U.S. dollars, and most of the dollars were reinvested in the West. Therefore, prices were relatively stable until the late '70s. It took most of that time for the West to adjust to the quadrupled prices; the costs were a drag on the Western economies.

In February, 1979, the Shah of Iran was overthrown by Islamic fundamentalists in a coup. During the uprisings, the flow of oil from Iran, OPEC's second leading producer at the time, slowed to a trickle. Later, adding to the pressures, a war broke out between Iran and Iraq in September, 1980. Once again, the West was faced with a production shortage. Once again, OPEC tripled prices in the face of large demand, from $13.80 per barrel in January, 1979, to $37.00 per barrel in June, 1980 (see Exhibits 3 and 4). And once again, inflation jumped to 12.4% in 1979 and 1980, from 7.6% in 1978, and the West tumbled into a recession. OPEC was at the height of its power to dictate world economic policy.

Market Pressures Strike OPEC

The 1980s

In mid-1980, Saudi Arabia was producing slightly over 10 million barrels per day of its "Arabian Light" crude oil at a posted price of $37.00 per barrel, representing the pinnacle of price and production for the "backbone" of the OPEC cartel. From this point on, oil suffered a precipitous slide in both production and price, reaching in early 1983 its first "bottoming out spike" for Saudi Arabia of 3.2 million barrels at a posted price of $29.00 per barrel (see Exhibits 4 and 5). Even this price was being widely bootlegged at prices as low as $20.00 per barrel. Production for OPEC as a whole was down to 14 million barrels per day from a 1973 peak of 31 million barrels, while weaker members were cheating on established quotas.

How did this startling change take place in less than two and one-half years? Very simply, market forces and the oligopoly model of the "kinked" demand curve began to function. Also, the demand curve for OPEC-produced oil had shifted to the left over the years. In reviewing the determinants of demand outlined earlier, we find there had been profound changes in all six factors. Regarding the changes in income, the 1970s had been a time of stagnation economically, and twice the economy had slipped into recessions. Thus, the lowered pace of economic activity spawned by the price hikes had lowered the demand for oil. Further, the U.S. economy had switched from a "manufacturing" mode to a "service" mode, further depressing demand. Next, the prices of other related energy sources had become more attractive relative to oil. This will be discussed more fully in a later paragraph. Fourth, changes in consumer preferences had vastly affected OPEC. During the late '70s and 1980, many countries and private companies had stockpiled oil as protection against future price shocks, preferring the stockpiling of oil at a relatively high investment price to an uncertainly of supplies. However, when interest rates skyrocketed in the early 1980s, with 20% rates available, the opportunity costs of holding these reserves had become overwhelming. From 1981 forward, these reserves were liquidated, flooding the market with previously stockpiled "old oil." Fifth, the great "baby boom" generation had passed out of the highly mobile 18-24 year old category, lessening demand somewhat. Finally, expectations greatly influenced consumer demand. As the realization struck home that long-term reliance on OPEC oil had declined (the U.S. in 1983 was importing 27% less oil, and OPEC imports were only 2.3% of America's needs), this realization reinforced the impetus to liquidate the "surplus" oil inventories.

The thinking regarding the price elasticity of oil changed dramatically. Until the early 1980s, it had been assumed oil was "price inelastic," and regardless of price, consumption would rise in conjunction with economic expansion. This concept was a casualty of the early 1980s. It can now be seen that the demand in an oligopoly is kinked when graphed (see Exhibit 6). At a high price, a whole range of substitute product options, which are marginal at low prices, become commercially viable. Those substitutes now even more viable were:

1965 – Great Britain discovers oil in the North Sea – 12 B barrels
1968 – The U.S. discovers oil near Prudhoe Bay – 9.7 B barrels
1974 – Mexico discovers oil in the Reforma fields
1974 – Technology toward shale oil recovery intensifies in the U.S.
1976 – Research into coal gasification intensifies in the U.S.

The OPEC analysts completely missed the significance of the economic concept of sunk costs. Costs that that have already been incurred as a result of past decisions will not necessarily be reversed when conditions change. When the decisions were made to build the Alaska Pipeline to pump oil from Prudhoe Bay to Valdez, to construct high technology North Sea oil platforms, or to build expensive transportation systems from the Reforma fields to the Gulf of Mexico, tremendous fixed costs were incurred. However, once these costs were incurred, it was relatively inexpensive to operate these capital assets. This significantly cut into the demand for OPEC oil.

OPEC misjudged the ability of the West to conserve. When oil prices were $34-$37 per barrel, it made sense to put additional insulation into homes and purchases fuel-efficient automobiles. When the price wars of the later 1980s took place, people did not rip the insulation out of homes or make a mass exodus back to gas-guzzling, less aerodynamic vehicles.

Next, and maybe most importantly, the United States government made tremendous strides toward reducing imports by abolishing price controls on domestically produced crude oil. The price of oil was allowed to rise fairly rapidly to the world level in the early '80s. The effect was immediately and dramatic. A total of 59,107 oil wells were drilled in the U.S. in 1980, shattering the previously mentioned 1956 record and immediately adding to U.S. reserves. Secondarily, allowing the price to rise added to proven reserves because the definition of "proven reserves" is "known reserves that can be recovered profitably using existing technology." With price at $37.00 per barrel, many of the existing fields in the U.S. which had already been "tapped" of "easy" oil became commercially viable once again.

I had a personal experience in this regard. In the early 1980s, I lived on 120 acres approximately 35 miles southeast of Ft. Wayne, Indiana, on the Ohio-Indiana border. In the 1880s, a large oil field had been discovered roughly 20 miles on either side of a line from Noblesville, Indiana, to Findlay, Ohio, in the Trenton subterranean layer at approximately 800-1200 feet below ground level. Our farm was directly on top of this pool. The pool was quickly exploited, and in the 1880s, Ohio became the leading oil producing state in the nation. Our farm had approximately 7 wells on it at the time, all powered with a single one-cylinder engine and pushrods (typical of the technology of that time). In the 1930s, with the onset of the Great Depression and the subsequent slide in aggregate demand, the wells were closed and capped. Geologists estimated only 10% of the oil had been recovered from the pool due to the archaic technology of the day. When prices rose to their astronomical early '80s level, I was contacted by an oil company, and the ground re-leased for oil exploration. The oil had once again become economically viable and recoverable with new, more efficient technology and a release from domestic price controls.

Finally, and possibly just as importantly, the laws of collusion in an oligopoly began to work as demand fell in '82-'83. Each individual oligopolist has an incentive to cheat on collusive price and production agreements. An undetected price cut will enable a firm to attract both customers who would not buy from any producer at a higher price and also those who would normally buy from other firms. At a lower price, there is incentive to increase production to maintain revenue. The demand curve facing the oligopolistic firm will be considerably more elastic that the industry as a whole. Each oligopolistic firm has two very conflicting tendencies when make cartels inherently unstable:

1.) To cooperate with others to maximize profits.
2.) To secretly cheat on agreements to increase its share of the joint profits.

Collusion theory states there are four obstacles to collusion which are relevant to the OPEC cartel:

1.) When the number of oligopolists is fairly large, effective collusion is less likely. (There are 13 members of OPEC, a large number for effective collusive agreement.)

2.) When it is difficult to eliminate secret price cuts, collusion is less attractive. (OPEC has no effective policing strategy, and contains such maverick members as Libya, Iran, and Iraq, which appear quite willing to cheat on agreements.)

3.) Low entry barriers are an obstacle to collusion. (With the elimination of U.S. domestic price controls and the willingness of the U.S., Great Britain, and Mexico to incur tremendous sunk costs to bring new oil to market, significant barriers to oil production in non-OPEC nations have fallen.)

4.) Unstable demand conditions are an obstacle to collusion.
(The Iran-Iraq war hung over OPEC's head throughout the
decade. This war held the mutually exclusive twin specters
of destruction of all oil facilities in the two countries, or
peace and a flood of new oil. OPEC in the 1980s faced
unstable demand for its product depending on which event
occurred. Further, the U.S. Strategic Oil Reserve, built up in
the late '70s, could always be liquidated, flooding the market
in the short term with a large supply of oil.

With rampant cheating on oil price and production, Saudi
Arabia twice rapidly increased production in the '80s (1986 and
1988) sending prices tumbling and enforcing quotas with is threat
as "swing producer" of OPEC. The first of these production
increases caused so much controversy that the brilliant Yemani lost
his job as coordinator of the cartel, and was replaced by Hisham
M. Nazer. During the writing of this report, OPEC once again
patched together an agreement on price and production between
such factions as Iran, Iraq, Nigeria, and the United Arab Emirates
(as of late November, 1988). As the 1980s draw to a close, it is clear
that OPEC operates in a significantly different and infinitely more
hostile economic climate than the heydays of the 1970s.

Conclusions On and Recommendations For the Future of OPEC…And the West

The 1990s and Beyond

Forecasting the future is always a matter of espousing an
informed opinion, and this section of the paper will be exactly this:
my opinions on OPEC's future, and the impact of OPEC's future
on the West. As OPEC moves into the 1990s, it can expect a three
stage future – a ten to fifteen year first stage, and two to three year
second stage, and an indeterminable but finite third stage.

The first stage of roughly 1989 to 2005 will be a time when the
"fabulous invalid still grasps in decrepit hands the keys to immense

possessions." OPEC will survive simply because it behooves many entities in the West for it to remain economically viable. Can one imaging saying this in 1973? The cartel will survive for three basic reasons. First, even though there has been widespread cheating on price and production quotas, this cheating has remained remarkably restrained in comparison with the history of previous commodity cartels. Even such mavericks as Libya and Iraq have been reticent in challenging the quota system too blatantly. And Saudi Arabia has been unbelievably pliant in its role as OPEC "swing producer," even considering the late 1980s production hikes to enforce quotas.

Secondly, it is in the best interest of such non-OPEC producers as Great Britain and Mexico to see the cartel survive. OPEC's survival helps keep the price of oil up to maximize the non-OPEC producers' profits, while enabling them to paint OPEC as the "bad guy."

Thirdly, Western bankers loaned billions of dollars, using projected oil revenues as security, to such seemingly rising powers as Mexico, Gabon, and Nigeria. The bankers have no desire to see these countries' economies founder and have the countries default on principal and interest payments.

So the invalid will stagger on like a boxer stunned in a middle round. But, like a boxer many times does, the cartel will gain strength almost imperceptibly as this stage wears on. This will occur because of the West's perplexing management style of focusing on sort-term results as the expense of long-term results. Over the past few years, a complacent America has taken the following steps:

1979-'88 – Environmentalists succeeded in delaying the construction and forcing the closing if numerous nuclear power plants

1981 – U.S. built auto fuel mileage requirements were relaxed to help the U.S. auto industry compete in world markets.

1983 – The Clinch River Breeder Reactor project was shut down.

1985 – There federally funded coal gasification plant in Beulah, ND, was closed.

1985 – Tax breaks for energy efficient home improvements were repealed.

1986 – The U.S. Synfuels Corporation was shut down.

The complacency of the U.S. and the West will allow OPEC to again become "swing producer for the world" as the fields at Prudhoe Bay, the North Sea, and Western Siberia wind down production. By the year 2000, OPEC will again hold a large percentage of the world's oil supply, and more importantly, will be making up shortfalls in domestic production for the Western countries. Around 2005, OPEC will be in a position to execute its third "oil shock." This period will only last approximately two years, as the West will be in a better position to react quickly to the shock (i.e.: oil leases on marginal oil fields are in place and infrastructures such as Mexico's pipeline to Monterrey are in place and can quickly be utilized).

Long-term, after the third price shock, OPEC's future will be dim. In 1906, a German economist named Robert Liefmann formulated the five rules of cartel theory, which have been validated by all subsequent experience. These rules were evidently overlooked or considered inapplicable by the founders of OPEC in 1960. Let's examine these rules as they apply to OPEC:

1.) **A cartel is always the product of weakness.** It would have been difficult to sell the West on the validity of this assumption in 1973, but from 1950 to 1973, the energy required to produce an additional unit of manufacturing output declined by 1.5% per year. Exhibit 8 shows that the decline from 1973 to 1983 was much more pronounced.

2.) **If a cartel succeeds in raising the price of a commodity, it will depress the prices off all other commodities of the same general class.** Foodstuffs, cotton, timber, metals, and minerals were at their postwar peak in the early-to-mid 1970s. Their prices have been depressed since that time.

3.) **A cartel will begin to unravel as soon as its strongest member – the largest and lowest cost producer – must cut production by 40% to support the smaller and weaker members.** I alluded to the unprecedented magnanimity of

Saudi Arabia as the most powerful producer earlier in this report. Reviewing Exhibit 5 again shows that Saudi Arabia has dropped production from a peak of just over 10 million barrels per day to a low of 2.5 million barrels per day. This unbelievable and willing flexibility has been the saving grace of OPEC thus far; however, even the Saudis have been exceeding their quota in 1988 in retaliation for widespread cheating. The agreement in November, 1988, should prove to save OPEC until the fearfulness of another price war dims, possibly in another 2 – 3 years.

4.) Any cartel undermines the market share of its members within 10 years or so. In 1973, OPEC supplied 60% of the oil supply of the industrialized nations; in 1982, this had fallen to 45%. The U.S.'s reliance on OPEC has dropped even more significantly (see Exhibit 9).

5.) A cartel permanently impairs the position of its product, unless it cuts prices steadily and systematically. As we have depicted with the discussion of the "kinked" demand curve, petroleum will lose markets quickly when it becomes more expensive, but will not regain markets by becoming cheaper.

I have no recommendation for OPEC. As can be seen from the conclusions drawn above, its fate is in the hands of oligopoly and cartel theory. OPEC <u>may</u> have one more era of glory, but long-term, it is bound to fail as have all commodity cartels before it. As for the West, I can make very strong recommendations. Do not become complacent. Use these next fifteen years to develop the technology to produce alternative fuels and sources of energy such as synthetic fuels, pure ethanol and methanol from grains, coal gasification, better nuclear reactors such as breeder and fusion reactors, and greater efficiency in buildings and vehicles. If the West fails to heed the warning and remains reliant on petroleum, one stark fact remains: there are 670 billion barrels of proven oil reserves in the world – and OPEC controls 450 billion of them.

Selected Bibliography

Gwartney, James D., Richard Stroup, and J.R. Clark. _Essentials of Economics_. 2nd ed. New York: Harcourt Brace Jovanovich, inc./ Academic Press, Inc., 1985.

Heilbronner, Robert L. and Lester C. Thorow. _The Economic Problem_. 2nd ed. Malvern, PA: American Institute for Property and Casualty Underwriters, Inc., 1981.

Leftwich, Richard H. and Ansel M. Sharp. _Economics of Social Issues_. 2nd ed. Malvern, PA: American Institute for Property and Casualty Underwriters, Inc., 1981.

Liefmann, Robert. _Cartels, Concerns, and Trusts_. New York: E.P. Dutton and Company, Inc., 1906.

McConnell, Campbell R. _Economics_. 5th ed. New York: McGraw-Hill, Inc., 1972.

Nault, William H., A. Richard Harmet, and Roy M. Fisher, Eds. _The World Book Encyclopedia Year Book, 1963-1988_. Chicago: World Book, Inc., 1963-1988.

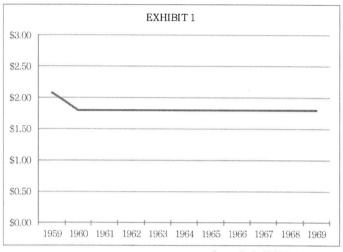

Source: Platt's OILGRAM Price Service

PRICE PER BARREL OF OIL – 1960s

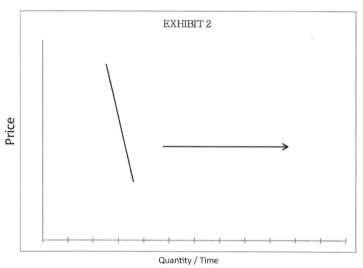

Source: Essentials of Economics

DEMAND FOR PETROLEUM IS **RELATIVELY INELASTIC**.
A PERCENT INCREASE IN PRICE RESULTS IN A SMALLER REDUCTION IN SALES.

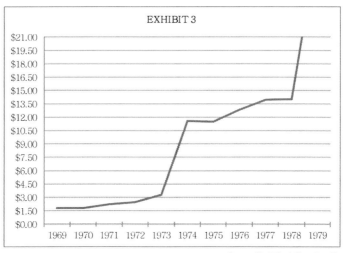

PRICE PER BARREL OF OIL - 1970s

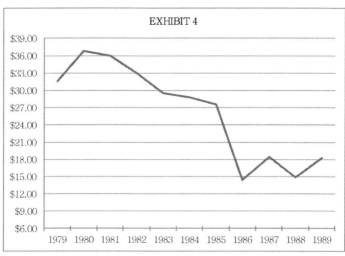

PRICE PER BARREL OF OIL - 1980s

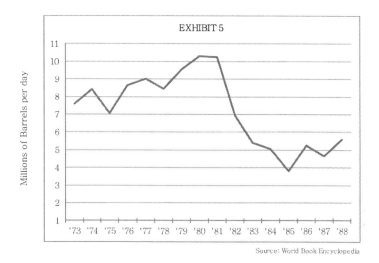

Source: World Book Encyclopedia

SAUDI ARABIAN OIL PRODUCTION: 1973 – 1988

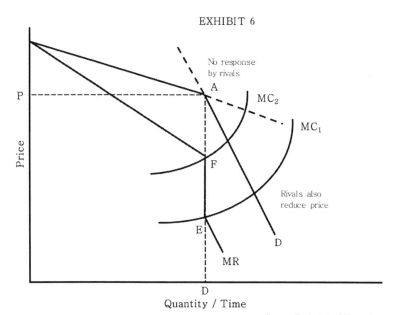

Source: Essientials of Economics

THE KINKED DEMAND CURVE

EXHIBIT 7

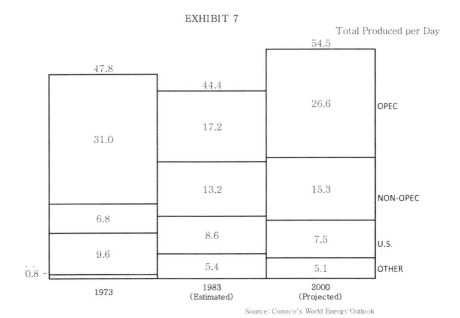

Total Produced per Day

WORLD OIL SUPPLY (IN MILLONS OF BARRELS PER DAY)

Source: Conoco's World Energy Outlook

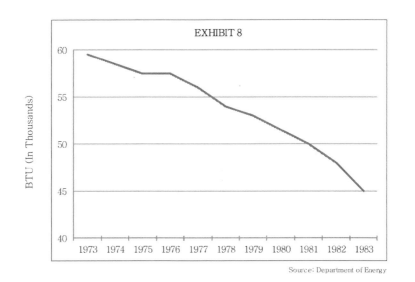

U.S. ENERGY CONSUMPTION PER GNP DOLLAR (1972 DOLLARS)

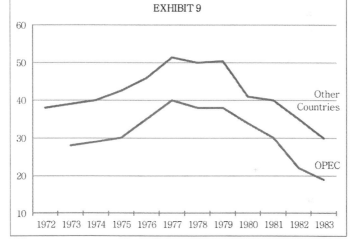

EXHIBIT 9

Other
Countries

OPEC

Source: Department of Energy

U.S. OIL IMPORTS (AS A PERCENTAGE OF CONSUMPTION)

POSTSCRIPT: THE (RISE AGAIN) OF OPEC

2013

(A follow-up to *"The Rise and Fall (and Rise Again) of OPEC"*, December, 1988)

By

John Eric Vining

It has been twenty-five years since John Vining completed his article on the varying fortunes of the Organization of Petroleum Exporting Countries (OPEC). At this anniversary, it is perhaps appropriate to review the historical results of the past twenty-five years in comparison with John's predictions.

John proved to be a very accurate prognosticator of the future, particularly as to the timing and effect of oil prices and production on the fortunes of OPEC and United States. However, he was only partially accurate as to specific causes of the various rises and falls in price and production. This may be understandable, given the vast array of factors that go into the pricing and production of petroleum. Let's take a look at some specific phrases from the 1988 article and some outcomes.

"As OPEC moves into the 1990s, it can expect a three stage future: a ten to fifteen year first stage, a two to three year second stage, and an indeterminate but finite third stage."

John hit the timing of the approximately fifteen year "lay-low" period of OPEC (from 1988-'90 to 2005) very accurately. Prices in historical, inflating dollars stayed relatively stagnant during 1990-2005. Notable exceptions to this period of relative stability were 1) a substantial price collapse following the end of the "Iran-Iraq War" in 1988 (with the subsequent resumption of significant oil production for both countries), 2) a price spike during the late 1990-early 1991 "Gulf War," and the uncertainty in supplies this engendered, and 3) another collapse caused by an unexpected and steep drop in demand due to the Asian Financial Crisis of 1997-'98.

"A cartel will begin to unravel as soon as its strongest member – the largest and lowest cost producer – must cut production by 40% to support the smaller and weaker members."

(Subsequent related quote:)

"Saudi Arabia has been unbelievably pliant in its role as OPEC "swing producer," even considering... [the recent] production hikes to enforce quotas."

During the twenty-five years since 1988, in continued defiance of a major rule of cartel theory, Saudi Arabia remained incredibly magnanimous in its role as "swing producer" of OPEC, and of the larger world. Many times during this period, the Saudis exercised an incredibly subtle, nuanced approach to commodity management to maintain the viability of OPEC's pricing and production, while facilitating relatively predictable oil production and prices for the industrialized world. The world in general and OPEC in particular owe Saudi Arabia a major debt of gratitude for its efforts and real contributions in promoting whatever modicum of economic stability the world has enjoyed in the past twenty-five years.

"...the cartel will gain strength almost imperceptibly as this stage wears on...because of the West's perplexing management style of focusing on short-term results at the expense of long-term results. The complacency of the U.S. and the West will allow OPEC again to become 'swing producer to the world'...By the year 2000, OPEC...will be making up shortfalls in domestic production for the Western countries."

The United States' oil production peaked at 9.5 million barrels per day in 1970, and fell steadily thereafter. In 1993, the number of barrels of oil produced domestically and the number of barrels of oil imported crossed paths at not quite 7 million barrels of oil per day. By the year 2000, the shortfall between U.S. domestic production and imports was approximately 3 million barrels of oil per day and climbing rapidly. OPEC made good a significant portion of this shortfall. Its ability to once again significantly influence world oil prices and production as "swing producer" was greatly enhanced.

The United States, as the largest and most diverse economy in the world during this period, was not as complacent as John had feared. True, nuclear power did not advance as an increasing venue of power for the West – the "Three Mile Island" and "Chernobyl" nuclear plant disasters were just too mentally grievous in the public's eyes for the industry and the world to overcome. However, the United States in particular made significant strides in extracting ethanol from grains, and particularly world-changing strides in drilling for and recovering shale oil from its Western and Rocky Mountain states. It has been predicted that the United States could turn from a net importer to a net exporter of petroleum by the 2020-2023 period, on the basis of shale oil recovery technology alone.

"Around 2005, OPEC will be in a position to execute its third "oil shock." This period will only last approximately two years..."

..."a two to three year second stage..."

As to the timing and duration of the second stage, John was very accurate once again. Oil prices were approximately $25.00 per barrel in January, 2005. Shortly thereafter, OPEC members cut the organization's crude oil production by 1.2 million barrels per day, effective November 1, 2006; and a further 500,000 barrels per day, effective February, 2007. With high demand from a galloping Western economy, coupled with huge demand from a rapidly developing Pacific Rim (particularly China), oil prices moved from approximately $25.00 per barrel in January, 2005, to a peak of just over $130 per barrel in July, 2008. (John opines that this qualifies as an oil shock!) OPEC's Net Oil Export Revenues peaked at approximately $525 billion in mid-2005 – only about $50 billion short of its previous 1980 high. Oil prices reached their high in July, 2008, and fell steadily thereafter, greatly affected by the onset of *"The Great Recession." "OPEC* [did] *have one more era of glory,"* as predicted.

In summary, John did not (and perhaps could not) predict several of the major factors that influenced world oil pricing and production in the 25 years between the end of 1988 and the end of 2013. Some factors were almost a given: political instability in the Middle East (and the larger Third World), highlighted by:

- Iraq's invasion of Kuwait
- The subsequent 1990-'91 Persian Gulf War
- The late-1991 dissolution of the Soviet Union (this particular instability was much unanticipated, heavily affecting non-OPEC production)
- The Nigerian oil workers' strike and overall unrest
- Continuing instability fostered by the rogue political regimes of Iraq, Libya, Iran, and Pakistan, highlighted by the September 11, 2001 terrorist attack on the World Trade Center in New York.
- Venezuelan political unrest

However, quite surprising was the major effect of natural and semi-natural disasters, which were relatively unforeseen or predicted:

- The shipwreck of the oil tanker *"Exxon Valdez,"* adding impetus to increased environmentalist concerns and costs.
- The effects of Hurricanes Ivan, Cindy, Dennis, Katrina, and Rita (plus a huge explosion of a Shell Oil rig) in the Gulf of Mexico, seriously disrupting the United States' ability handle and process oil.

And finally, the greatly surprising effect of one factor which John only briefly alluded to in his 1988 report, and had relatively discounted as a management tool:

- The political will and ability of the United States to manipulate its Strategic Petroleum Reserve (SPR) to offset the effect of OPEC production cuts. The extent of the use of this factor had a relatively unforeseen (but positive, for the U.S. and the West overall) impact in keeping oil prices and production from gyrating wildly during the periods of the greatest political and natural instability.

To close, John Vining's 1988 report, *"The Rise and Fall (and Rise Again) of OPEC"* was a reasonably accurate foretelling of the period from 1988 to 2013. John adds a personal note that he had hours of enjoyment in the past 25 years, gathering articles and assessing the progress of his predictions.

"...and an indeterminable, but finite third stage." History is being recorded as we read these pages!

Setting the Stage for "Historical Characters"

History was always important for both Bob and John. During the years they farmed together on the small farm in northern Mercer County, Ohio, they spent many hours discussing history while completing the various chores around the farm. Bob and John tended to approach problems from different vantage points, so the discussions were always lively, and sometimes bordered on "heated."

Our father was also interested in history, having been a participant in the greatest war the world has ever known, World War II. As soon as John learned to read with a degree of comprehension, Dad started to bring home history books as gifts for him to read. Two of the first, for John's 11th birthday, were *"Heroes in Blue and Gray,"* by Robert E. Alter and *"The Civil War – A History,"* by Harry Hansen. The die was cast. Soon John was using some of his own cash to buy military history books – the first being *"The Balloon Buster,"* by Norman S. Hall. John soon found that certain historical characters caught his attention and fascination. He studied about their lives and careers, and sometimes wrote about what he had discovered.

A few of those character studies are included in this compendium of works. I hope you find the diversity of subjects and stories interesting and entertaining.

Book Review: "American Capitalism"

By

John Kenneth Galbraith

Reviewed By

John Eric Vining

1976

John Kenneth Galbraith is one of the most respected economists in the world today. His other written works include "The Affluent Society" and "The Great Crash."

This book deals with the fall of the classical system of economics and the rise of Keynesian economics.

Picture yourself in the late 1940s and early 1950s. Business is great and the newly restructured economy is working fine. But deep down inside there is a fear – the fear that the United States' economic system is inherently unstable. This is the fear that *many* businessmen had at this time. The Great Depression still was an ugly blot on their memories. Therefore, although business was stable, it was growing very slowly. Many businesses held a lot of liquid assets and feared rapid expansion.

Let us look at the political aspects of this fear. The liberal has always feared that too much power was in the hands of too few businesses. This fear produced the Sherman Anti-Trust Act in the late 1800s and early 1900s. After a government study was released in 1947 saying that the 113 largest businesses in the United States controlled 46% of all property, plants, and equipment, his fears were once again aroused.

The conservative fears government intervention of private enterprise. During the '30s and early '40s, he saw government power over business reach astronomical proportions. He feared socialism was near. Therefore he was reluctant to give up any power he had.

To understand these fears more fully, let us now examine the basis on which our economy was built. It was called the classical system. The classical system of economic theory had been imported from England in the 1870s to give some rhyme & reason to our rapidly expanding economy. It was based on four basic beliefs. The first and probably most important belief was that the economy had to have competition to survive. Competition in its purest sense meant that there were so many buyers and sellers that no one buyer or seller could influence the market price to any great extent. The second cornerstone of the classical system was Say's Law. Say's Law stated that the act of producing goods automatically produces purchasing power for buying them. If saving happened to take place, the interest rate served as a device for controlling it. The third basic theory was that the price set by free competition is the lowest that is possible. Since no individual buyer or seller can influence the market, the producer must adapt his own business costs so he can charge the going rate. The final belief was that labor would always be at full employment because if somebody was out of work, he could always find another job by lowering the wage he charged to the employer.

The competitive model had two inherent flaws which caused the final downfall in the 1930s. However, the roots of these problems went back many years before that. The problems were the lack of precise performance by the competitive model and the lack of competition.

In the late 1800s the first of the great industrial giants came into being. Soon three or four of these giants came to control certain industries and an oligopoly was started. An oligopoly is defined as imperfect competition where there is something less than complete monopoly and something less than pure competition. This in later years would become a characteristic of big business in the United States. An industry would be dominated by 3 or 4 industrial giants surrounded by a small fringe of successful but very small businesses. Slowly the giants would pull away because they had the advantage of volume pricing and technological innovativeness. The small businesses would slowly die out until just the big three or four were left. A good example of this was the auto industry. In 1947 the market was dominated by General Motors, Ford Motors, and Chrysler, surrounded by Packard, De Soto, Kaiser, Nash, Hudson, and Studebaker. Now all that is left is General Motors, Ford, and Chrysler, along with a conglomerate called American Motors.

In the 1920s business thinking changed in the area of price-making. Competition had once been relied upon to set prices. However, free competition had long since departed the American business scene and a new way had to be found to set prices. Since there were only 3 or 4 sellers, a price cut by one might be followed by a price cut by others. In fact, it was entirely possible that all would "follow the leader." This could be financially ruinous to the industry because eventually the selling price would not cover the expenses and the businesses would go under. Therefore, the industrial giants got together and set a price that gave them all a profit and mutually benefited them all. This raised a storm of controversy and many of the businesses were prosecuted. However, the monetary fines that were leveled against them were a small price to pay for financial solvency.

Now that price cutting was no longer a means of attracting customers, a new way had to be found. This came in the form of advertising. Since a Ford is basically the same as a Chevy and they are priced essentially the same, the only way to sell a Ford is to advertise all the extras that come with it in the hope of attracting customers.

The American businessman was profiting, even though his power and economic structure had been exposed. He was safe mainly because there was nothing anyone could do to stop him. The anti-trust acts were comparable to a slap on the hand and the liberals were too weak in Congress to get much of anything done.

The Great Crash of 1929 caught many businessmen by surprise. Many were so-called paper-millionaires who had built their millions on speculation and had very little liquid assets. Other businessmen found that they could no longer finance their operation because of receivable lag and the tight money crunch. The classical system had fallen because its two greatest faults had been exposed. Competition had long since become a thing of the past and businessmen had failed to pay strict attention to the details of the precise classical system.

Economists continued to follow the classical thinking until well into the 1930s, when John Maynard Keynes wrote a book called "The General Theory of Employment, Interest, and Money." In this book he offered a new theory to replace the classical theory of economics. It differed greatly with the traditional beliefs and at first was ridiculed. However, it gained wide acceptance in the Executive Branch of the United States government and was put into practice.

The Keynesian theory was based on the following points. First, Keynes stated that depression, unemployment, and inflation were in no way abnormal to our economy. This sharply differed with the classical theory which said that depression and unemployment were virtually impossible. Since the classical system had been set up, however, trade unions and workers' unions had been set up which made it hard for workers who were unemployed to cut their wage. Therefore unemployment, and eventually, large scale depression were entirely possible.

Secondly, the act of producing and selling goods does put money into someone's hands, but it does not always get into the individual worker's hands. At the time of the inception of the classical system, huge corporations were virtually unheard of. Much of the profit of a corporation takes the form of retained earnings, or stockholders' dividends, which are not immediately put back into circulation. There is a great possibility that a cash flow lag may occur.

The third point Keynes made was that the interest rate does not influence saving and borrowing as greatly as the classical economists said it did. If an individual has money, he is not going to spend it just because interest rates are low at the current time. Conversely, if a business is on an expansion schedule, they are not going to hold up everything because of high interest. Thus the possibility of a money crunch was clearly stated.

Fourth, Keynes stated that technological advance had slowed because all the simple things that merely required innovative thought had been invented. Only the huge businesses had the excess resources to construct laboratories. Therefore, when a small business's market slowed, he had nothing to do but go out of business because he could not research out a new product. This business failure, on a large scale, was potentially damaging to the economy.

Strangely, liberals were the first group to accept this theory. The Keynesian theory openly stated that oligopoly was rampant in our economy, and that much power was in the hands of a very few people. However, the liberal was more open-minded at this time, and was willing to try anything to break the depression. Liberal-minded President Franklin D. Roosevelt was in office at this time, and his acceptance of this theory and its use in the economy were instrumental in breaking the depression's back.

John Kenneth Galbraith came up with a solution on how to deal with the oligopoly which was now an accepted part of the United States economy. He called it the theory of countervailing power. This theory states that a small group of sellers is counteracted by a small group of buyers. This theory came into being because the competitive model, on which there were many sellers and many buyers, could no longer be counted upon to set prices. By banding together, buyers could demand certain things and the seller was compelled to listen, or lose an important share of his market.

A good example of this theory of countervailing power was the American labor market. When industry dealt with each worker personally, it treated him badly (seventy-two hour weeks, 12-hour days). However, when labor banded together, the businessman had to listen or he had a strike on his hands.

An opposite example is American agriculture. For years farmers had tried to band together to influence the market. Due to the acts of independents, the union effort has failed and farmers have very little more power over markets than they did decades ago.

Strangely enough, government in the United States was slow to accept the concept of countervailing power. Whenever a case went to court, the rulings usually favored the holders of original power;

namely, the industries. An exception to this rule has been the Taft-Hartley Act, which set up boundaries on how far both industries and unions could go.

Galbraith also dealt with the power structure of United States business. He called the "decentralized decision," decisions made by individual business heads, the backbone of free enterprise. As long as business heads made wise and fair decisions, there would be no reason for government intervention; therefore, businessmen's rights would be protected. However, the more government intervention, the greater the chance for creeping socialism to take over.

Galbraith also emphasized the importance of the "governmental" (or "centralized") decision. The centralized decision is important because faulty decision-making on the part of the government could lead to the emergence of huge monopolies. These monopolies would be financially disastrous to the economy.

In the final part of the book, Galbraith voiced a warning. The warning was that too much demand for goods is a fault of Keynes's theory. Countervailing power is useless in a heavy demand situation and spiraling inflation is the result. In the late forties, businesses held a lot of liquid assets in fear of another depression. Business growth was slow but steady. Then, as the fear of depression lessened, business expanded rapidly and the demand for capital goods increased. The result was slow but steady inflation. Galbraith advocates restraint in demand to help maintain a healthy economy.

This book impressed me in many ways. One way was its detailed analysis of the classical and Keynesian systems. The book, although at times very deep and consequently boring, was very detailed and exact. Another part of the book that intrigued me was the last part of the book. Here is John Kenneth Galbraith in 1950, telling what is happening in the 1970s, and doing it with striking accuracy. But even Galbraith couldn't have seen the materials shortages and freezes which have led to the current recession. However, for analyzing a problem and tackling it, John Kenneth Galbraith stands among the giants.

WILLIAM O. DOUGLAS

2002

By

John Eric Vining

William Orville Douglas was, in my opinion, the most influential Supreme Court Justice in American history. Just the fact that Mr. Douglas served on the Court longer than any other in history (36 years) would qualify him as influential, given the sheer volume of decisions a jurist would render in such an extended time. However, the period over which Justice Douglas presided (1939 to 1975) was one of the most controversial in America's history. That Douglas played such a pivotal role in the dramatic decisions of such a period qualifies him as the most influential justice in history.

Interestingly, Mr. Douglas would have played a vocal role in the development of the philosophies in the middle part of the 20th Century even had he not been a Supreme Court Justice. As an author, Douglas' books included *The Anatomy of Liberty* (1963) and *Points of Rebellion* (1970). Each in its own way was a significant contribution to the development of mid-20th Century liberal thought.

It was as a Supreme Court Justice that William O. Douglas had his greatest impact on American history. If one word could describe Mr. Douglas' approach to American legal theories, that word would be his espousal of the concept of "*freedom*." Douglas commented upon some of the most important definitions of freedom this country has ever seen, being noted as a staunch supporter of civil rights and civil liberties.

Douglas assumed his place on the Court during the far-reaching events of the mid-20th Century. During the early-1940s, Douglas viewed World War II - the great contest between democracy and freedom versus fascism and suppression – from the Court bench. His legal work in support of the United States helped affirm American freedoms while contributing to final victory. In the late-1940s and 1950s, Douglas helped define freedom and civil liberties for organized labor through interpretations of such legislation as the *Taft-Hartley Act of 1947*. Upon the publication of Rachel Carson's *Silent Spring* (1962), Douglas became a rare early high-profile supporter, calling it "the most important chronicle of this century for the human race." He anticipated the coming environmental movement, which sought to guarantee the freedom of future generations to enjoy clean and abundant natural resources, by a full half-decade.

However, it was Douglas' decisions in what I feel were the two most monumental Supreme Court cases of the 20th Century which secured his place in history. Douglas supported the unanimous Court decision in the landmark *Brown vs. Board of Education of Topeka* (1954). In this decision, the Court found that racial segregation in public schools was unconstitutional, giving momentum to the civil rights movement for African-Americans – a substantial portion of United States' citizenry.

Near the end of his career, Justice Douglas voted with the majority in another landmark decision. *Roe vs. Wade* (1973) paved the way for women in the United States to have the freedom to choose whether to carry a pregnancy to full term. The decision was a testament to Douglas' dedication to individual civil liberties, yet it aroused such passions and was so controversial that it is still hotly debated today, 29 years later.

William O. Douglas was devoted to civil rights, civil liberties, and personal freedom, even in the face of popular resistance to his decisions. For this reason, he was the most influential justice in American history.

MAJOR GENERAL JOHN E. WOOL

1784-1869

First in War, First in Peace, and…Forgotten
in the Eyes of His Countrymen!

The Life of an American Military Hero

By

John Eric Vining

Who laments for the second-in-command? For generations, Winfield Scott has been immortalized as one of the greatest generals this country ever produced. Yet, John Ellis Wool was an almost exact contemporary of Winfield Scott. Like Scott, Wool emerged from the War of 1812 a national hero, struggled in battles with Native Americans on the U. S. frontiers, held command of large units in the Mexican War, and remained a general officer through the first years of the Civil War. Unlike Scott, who is enshrined in the minds of military historians as an American icon, Wool has been forgotten to the extent that his name does not even warrant an entry in many encyclopedias and histories. Perhaps because Wool, though a "spit-and-polish", by-the-book professional through and through, leavened his various commands with compassion at appropriate times, his star faded in comparison to other possibly more successful generals.

John E. Wool was born February 29, 1784, and pursued several occupations until the outbreak of the War of 1812. He received his commission as a military officer in 1812, being commissioned as a captain in the 13th New York Regiment shortly after the onset of the War of 1812.[1] Wool's unit was assigned to the Niagara front at Lewiston, New York, under the command of Major General

Stephen Van Rensselaer[2]. On October 10th, 1812, the Americans began fording the Niagara River in preparation for an assault of the British positions on Queenston Heights to the west[3]. British resistance to the landing and assault on the heights was fierce, with many of the American senior commanders receiving incapacitating wounds[4] fairly early in the assault. Command devolved upon Captain Wool[5], who gallantly remained at his post as commander of the assault even though severely wounded in the upper thigh[6]. Wool led a charge that captured several British cannon, and came within a hair's breath of routing the enemy[7] before reinforcements arrived to stabilize the faltering British lines. Growing progressively weaker from a substantial loss of blood,[8] Wool was evacuated to the American side of the Niagara River. The battle went against the U.S. forces later in the day, but this ultimate reverse in no way tarnished the luster of Captain Wool's accomplishments. Both he and Lieutenant Colonel Winfield Scott emerged from the Battle of Queenston Heights as heroes.[9]

John Wool quickly recovered from his wounds, was promoted to major for his success at Queenston Heights, and was reassigned to the 29th Infantry Regiment in April, 1813.[10] The 29th was posted to the northern New York frontier, where once again Wool heroically participated in a large battle. On September 5th, 1814,[11] commanding only 280 soldiers, Wool and his unit successfully ambushed a 12,000-man British army wing invading Plattsburg, New York, from Canada. Wool's unit significantly slowed the advance[12] and inflicted numerous casualties on the column, materially aiding the American victory in the Battle of Plattsburg/ Lake Champlain. For his contributions in assisting in the defeat of the invasion that Winston Churchill would later call "the most decisive engagement of the war,"[13] Major Wool was promoted to lieutenant colonel.[14]

John E. Wool stayed in the army after the War, was promoted to full colonel, and was named Inspector General of the Army in 1821.[15] It was a post in which Wool would remain, with brief interludes of field command, for some twenty-five years. On April 26, 1826 he was brevetted brigadier general for faithful service.

Wool visited Europe during this period to inspect foreign military establishments.

One of the interludes in his tenure as inspector general showed Wool's stature as a man of peace. In 1835, General John E. Wool was sent to the Cherokee Nation to enforce the removal of the Cherokees from the Tennessee/Georgia/Alabama border area to Arkansas and Oklahoma Territory.[16] Wool arrived as a "my-country-right-or-wrong" officer, bent on enforcing the laws of the land and the intent of his commander-in-chief, Andrew Jackson. Before a year had passed, his qualities as a human showed through, and on September 10, 1836, General Wool wrote Secretary of War Lewis Cass the following:

"...The duty I have to perform is far from pleasant...Only made tolerable with the hope that I may stay cruelty and injustice, and assist the wretched and deluded beings called Cherokees, who are only the prey of the most profligate and most vicious of white men...The whole scene, since I have been in this country, has been nothing but a heart-rending one, and such a one as I would be glad to be rid of as soon as circumstances will permit...If I could, and I could not do them a greater kindness, ***I would remove every Indian tomorrow, beyond the reach of white men***, who like vultures, are watching, ready to pounce upon their prey, and strip them of everything they have or expect to have from the government... nineteen-twentieths, if not 99 out of every hundred, will go penniless to the west."[17]

Wool was not relieved of his burdensome command immediately. His compassion toward the Native Americans led to frequent clashes with corrupt Indian commissioners Benjamin Curry, John Kennedy, and Wilson Lumpkin – men whose every official move was calculated to strip as much wealth as possible from the departing Cherokees. In contrast, Wool's attitude toward the Cherokees became more compassionate and paternalistic as time progressed. His orders contained the following phrases (among others) during the evacuation of the Cherokee Nation:

March 15th, 1837: "You will treat the Cherokees kindly and give them all the protection guaranteed by the late treaty..."[18]

March 30th, 1837: "After they are taken (to Ross's Landing), they must be treated with kindness, and on no account must the soldiers be permitted to offer any insult to them, or allowed to commit any depredation on their property."[19]

April 20th, 1837: "Those (Native Americans) found in Cherokee country (are) generally in wretched condition. I ordered sufficient clothing to cover their nakedness."[20]

General Wool was particularly harsh with whiskey peddlers and gamblers, who preyed upon and weakened Cherokees and soldiers alike.[21] Perhaps because of his clashes with the corrupt power structure (as embodied by the civilian co-commissioners) which generally fostered and condoned anything that helped destroy the Cherokee Nation, General Wool was relieved of his command in midsummer, 1837.[22] This does not seem to have affected his rise in the army, as he was promoted to full brigadier general on June 25th, 1841.[23]

President James K. Polk's intrigues and General Zachary Taylor's provocative moves in the disputed territory on the Texas/Mexico border between the Nueces and Rio Grande Rivers helped precipitate the Mexican War in 1846. After the declaration of war, the United States military leadership engineered a four-army assault on Mexico. General Zachary Taylor would move from the mouth of the Rio Grande River to the northwest and eventually west into the interior of north-central Mexico. General Stephen Watts Kearny would move from Fort Leavenworth, Kansas Territory to the southwest to Santa Fe, and eventually west to conquer California. General Winfield Scott would launch an amphibious assault from Vera Cruz on the Gulf coast to eventually conquer Mexico City.

The campaigns of these three armies are well known in history, but due to a quirk of political fate, the fourth army and its campaign essentially have been forgotten. This fourth army was to gather at

San Antonio, Texas, cross the Rio Grande River at Presidio, and invade the Mexican province of Chihuahua. The army was called the *Army of the Centre*[24] (also known as the *"Centre Division"*[25]) and was commanded by General John Ellis Wool.

The *Army of the Centre* gathered in Texas in August 1846. It consisted of two regiments of volunteer infantry from Illinois, 600 Regular Army infantry, a Regular Army light artillery battery; a unit of Texas Rangers, and a unit of Arkansas cavalry.[26] This army left San Antonio on September 26th, 1846,[27] crossed the Rio Grande River into Chihuahua, occupied Santa Rosa and Monclova, then edged south into the province of Tamaulipas. It finally reached Agua Nueva (near Buena Vista) on December 21st, 1846.[28]

At this time, the endless intrigues of President Polk touched General Wool and cost him his date with immortality. Alarmed that General Taylor, a Whig, was gaining too much popularity, Polk ordered U.S. Army Commander Winfield Scott to activate the third prong of the planned attacks and invade Mexico from the Gulf. Scott was to draw experienced soldiers from Taylor's existing army, thus weakening Taylor so he would not attempt to move deeper into Mexico and gain more victories to further enhance his reputation. In early January, 1847, Scott issued orders stripping the experienced core of Taylor's army and sending it south to meet him.

Polk's plan came apart, however. Polk manipulated the reentry of exiled former strongman General Antonio Santa Anna into Mexico to once again become Mexico's president/dictator, with the understanding that Santa Anna would then help negotiate a peace treaty. However, Santa Anna, the self-styled "Napoleon of the West," realized through intercepted dispatches between Taylor and Scott that the northern army had been weakened and the transferred divisions had not yet reached Scott. He determined to strike the weakened Taylor and destroy him before turning on Scott.[29]

By a twist of fate, Wool's *Army of the Centre* reached Taylor just after Scott requisitioned Taylor's experienced Regulars and just as Santa Anna approached. Wool was ordered to dissolve the structure of the *Army of the Centre*, give most of his troops to Taylor, and become commander of a division within Taylor's army. (Wool also assumed the roles of second-in-command and chief tactician for Taylor's army[30]).

In late January, 1847 Wool's Division led the advance force of Taylor's 4,750-man army[31] toward the south, while Santa Anna advanced north with 21,553 soldiers[32] (due to the hard march, only 15,142 remained available for the battle[33]). As chief tactician, General Wool was responsible for selecting the battleground for what would become the Battle of Buena Vista. This battleground was characterized as "the best location in all the country for a battle of few against a superior force."[34] Wool was charged with the deployment of the American forces,[35] and also selected a very strong position for his own division. Because this position was so strong, Santa Anna chose to slide to the east of this position and attack Taylor's other divisions. Taylor's successes in turning back these attacks led to further fame for him as the "David versus Goliath" victor over Santa Anna at Buena Vista.

President Polk subsequently ordered Zachary Taylor back to the United States before he could win further military laurels and become an even stronger Whig candidate for president. Ironically, Wool's skill in selecting a position and protecting the troops under his command cemented a hero status for Zachary Taylor, and also cemented his own relative anonymity. Thus, John Ellis Wool had at least some influence in the election of Zachary Taylor as President of the United States.

Wool's unit emerged from the Battle of Buena Vista relatively intact. As his division was in good shape, and he was second-in-command and ranking officer of the army at this point, General Wool's division was chosen to occupy Saltillo, Mexico,[36] near the Buena Vista battlefield. The remainder of the army was sent to General Scott at Vera Cruz, and he was now commander of what was left of the *Army of Occupation*. In effect, Wool was left to stabilize the relatively idle northern front via the static occupation of Saltillo.

Once more, Wool followed orders and proved to be a strict, careful officer. Wool, in the midst of enemy territory in northern

Mexico, struggled with guerrillas who were sniping at his occupation troops. He resourcefully curbed this practice by fining the guerrillas' Mexican sympathizers.[37] In just a few months he reported the collection of $8,000 in fines.[38]

Wool also reinforced his reputation as a moralistic disciplinarian by ejecting from Saltillo all Americans "who cannot satisfactorily account for themselves, as well as gamblers" in January, 1848.[39] He emerged from the war with his administrative reputation enhanced.

John E. Wool was brevetted major general dating from February 23, 1847, (the date of the end of the Battle of Buena Vista). He was voted the thanks of Congress and presented with a ceremonial sword for his service in the Mexican War.[40]

In 1854, John E. Wool headed the Army's Pacific Department,[41] and once more found himself embroiled in the festering wounds that were the Nineteenth Century's wars of Native American suppression. In the mid-1850s, farmers and fortune seekers poured into the Pacific Northwest. As conflicts between the Native Americans and the immigrants increased, the attitude of the settlers hardened into enmity.[42] The Army was called in to keep the peace, however, many of the regular soldiers sent to this area viewed the Native Americans with compassion.[43] Wool himself openly sympathized with the Indians.[44] As he had done with the Cherokees nearly twenty years earlier, Wool directed his field officers not to fight the Native Americans unless forced to do so, and at all other times respect the Indians and persuade them to live peacefully. He felt the settlers' propensity to fight the Native Americans sprang less from genuine fear and concern over self-defense and more from a cynical intent to plunder the Indians of stock and other property.[45] A stiff professional soldier, Wool did not work well with civilians,[46] particularly when he felt they were self-serving and corrupt, as he had previously demonstrated with the Cherokee commissioners. Once more, this moralistic trait came to the fore. Wool considered Washington Territorial Governor Isaac I. Stevens a scoundrel and Oregon Governor George Curry little better. Opinionated and combative, Wool did not shrink from publicly and vitriolically feuding with them.[47]

Open and bitter warfare between the white immigrants and Native Americans in the Pacific Northwest exploded on two fronts in the fall of 1855. General Wool, having few men and many needs, could not cover all areas of conflict. Consequently, the war spun out of control. Wool characterized the fighting with the following statement: "It has become a contest of extermination by both whites and Indians."[48] Governor Stevens, involved in treaty-making deep within Indian territory (with the intent to extract more land from the Indians), was captured. When Wool delayed in immediately sending federal troops to rescue him, the territorial militia engaged in a bloody expedition to secure the freedom of the governor, which they did after several savage incidents. Eventually, in the spring of 1856,[49] Wool was able to send regular troops on a pacification mission among the Indians, but the mission found few Native Americans and was generally uneventful. Perhaps the general's heart was not in his work on this occasion.

The subsequent war of words flamed to a high degree, however. Governor Stevens denounced Wool for mis-deployment of the armed forces and demanded his removal for "utter and signal incapacity" and "criminal neglect of my safety."[50] On his part, Wool excoriated "the two war governors" for pursuing a needless and expensive war solely for the purpose "of plunder of the Indians and the treasury of the United States."[51]

Once more, the corrupt civilian power structure placed a black mark beside the name of John E. Wool. The people of Oregon and Washington were scandalized at the federal army's sympathy with the Indians and outraged at Wool's forceful and public verbal attacks on Stevens and the militia.[52] The two governors, savvy in the manipulation of public opinion, conducted an effective lobbying campaign with the authorities in Washington. General Wool was relieved of duty as commander of the Department of the Pacific in May, 1857.[53]

A soldier of Wool's obvious administrative and martial abilities could not be ignored, though. In the spring of 1861, war broke between the United States and the newly formed Confederate States of America. John E. Wool, maintaining his peacetime rank as a senior brigadier general in the regular army,[54] was now seventy-seven years old. He showed signs of aging; his hands trembled and he frequently repeated comments he had said a short while back.[55] Nevertheless, he retained the same pride and feistiness he had displayed throughout his then forty-nine-year career with the U.S. Army. As younger (and now more capable) junior officers were promoted around him in 1862, Wool successfully lobbied for command of Fort Monroe, which dominated the approaches to Hampton Roads. Wool commanded the ten infantry regiments and four artillery batteries stationed at Fort Monroe[56] (10,000 troops[57]), which comprised the Union Department of Virginia. He then succeeded in having this fort and department exempted from overall Union commander General George B. McClellan's territorial jurisdiction. In this way, General Wool avoided having to take orders from General McClellan,[58] whom he detested. The old general, so deficient in the nuances of civilian politics, was still deft in the art of military politics.

General Wool soon played an important role in one of the most dramatic events of the Civil War. The Gosport Naval Yard at Norfolk fell at an early date to Confederate forces in the area. Most loyal Union dockworkers left shortly thereafter, but one, William Lyons, stayed.[59] He pretended to sympathize with the South, and thus was allowed to remain at work in the navy yard. Lyons established contact with General Wool at Fort Monroe, and kept the Union appraised of Confederate activities at Norfolk, particularly the progress the Confederates were making in rebuilding the stricken Union warship *Merrimack* into the Confederate ironclad *Virginia*. In February, 1862, Lyons informed Wool that *Virginia* would sail within a month[60] and that the Confederates intended to attack several Union wooden blockading vessels as soon as possible. As Wool gathered information, he relayed it to Washington, in the latter stages by the recent addition of new technology in the form of a telegraph installed at Fort Monroe.[61] The information Wool forwarded helped speed the completion and transfer of the Union ironclad *Monitor* to Hampton Roads (Wool was not too old to recognize the value the new telegraph could render in speeding military communications). Thus,

Wool played a signal role in the dramatic battle of a new age of sea warfare – the first battle between iron ships.

Brevet Major General Wool had one last chance to possibly lead troops into a Civil War battle. In early 1862, as General McClellan's ponderous Army of the Potomac moved up the opposite side of the York Peninsula, its movement effectively outflanked Norfolk.[62] The Confederates stationed there were in danger. As luck would have it, President Lincoln and Secretaries Chase and Stanton were visiting Fort Monroe[63] to view the progress of the war from that vantage point as McClellan's advance occurred. Lincoln immediately grasped the significance of McClellan's move, and was amazed that McClellan had made no plans to capitalize on this and capture Norfolk.[64] The President decided to do it himself, employing the fortress garrison[65] of the ten regiments of infantry under John E. Wool (now up to 14,007 troops[66]) . Despite the physical infirmities of age, there was no lack of courage on the part of the seventy-eight-year-old hero of the War of 1812. With gusto, Wool stated he would gladly undertake the movement[67] under the orders of his Commander in Chief.

The first problem centered on the Navy. Bluff, much-disliked Commodore Louis M. Goldsborough, every bit as irascible as Wool (whom Goldsborough regarded as "that inflated fool"[68] and probably had no wish to aid in any way), thought it too dangerous to ferry soldiers across Hampton Roads without knowing the exact whereabouts of the *Virginia*. The President overruled Goldsborough and directed the reconnoitering of the opposite shore for a landing place. However, efficient General Wool had already studied maps and river charts and chosen a spot – soldiers were already embarking on small boats to begin the operation when the President returned.[69]

Although both the Commander in Chief and the operational commander were fully prepared for a set-piece battle, none occurred. The Confederate garrison at Norfolk, realizing their danger, abandoned the city shortly before General Wool's arrival. Wool, with Secretary Chase in attendance, accepted the keys to the city on May 10, 1862.[70] This action earned Wool a promotion to full major general, effective May 16, 1862.[71]

General John E. Wool contributed further to the drama that was the Civil War. Transferred from Fort Monroe to Maryland[72] as commander of the Middle Department and VII Corps later in 1862,[73] old General Wool conferred with brash, arrogant General John Pope on the eve of the Second Battle of Bull Run. Pope boasted that if the highly touted Confederate General Thomas J. "Stonewall" Jackson wanted to fight, Pope would be happy to accommodate him. General Wool had maintained a full awareness of the capabilities of the pre-war officer corps and the instructors at the various military academies. Wool still possessed a sharp military mind and carefully assessed the troop dispositions as the battle approached. Noting Pope's lax attitude in directing the concentration of his troops at the approach of the Confederates, Wool warned Pope: "Jackson is an enterprising officer. Delays are dangerous."[74] The foolish Pope ignored this and other warnings. The result was that the rapidly moving Jackson and the coolly calculating Lee crushed Pope at Second Manassas in one of the worst defeats the Union suffered in the Civil War.

John E. Wool had one last act to play in the physical and political carnage of the Eastern Theater. In January, 1863, Wool once more assumed command of the Department of the East, with headquarters in New York.[75] From this post he oversaw the Federal crushing of the New York City draft riots of July 13-16, 1863. The riots were in response to President Lincoln's **Enrollment Act of Conscription**, widely seen as unfair to the immigrant and working classes. Perhaps 50,000 rioters smashed business windows, draft centers, telegraph facilities, and attacked blacks and abolitionists. Wool initially called up 4,000 troops,[76] and by the end of the riot 10,000 troops had poured into the city.[77] By the evening of July 16th, the riot had subsided. At the climax of the riot, 119 people had been killed, 306 injured,[78] and damage to the city was estimated at 1.5 million dollars.

Wool was tenacious in putting down the unrest and was among those investigated after the riot.[79] The veterans of the Army of the Potomac imposed a hard peace.[80] Soldiers broke down doors, bayoneted all who interfered, and drove occupants to the roof, from which many jumped to certain death below.[81]

Wool's reputation was permanently sullied because he commanded the Union forces during those disastrous riots.[82] The popular press excoriated Wool. The **Philadelphia Weekly Times** blazed: "Old age and consequent infirmity rendered the removal of General Wool from so responsible a command a matter of perfect propriety…General Wool, in his temporary office at the St. Nicholas Hotel, unconscious of the real conditions of things and issuing orders contrary to reason and to military precedent…"[83] was characterized as "muddleheaded and indecisive."[84]

John Wool was perhaps viewed as an early and convenient scapegoat by the U.S. military establishment. Navy Secretary Welles wrote as early as July 15: "General Wool, unfitted by age for such duties, though patriotic and well-disposed, has been continued in command there at a time when a younger and more vigorous mind was required."[85] Regarding his replacement, "the influences that bring it about are evident. [Secretary of State William E.] Seward and [Secretary of War Edwin M.] Stanton have arranged it."[86]

Wool was 79 years old at the time of the New York Draft Riots. He responded to the question of whether or not he would command more troops in the war by saying, "They don't want me, they think of me too old."[87]

John Ellis Wool retired from active service on August 1st, 1863.[88] He was the oldest officer to execute active command in the army at the time.[89] Wool had served his country as an officer in its armed forces for 51 years, including 37 as a general. Proving tough to the end, John E. Wool survived another six years, dying on November 10, 1869.[90] He was born shortly after his country's birth, defended it in three major wars and several frontier struggles, lived to see it divided and then reunited, and lived nearly long enough to see it reconstructed. He made a significant contribution to his country's defense at a time when its military was unappreciated, its officers slowly promoted, and its entire force underpaid. Hopefully, General John Ellis Wool's contributions to our nation's history and well-being will be unappreciated no longer.

NOTES

1   David S. Heidler and Jeanne T. Heidler, eds., <u>Encyclopedia of the War of 1812</u> (Santa Barbara, CA: ABC-CLIO, Inc., 1997), s.v. "Wool, John Ellis," by Robert Saunders, Jr., p. 561.

2   Ibid.

3   Ibid., p. 562.

4   David S. Heidler and Jeanne T. Heidler, eds., <u>Encyclopedia of the War of 1812</u> (Santa Barbara, CA: ABC-CLIO, Inc., 1997), s.v. "Queenston Heights, Battle of," by Heidler and Heidler, p. 438.

5   Ibid.

6   Heidler and Heidler, eds., s.v. "Wool, John Ellis," by Saunders, p. 562.

7   Chuck Lyons, "Disaster at Queenston Heights," <u>Military History</u>, 10, No. 3, (December 2008), p. 43.

8   Heidler and Heidler, eds., s.v. "Wool, John Ellis," by Saunders, p. 562.

9   Heidler and Heidler, eds., s.v. "Queenston Heights, Battle of," by Heidler and Heidler, p. 438.

10   Heidler and Heidler, eds., s.v. "Wool, John Ellis," by Saunders, p. 562.

11   David S. Heidler and Jeanne T. Heidler, eds., <u>Encyclopedia of the War of 1812</u> (Santa Barbara, CA: ABC-CLIO, Inc., 1997), s.v. "Plattsburg, Battle of," by John M. Keefe, p. 420.

12   Heidler and Heidler, eds., s.v. "Wool, John Ellis," by Saunders, p. 562.

13   Heidler and Heidler, eds., s.v. "Plattsburg, Battle of," by Keefe, p. 420.

14   Heidler and Heidler, eds., s.v. "Wool, John Ellis," by Saunders, p. 562.

15   Ibid.

16   John Ehle, <u>Trail of Tears, The Rise and Fall of the Cherokee Nation</u> (New York: Anchor Books, a division of Random House, Inc., 1988), p. 300.

17   Ibid., p. 302.

18   Ibid., p. 310.

19   Ibid.

20   Ibid.

21   Ibid., p. 309.

22   Ibid., p. 311.

23   "John E. Wool," http://fortwiki.com/John_E._Wool, page 3 of 4.

24   Horatio O. Ladd, <u>History of the War with Mexico</u> (New York: Dodd, Mead and Company, 1883), p. 75.

25   K. Jack Bauer, <u>The Mexican War 1846-1848</u> (Lincoln, NE and London: University of Nebraska Press, 1974), p. 146.

26   David A. Clary, <u>Eagles and Empire</u> (New York: Bantam Books, 2009), p.165.

27   Bauer, p. 146.

28   Clary, p.228.

29   David Nevin, <u>The Mexican War</u> (Alexandria, VA: Time-Life Books, Inc., 1978), pp. 78-79.

30   Heidler and Heidler, eds., s.v. "Wool, John Ellis," by Saunders, p. 562.

[31] Clary, p. 274.

[32] Ibid., p. 272.

[33] Ibid.

[34] Ladd, p. 186.

[35] Mike Haskew, "Old Rough and Ready at Buena Vista," <u>Military Heritage</u>, 8, No. 6 (June 2007), p.29.

[36] Nevin, p. 91.

[37] Ibid., p. 92.

[38] Ibid.

[39] Ibid., p. 91.

[40] "John E. Wool," http://fortwiki.com/John_E._Wool, pages 2 & 3 of 4.

[41] Robert M. Utley & Wilcomb E. Washburn, <u>Indian Wars</u> (Boston: Houghton Mifflin Company, 1977), p. 179.

[42] Ibid., p. 177

[43] Ibid.

[44] Ibid., p. 179

[45] Ibid.

[46] Ehle, p. 308-9.

[47] Utley & Washburn, p.179.

[48] Ibid., p. 180.

[49] Ibid., p. 181.

50 Ibid.

51 Ibid.

52 Ibid., p. 183.

53 Ibid.

54 Webb Garrison, <u>Civil War Trivia and Fact Book</u> (Nashville, TN: Rutledge Hill Press, Inc., 1992), p. 38.

55 Shelby Foote, <u>The Civil War – A Narrative: Fort Sumter to Perryville</u> (New York: Random House, Inc., 1957), P. 414.

56 William C. Davis, <u>Duel Between the First Ironclads</u> (Baton Rouge, LA: Louisiana State University Press, 1975), p. 70.

57 Harry Hansen, <u>The Civil War – A History</u> (New York: Penguin Books USA, Inc., 1961), p. 179.

58 Garrison, p. 38.

59 Davis, pp. 55 and 73.

60 Ibid., p. 73.

61 Ibid., p. 108.

62 Foote, p. 414.

63 Ibid., p. 413.

64 Ibid., p. 414.

65 Ibid.

66 Hansen, p. 185.

67 Foote, 414.

[68] Ibid.

[69] Ibid.

[70] Ibid.

[71] "John E. Wool," http://fortwiki.com/John_E._Wool, page 3 of 4.

[72] Foote, p. 598.

[73] "John E. Wool," http://fortwiki.com/John_E._Wool, pages 2 & 3 of 4.

[74] Foote, p. 598.

[75] "John E. Wool," http://fortwiki.com/John_E._Wool, page 3 of 4.

[76] William K. Klingaman, ***Abraham Lincoln and the Road to Emancipation, 1861-1865***, p. 264. http://www.mrlincolnandnewyork,org/inside.asp?ID=94&subjected=4.

[77] Edward Robb Ellis, The Epic of New Your City: A Narrative History (Kondansha International, N.Y. 1966). http://clevelandcivilwarroundtable.com/articles/society/nyc_riots.htm.

[78] Laurence M. Hauptman, "John E. Wool and the New York City Draft Riots of 1863: A Reassessment." Civil War History 49.4 (2003), p. 373.

[79] "John E. Wool," http://fortwiki.com/John_E._Wool, page 2 of 4.

[80] Ellis, http://clevelandcivilwarroundtable.com/articles/society/nyc_riots.htm.

[81] Ibid.

[82] "John E. Wool," http://fortwiki.com/John_E._Wool, page 2 of 4.

83 ***Annals of the War Written by Leading Participants North and South, Originally Published in the Philadelphia Weekly Times,*** p. 302-303 (T.P. McElrath, "The Draft Riots in New York").

http://www.mrlincolnandnewyork,org/inside. asp?ID=94&subjected=4.

84 Ellis, http://clevelandcivilwarroundtable.com/articles/society/nyc_riots.htm.

85 Gideon Welles, ***Diary of Gideon Welles,*** Volume I, p. 373 (July 15, 1863).

http://www.mrlincolnandnewyork,org/inside. asp?ID=94&subjected=4.

86 Ibid.

87 Hauptman, P. 373.

88 "John E. Wool," http://fortwiki.com/John_E._Wool, page 2 of 4.

89 Ibid.

90 Ibid.

2ND LIEUTENANT FRANK LUKE, JR.: CLEARING THE CONTROVERSY

1984

By

John Eric Vining

2nd Lieutenant Frank Luke, Jr. was one of the most fascinating and controversial fighter pilots ever to wear an American uniform. He was what was then known as a "pursuit" pilot for the United States Air Service in World War I. None other than America's World War I "Ace of Aces," Eddie Rickenbacker, called Luke "the greatest fighter who ever went into the air."[1] Luke was one of four fighting flyers in World War I to win the Congressional Medal of Honor. Yet he was so insubordinate that, had he lived, he would have been recommended for a general courtmartial.[2]

Frank Luke was characterized as arrogant, swaggering, and brutal[3] – also as aggressive, shy, yet braggardly.[4] He was so effective as a pilot that he obtained aerial victories over his enemies in prodigious and rapid quantities: eight in five days,[5] seventeen in fifteen days,[6] and eighteen in seventeen days.[7] Most of these victories (14) were over German aerial observation balloons, earning him the moniker *"The Balloon Buster."* Yet the very rapidity of this accumulated glory contributed to the most lasting controversy of his legacy.

Ever since Frank Luke's death in combat on September 29, 1918, there has been uncertainty over just how many victories Luke achieved in World War I. Even as late as the 1980s, publications such as the following are quoting varied totals for the American ace:

21 victories, *"Wings,"* copywrite: 1983
21 victories, *"Winged Warfare,"* copywrite: 1967[8]
19 victories, *"The Balloon Buster,"* copywrite: 1928
18 victories, *"Air Aces,"* copywrite: 1983
18 Victories, *"Knights of the Air,"* copywrite: 1980

"Knights of the Air" even goes one step further in contributing to the controversy: It quotes a calculation of Luke's total as "20" in the body of the book,[9] and "18" in a listing of aces in the Appendix in the back of the book![10]

Why would there be so much variation in what would seem to be the simple task of counting of the number of enemy aircraft to fall to Lieutenant Luke's guns? Actually there are several very good reasons.

First, the very rapidity of the accumulated victories contributed to the problem. Luke gained all of his eventually confirmed victories in just less than a month-and-a-half, and eighteen of the eventual total in seventeen days. The sheer speed needed to process and confirm the claims would seem to guarantee that errors would be made. After all, the main war effort must be to combat the enemy; such niceties as confirming aerial victories must necessarily be of secondary importance.

Second, the confirmation process was complicated by the World War I accounting practice of "shared" victories. Two or more pilots, both contributing to a kill of an enemy aircraft, may both be credited with a full victory over a foe. Luke had several "shared" victories; so did Rickenbacker and virtually every other American ace. Though a standard practice, it did introduce a measure of uncertainty to the entire confirmation procedure.

Finally, some professional pettiness might have crept into the picture. Luke "was not popular because of his attitude."[11] To some extent, he considered himself a prima donna and acted like one. There may have been some reluctance to credit to him any victories of which there was any doubt whatsoever. In fact, Luke's very first confirmed victory might be considered the pattern for this particular factor.

The following is a list of every victory that could be attributed to Frank Luke by visual or verbal affirmation:

August 16, 1918	1 plane	Confirmed: status considered questionable
September 12, 1918	1 balloon	Confirmed
September 14, 1918	2 balloons	Confirmed
September 15, 1918	3 balloons	Confirmed
September 16, 1918	2 balloons	Confirmed
September 18, 1918	2 balloons	Confirmed
"	3 planes	Confirmed
September 26, 1918	1 plane	Confirmed
September 28, 1918	1 balloon	Confirmed
September 29, 1918	3 balloons	Confirmed
"	2 planes	Unconfirmed

The total of this "gross" listing comes to 21 victories.

One publication stated that "on 16 August [Luke] broke away alone to attack an aircraft, claiming a victory which apparently was not confirmed."[12] However, Norman S. Hall, writing Luke's biography in 1928, had the following to say about this particular victory:

> "Luke couldn't locate precisely where this combat had taken place, with the result that it became the greatest controversial air battle in the American Air Service"...The August 16 report "– which I have seen – is Luke's first combat report. Unquestionably, this account...is the one he rendered:[13]
> *"Combat Report – August 16, 1918"*

"Lieutenant Frank Luke reports:

"...Opened fire at about 100 feet, keeping both guns on him until within a few feet, then zoomed away. When I next saw him he was on his back, but looked as though he was going to come out of it, so I dove again, holding both guns on him. Instead of coming out of it, he sideslipped off the opposite side, much like a falling leaf, and went down on his back…My last look at the plane shot down convinced me that he struck the ground, for he was still on his back about 1,500 meters below.

"The machine was brought down northeast of Soissons in the vicinity of Jouy and Vially. Do not know the exact location as, this being my first combat, did not notice closely, but know that it was some distance within German territory…"[14]

"Major [Harold] Hartney accepted this report and Luke was credited officially with the plane, for it was the first on the list which the War Department provided me.[15]

"Hartney, in discussing this phase of Luke's career, said:

"I am firmly convinced the boy got the plane. His account of the battle contained those little differences that give such a report the touch of verisimilitude. But the squadron didn't believe him and that made Luke bitter."[16]

There are comparatively minor controversies in at least two other situations. On September 16th, one source states that Luke shot down one balloon during the day and two more that evening.[17] However, both Luke's biography[18] and official US records make clear his total for the day was two: one alone and another credited under the "shared"[19] scoring convention described above. On September 26th, Luke was (apparently erroneously) reported to have flown a combat mission but returned with no victories, while on the 28th to have scored victories over both a plane and a balloon.[20] A review of Luke's combat reports shows he was credited with a plane on September 26th and a balloon on September 28th.[21] Neither of these incidents would seem to contribute to the overall uncertainty over Frank Luke's final score.

Perhaps the controversy lending the most weight to the disparity in his final score arose from Lieutenant Frank Luke's last combat, the one for which he was awarded the Congressional Medal of Honor, but one from which he did not return. As a consequence, he was not able to file an official combat report. In this mission, it is unquestioned that he single-handedly attacked and destroyed three German observation balloons in the face of heavy and incessant anti-aircraft fire. This fire heavily wounded and, in the accounts of many, killed Luke (the exact circumstances of his death are controversial as well).

However, on the basis of the following report, there was some evidence that Luke scored two additional victories that Sunday evening:

January 3, 1919

"FROM: Graves Registration Officer, Neufchateau Area NO. 1

TO: Chief of Air Services, A.P.O. [American Post Office] 717

SUBJECT: Grave, Unknown American Aviator

1. Units of this service have located the grave of an unknown aviator killed on Sunday, September 29, 1918, in the village of Murvaux.

2. From the inspection of the grave and interview held with the inhabitants of this town, the following information was learned in regard to this aviator and his heroism. He is reported as having light hair, young, of medium height, and of heavy stature.

3. Reported by the inhabitants that previous to being killed this man had brought down three German balloons, two German planes, and dropped hand bombs, killing eleven German soldiers and wounding a number of others.

4. He was wounded himself in the shoulder and evidently had to make a forced landing. Upon landing he opened fire with his automatic and fought until he was killed.

5. It is also reported that the Germans took his shoes, leggings, and money, leaving his grave unmarked.

CHESTER E. STATEN
Captain of Infantry
G.R.S. Officer"[22]

"…everyone at air headquarters believed this to be Luke's grave…"[23]

This is the only record I have found that states Luke brought down two planes in addition to the three balloons. Just prior to his final combat, Luke had dropped a note to a forward observation station to "Watch three Hun balloons on the Meuse,"[24] followed by these observers viewing the aforesaid three balloons promptly go up in smoke, one after another. There is no question of their destruction or of the confirmation of this by trained observers. But the only affirmation of the two additional planes came from untrained civilians. This was not considered sufficient evidence, and these two alleged victories (in my opinion) were never confirmed. However, it appears to me that some sources have credited Luke with them; this is the only way I can see for his final total to be listed as 21 victories.

2nd Lieutenant Frank Luke was a brave, daring, and skillful pilot, still a legend in the United States Air Force. To the best of my knowledge, based on a substantial review of records and accounts, his fighting career ended at his death on September 29, 1918, with a total of 19 confirmed aerial victories.

2015 Addendum to *Clearing the Controversy*

July 3, 2015: I just completing reading *Terror of the Autumn Skies; The True Story of Frank Luke, America's Rogue Ace of World War II*, by Blaine Pardoe (New York: Skyhorse Publishing, Inc., 2011). Mr. Pardoe does an outstanding job of researching Luke's life in this book. As a part of this study, Pardoe discusses Frank Luke's August 16, 1918 "victory," which he maintains is unconfirmed. Mr. Pardoe makes the following statements:

1) On page 240, he states, "There is ample evidence from Frank's account of the battle, Hartney's corroboration of the account, and the German records of a downed aircraft at the location that Frank identified in his report to suggest that Frank scored a kill on the 16th."

2) On page 270: "Leutnant Alex Jagenberg was recorded as dead at Noyon, which is in the Soissons valley within a dozen kilometers of the vicinity that Frank's combat report references"…"The proximity of Jagenberg's downing to the region Luke outlined in his August 16 combat report, however, makes it seem likely that Leutnant Jagenberg was Luke's first true combat victim."

3) On page 10: "For a time there would be claims by the Army that it [the August 16 claim] was indeed an official kill for Frank." Page 203: "…the Air Force opened the door for dispute when it recalculated the kills for World War I pilots in the 1960s." Page 204: "Frank's records were adjusted in an effort to level the playing field for pilots who had fought under the newer shared-kill system. Frank's victory count was reduced as a result of this new system…"

4) In 1928, on page 67 of *The Balloon Buster*, regarding the August 16 claim, Norman S. Hall states, "Luke was credited officially with the plane, for it was the first on the list which the War Department provided me." Pardoe had ample opportunity to refute this statement, as he did with many of Hall's other assertions, but chose to be silent on this particular phrase.

Thus, I continue to maintain that 2nd Lieutenant Frank Luke, Jr. was credited, at least initially, with a confirmed victory over a German aircraft on August 16th, 1918. The conceptual validity of an official recalculation of a pilot's victory total, which is conducted over forty years after the fact, is up to the reader to assess. In my opinion, Luke's total of official victories at the time of his death on September 29th, 1918, was 19 confirmed victories.

Footnotes

1   Norman S. Hall, *The Balloon Buster* (New York: Bantam Books, 1966; Original copywrite 1928; Renewed 1956), p .124.

2   Ibid.

3   Ibid.

4   Christopher Shores, *Air Aces* (Novato, CA: Presidio Press, 1983), p. 32.

5   Ezra Bowen, *Knights of the Air* (Alexandria, VA: Time-Life Books, 1980), p.171.

6   Karl Schneide, "The Great War," *Wings*, 13, No. 6 (Dec. 1983), 46.

7   Shores, p. 32.

8   Lt. Col. William A. Bishop, *Winged Warfare* (New York: Doubleday & Company, 1967), p. 255.

9   Bowen, p. 171.

10   Ibid., p. 186.

11   Hall, p. 124.

12   Shores, p. 32.

13   Hall, p. 66.

14   Ibid., pp. 66-67.

15   Ibid., p. 67.

16   Ibid., p. 68.

17 Shores, p. 32.

18 Hall, pp. 87-91.

19 Shores, p. 32.

20 Ibid., p. 32.

21 Hall, p. 105, 107.

22 Hall, pp. 114-115.

23 Ibid., p. 115.

24 Ibid., p. 109.

Bibliography

Bishop, Lt. Col. William A. *Winged Warfare*. New York: Doubleday & Company, 1967.

Bowen, Ezra. *Knights of the Air*. Alexandria, VA: Time-Life Books, 1980.

Hall, Norman S. *The Balloon Buster*. (New York: Bantam Books, 1966; Original copywrite, 1928; Renewed, 1956.

Schneide, Karl. "The Great War." *Wings*, 13, No. 6 (Dec.1983), 46.

Shores, Christopher. Air Aces. Novato, CA: Presidio Press, 1983.

A TALE OF TWO ERAS

2003

By

John Eric Vining

It was a tale of two eras.

<u>Era # 1:</u> The costs of expanded governmental largesse and a foreign war, financed through deficit spending, create a new and unpleasant economic phenomenon called "stagflation." Wage and price controls, a weak dollar, poor quality products, rioting at colleges over involvement in foreign military adventures, oil shortages from OPEC embargoes, Communism on the march in the Third World. The Pentagon Papers and an administration's "Enemies List." <u>Bottom Line:</u> *Distrust of the people in their government, and of the government in its people.*

<u>Era # 2:</u> Virtual free-market hedonism, the dollar is king, "Quality is Job 1," tailgate parties before the big game on Saturday afternoon, OPEC stimulating production to maintain revenues, the arms build-up insuring the implosion of the U.S.S.R. A renewed destination for high school field trips: Washington, D.C. <u>Bottom Line:</u> *The president is our leader and "can do" is the name of the game.*

Visualize *1974*: The economy is so bad and the dollar so weak that a Canadian disk-jockey feels compelled to write an ode in defense of the poor Americans, whom everybody is trampling under foot. Consumers are virtually forced to look to foreign-built alternatives to obtain quality products (remember the Vega and the Pinto?). You may be listening to the news of the latest protest march or the growing war in Angola on your car radio as you're waiting in line at your local gas station.

Now visualize *1984*: Inflation is at historically low levels. The dollar is so strong that United States uses its financial power to prop up foreign currencies. A renewed Chrysler Corporation is taking the domestic auto market by storm with its new line of mini-vans. You may be listening to your new CD player in your recently-reintroduced American-built convertible. Hollywood is contemplating the filming of the movies *Wall Street* and *Top Gun*.

What happened in between? ***Nixon resigned!*** The actual resignation may have been just symbolic or truly substantial, but regardless, the results were stunning. Following the hamstrung Ford Administration and the backlash election of Jimmy Carter, America shook off its torpor, flexed its muscles, and destroyed Communism. By the early 1990s, America as the only remaining superpower (both politically and economically) had an economy nearly double the size of the rest of the world combined.

The only other sudden transition that came close to the Nixon resignation in impact on the country was the death of William McKinley. McKinley was succeeded by one Theodore Roosevelt, whose personal dynamism was responsible for transforming America from a sleepy former colony "over there" to sharing the world's center stage with the old European powers.

Other sudden presidential transitions resulted in the smooth operation of the Constitution in facilitating the transfer of power from one executive to another. The Nixon transition was the only one involving grave Constitutional issues of transferring presidential power to a potential non-elected chief executive. For these many reasons, the resignation of Richard Nixon was the greatest presidential transition in America's history.

Setting the Stage for "Historical Topics"

As the years went by, John continued to read history in his spare time while he pursued his career as a manager. The education, training, and experience John accumulated while managing people and functions began to influence John's avocation of studying history. Instead of merely reading *about* historical facts, he began to ask *why* events happened as they did and *how* various facts affected history.

Several of the shorts stories that follow reflect this questioning attitude. Some of these stories reflect original thoughts that perhaps other historians had not considered (such as *In Defense of the Allied Strategic Bombing Campaign* and *American Super-Frigates*), while others stories really just compiled facts in ways that helped John understand some very complicated scenarios (such as *A History of Labor Laws*). I hope you enjoy a little reading that may be somewhat out of the ordinary.

BACKGROUND TO: THE RUSSIAN INVASION OF CZECHOSLOVAKIA

"Seeds of 'Prague Spring' Taking Hold 20 Years Later"

Excerpt from <u>The American</u>, the afternoon
daily newspaper of Waterbury, CT

September 2, 1988, page 7.

The recent 20th anniversary of the Soviet invasion of Czechoslovakia has sparked renewed political activism that augments the ongoing struggles in Poland. In Prague, 10,000 demonstrators chanted "Dubcek, Dubcek" and demanded the withdrawal of Soviet troops and free elections. In Moscow, 500 activists, organized by the fledgling Democratic Union, called for a return to a multi-party government and shouted "Prague, Prague."

On the evening of August 20, 1968, over 500,000 Soviet and other Warsaw Pact troops invaded Czechoslovakia, a treacherous and brutal act that shattered the reform movement which had generated worldwide interest. In order to avoid senseless bloodshed, the Czechoslovak government decided against a futile military response and instead ordered peaceful civilian resistance.

By the next day the entire country had been occupied, and tanks rolled down the streets of the major cities. Alexander Dubcek, the first secretary of the Czechoslovak Communist Party, and other reform leaders were handcuffed and flown to secret locations. The emotional oral confrontations between the unarmed civilians and the edgy soldiers and tank crews provided a dramatic spectacle on the evening news.

The "Prague Spring" began in January 1968 when the stalinist Antonin Novotny was forced to resign as first secretary of the Communist party. The reformers embarked on a "new course" that that was based on the recognition and public admission that twenty years of stalinist rule had been a dismal failure. This "new course" called for a return to "socialism with a human face" and "democratic socialism." In less than eight months, profound political and economic changes were implemented, creating a sensation on both sides of the iron curtain.

In 1946 the Czechoslovak Communist Party received a plurality of 38.7% of the vote in a relatively free and open election. In February 1948, a political crisis arose, and the Communist Party seized absolute power. As a result of Soviet dictator Josef Stalin's machinations, from 1948 to 1953 there followed a series of purges, arrests, show trials and executions. The Czechoslovak Communist Party was recast in the form of the perverse apparat, the brutal secret police-based system that Stalin had created twenty years earlier. Novotny was a prime mover and beneficiary of the purges, becoming first secretary in 1953 and president in 1957. He ruled as a virtual dictator making effective use of the secret police, political intrigue and patronage.

Novotny was able to keep a tight lid on the ferment that erupted within the Soviet bloc during his tenure. In 1953 Stalin's death led to a wave of riots and strikes in Eastern Europe. In Hungary, Imre Nagy became prime minister of a reform government that lasted until the stalinists ousted him in 1955. In February 1956, Nikita S. Khrushchev delivered his famous "secret speech" that denounced some of Stalin's crimes and launched his destalinization campaign. Political crises soon erupted in Poland and Hungary. In Poland, Wlawdyslaw Gomulka established a "national communist" government following a personal confrontation in which he convinced Khrushchev to halt the Soviet forces that were heading for Warsaw. In Hungary, continued stalinist rule led to large popular demonstrations that erupted into full-scale revolution that toppled the communist regime and returned Nagy to power. Nagy's inability to control the revolution and his plans to withdraw from the Warsaw Pact and declare neutrality contributed to the bloody Soviet invasion in November 1956.

In 1964 Khrushchev was deposed and replaced by Leonid I. Brezhnev as first secretary and by Aleksei N. Kosygin as prime minister. Destalinization and liberalization came to an abrupt halt, and an official program to rehabilitate Stalin was begun.

By 1967 Czechoslovakia faced enormous problems: a population crippled and powerless after twenty years of submission to stalinist rule; economic stagnation arising from dogmatic stalinist "iron and steel" central planning; a work force without initiative and demoralized by incompetent managers and political hacks who controlled the trade unions; cynical students staging periodic demonstrations and following silly western fads; intellectuals unhappy with strict censorship and constant repression; a civil service stifled by the absurd stalinist dual bureaucracy whereby every government ministry had a duplicate entity with the Communist Party apparatus; a moribund Communist Party controlled by a collection of mediocre bureaucrats known as apparatchiks, corrupt political insiders and ruthless opportunists.

In the autumn of 1967 discontentment with Novotny's rule was widespread even within his handpicked central committee which was trying to engineer his resignation. In December Novotny's last two schemes — a personal appeal to Brezhnev and a military coup — both fell flat. When the central committee reconvened in January, Novotny had no option but to resign as first secretary, although he was allowed to retain the ceremonial office of President. Dubcek, a centrist among the reformers, was unanimously elected first secretary on Jan. 5.

The censored press had not informed the public about the intense power struggle within the central committee, although bits and pieces had filtered through foreign sources. The cautious public was unsure about what to expect from Dubcek's election. On the surface, his personality and background indicated nothing more than an honest, clean apparatchik. There was, however, a strong underlying feeling that profound changes were to follow. This was demonstrated on January 7 when Dubcek attended a soccer match and received prolonged, spontaneous applause from the spectators.

The reformers had definite objectives; revitalization and democratization of the entire Communist Party apparatus, with all deliberations and debates made public; dismantling the dual bureaucracy and entrusting the day-to-day government operations to the professional civil service; establishing an independent judiciary; eliminating censorship; decentralizing economic planning; and overall emancipation of all sectors of society.

There was no set plan for achieving these objectives and no way of determining the ultimate results. The reformers went out of their way to reaffirm repeatedly their loyalty to the Soviet Union and their adherence to the Warsaw Pact. They remembered the Soviet invasion of Hungary and wanted to avoid a similar fate. However, they felt that the reforms were essential and inevitable in order to establish a viable claim for retaining power.

Events soon started following their own course. Public opinion and the press became the key instruments for dislodging conservatives from their posts. Government archives were opened to investigators. Renewed interest in political developments led to a phenomenal increase in sales of newspapers and magazines. Public disclosures about corruption, abuses of power and the political trials of the 1950s aroused immense public anger and forced many resignations. Some officials committed suicide. The corrupt general Jan Sejna fled and was given political asylum in the United States.

In March the censors voluntarily ceased to function, although the law ending censorship was not passed until June. Novotny resigned as President and was replaced by Ludvik Svoboda who had commanded the Czechoslovak corps that had distinguished itself in the Eastern Front during World War II. Svoboda had been awarded numerous Soviet military decorations. After the war, he became a victim of the purges, was jailed and was later assigned as a bookkeeper to a remote cooperative. Subsequently, he was rehabilitated at Khrushchev's personal insistence and was appointed to the army's historical institute. The intent of his appointment was to reassure the Soviet leaders.

By this time, the Soviet leaders were having grave concerns about the startling developments in Czechoslovakia. To the

Czechoslovaks the reforms strengthened the power of the Communist Party. The Soviet leaders felt that the Communist Party, and therefore the Soviet Union, was losing control. The continued assurances by the reformers that they were loyal to the Soviet Union and the Warsaw Pact did not offset the fact that most of the men who were obedient to Moscow had been removed from office. The elimination of censorship had led to the publication of some articles that criticized the Soviet Union, proposed leaving the Warsaw Pact and declaring neutrality, and asked for a return to a multi-party system. The reformers would not yield to Soviet pressure for halting the reform process and restoring censorship. Many meetings were held between Czechoslovak and Soviet officials, culminating in a heated three day confrontation at the end of July. The Bratislava agreement that followed gave the impression that the crisis had been resolved.

In setting the stage for the invasion, the Soviet bloc press had been publishing a barrage of bogus articles giving the impression that the Czechoslovak party had been taken over by a small group which was under the spell of West German "revanchists" and other "imperialists." The official communiqué following the invasion stated that the troops were sent in response to an appeal from "statesmen and party representatives" requesting assistance against "the threat of counterrevolutionary forces who were plotting with foreign forces hostile to socialism."

The Soviets planned to set up a puppet "revolutionary government of workers and peasants." This plan was foiled by President Svoboda who secured the release of the arrested reformers and forced the Soviets to negotiate with them. As a result of these Moscow negotiations, Dubcek and other reformers were reinstated. However, the Soviets regained control of the secret police and proceeded to dismantle the "Prague Spring" from the inside. Dubcek was ousted as first secretary in 1969, expelled from the party in 1970 and given a job as a forestry inspector.

The "Prague Spring" became a historical footnote. Dubcek and the other reformers faded into obscurity, depicted in the West as naïve dreamers who expected to convince Brezhnev and Kosygin that the apparat could be successfully converted to democratic socialism.

Eventually, Brezhnev and Kosygin became captives of the apparat. Kosygin's proposed limited reforms were shelved by the party bureaucracy, and he was permitted to retire as prime minister only a few months before his death. Brezhnev ushered in an era of unprecedented privileges, perks and corruption for the bureaucracy, although the overall standard of living declined. During the last years of his life he was almost totally incapacitated, but he had to be retained as a front-man and died in office in Nov. 1982.

Today Brezhnev is in disgrace and is blamed for the "era of stagnation." Soviet novelist Daniel Granin has described Brezhnev's cabal as a bunch of "money-grubbers, fleecers, high-flown con men, heros of cynicism and black marketers."

The course of history has intervened. References to the "Prague Spring" are being made in the world press in conjunction with Soviet leader Mikhail S. Gorbachev's programs of "glasnost" and "perestroika" involving openness and economic restructuring. Last January, the Italian newspaper, L'Unita', published a startling interview with Dubcek, his first since being deposed. Dubcek referred to "perestroika" as being "indispensable" and of having a "profound connection" with his own reform program of 20 years ago.

Dubcek lamented the loss of 20 years and pondered "about what could have been accomplished in these years with the 'new course' and about the advantages which there would have been for our country and for socialism."

Not many reformers have been able to survive. Dubcek has lived to see the seeds of the "Prague Spring" take root in the heart of the apparat that crushed him 20 years ago.

THE RUSSIAN INVASION OF CZECHOSLOVAKIA

1975

By

John Eric Vining

The facts of the Russian invasion of Czechoslovakia are now history. The whole story can be looked up in any library in the United States. However, in my opinion, the most important motives behind the invasion were political motives.

When I first started studying about Czechoslovakia, I thought that everybody from the First Secretary down to the neighborhood blacksmith was a rabid Communist, ready to make everyday sacrifices to stamp out the imperial capitalist pigs. I hadn't known that the Czechs had once been a part of a great empire, and had a proud heritage behind them. I hadn't known that Czechoslovakia had been one of the most industrialized and progressive democracies in Europe. In fact, I knew very little about Czechoslovakia except that it was one of those terrible Communist monsters in eastern Europe, ready to start armed revolts everywhere, stamp out capitalism, and replace it with that cure for all evils, communism.

Now I realize that the people of Czechoslovakia are much like me. All they want is to have the simple pleasures in life and be allowed to live with dignity. Unfortunately, that hovering specter, the Soviet Union, seems to feel that to let a person live with dignity is to invite capitalism. All such reactionary ideas must be crushed in order to save the pure form of communism.

Further, I realized that the invasion of Czechoslovakia in August, 1968 was not merely to crush the regime of Alexander Dubcek, with its democratic undertones, but to set an example to other Communist Bloc countries. Ever since the founding of the empire in the late 1940s, the Communist Bloc had been developing cracks. In 1948, Yugoslavia had achieved a sort of neutrality. In 1955, Austria achieved neutrality. In 1956, a revolt was bloodily crushed in Hungary. In 1961, the Berlin Wall had to be put up to keep people from slipping over into West Berlin. And during the early '60s, Romania began slowly to slip away. Clearly something had to be done to impress upon the Communist Bloc countries the importance of solidarity. The Czechoslovakian liberalization provided the perfect excuse to show off Soviet military might.

Finally, I was convinced that the Soviets are completely deceitful. At Cierna, Dubcek was promised that the Soviets would not interfere with his reforms. Yet not a month later the Soviets and other Communist Bloc countries rolled into Czechoslovakia, using the excuse that they had found American military arms on the Czechoslovakian border. This leads me to wonder whether there can ever be true détente between the Soviet Union and any other country because of this inherent deceit.

And what of Czechoslovakia today? Its people are demoralized and its economy is failing. The people are trying to use a kind of passive resistance against the Russians, featuring a work slowdown which has a direct bearing on the economy. There is a sort of hopelessness, and the gay mood of Spring, 1968 is replaced by a sullen grayness. The Soviet Union has installed a puppet as First Secretary, and takes increasing interest in everything connected to the Czech political scene. My feeling is that there is little hope of the Czechs ever controlling anything important politically, and that the Prague Spring was on the beginning of a new and even more grim future.

A Short History of the U.S. Labor Movement

And the Rise of Labor Law

1990

By

John Eric Vining

Introduction

The labor movement in the United States has enjoyed a checkered history. From the movement's earliest beginnings, shortly after the Revolutionary War, to the most current federal legislation, the movement has been surrounded by controversy. The pendulum of activity has swung from the first timid requests for recognition to violent strike activity; from the "laissez faire" attitude of the government during the second phase of the Industrial Revolution (circa 1790s) to the activist legislation of the 1930s; from great internal schisms among the individual unions to awesome displays of united power. Is it any wonder the labor movement is viewed today with a mixture of deep distrust and unbridled respect?

In this report, we will examine the rise of labor unions in the United States, which are a prerequisite for understanding the need for and structure of the great labor legislation which basically began in the 1930s. We will then profile the major laws which have had a profound effect on labor-management relations. Finally, we will chart the progress of the labor movement, and consequently labor law, in the past 30 years. These studies will enable us to evaluate the reasons labor law was necessary, along with discussing ways in which management may interact productively with labor in the future. Only by foreseeing the future by learning from the past can

America compete in a global economy. Smooth labor-management relations are a key aspect of America's future economic viability in this global competition.

A Condensed History of the United States Labor Movement

As mentioned earlier, the United States labor movement had its beginnings in the 1790s. In 1792, shoemakers in Philadelphia organized the first local trade union. Later in the decade, in 1799, this union won the first contract granted to a union in the United States after a two week strike. Bargaining during this period was tentative and crude. The activists would post a sign outlining their demands on the employer's premises, then conceal themselves near the sign. They would watch the employer's reaction to their demands. If the employer rejected them, the workers would go on strike by failing to report for work.

Local unions, and somewhat larger associations of related craft unions, sprouted during the 1820s and 1830s. The first big break for labor came in 1842, when a Massachusetts court ruled that labor unions were legal.

The Massachusetts ruling opened the floodgates for the formation of labor unions. National unions began to spring forth in the 1850s and 1860s. These nationals banded together for the first time in 1865 to form the International Industrial Assembly of America, to become known the next year as the National Labor Union. With Ira Stewart and William H. Sylvis as its leaders, the National Labor Union pushed for such innovative features as the 8-hour day and the abolition of child labor. However, an activity which was to thwart the growth of unions in America now afflicted the National Labor Union. The organization became involved with various political-reform movements in the late 1860s. America at that time was very concerned about the influence of European anarchists in U.S. affairs. The NLU was linked to these anarchists, and this first association of national labor unions disappeared by 1872.

At the same time the National Labor Union was maturing and engaging in self-destructive political activities, a second national association was growing in power. The Noble Order of the Knights of Labor was organized in Philadelphia in 1869, led by a tailor, Uriah Stephens. The organizational emphasis of the National Labor Union had been that it was an association of local and national unions. However, the Knights of Labor was organized differently. It was the first American attempt to found a union for all workers – skilled or unskilled – individuals, local unions, or national unions.

The Knights of Labor grew slowly, and did not have a significant power base or large membership until 1877. Higher wages were the major concern of the era, and unions increasingly supported this demand. Industrialists, naturally, resisted this development. In July 1877, four eastern railroads cut wages by 10%. This was widely interpreted as a contemptuous moved on the part of management. A strike by railroad unions, supported by the Knights of Labor, immediately erupted. The strike so paralyzed the nation's transportation that, for the first time in United States history, federal troops were called out to break the strike. Troops and strikers battled for nearly three weeks. When the strike ground to a halt, more than fifty people had been killed and more than one hundred wounded. In an angry retaliation for what labor saw as the industrialists' and the government's collusion to break the strike, workers flocked to join the Knights of Labor, creating a power base of approximately 100,000 members.

Not coincidently, the Knights were able to flex their newfound muscle in the mid-1880s. In March, 1885, organized labor scored one of its first major successes. The Knights led a strike against a group of railroads owned by Jay Gould. Gould had once again defied the major rallying point of organized labor (wage enhancement) by instituting a 10% pay cut. Gould had boasted, "I can hire one half of the working class to kill the other half." Again, as he had in 1869 when trying to corner the gold market, Gould had overestimated his ability to manipulate power. The strike nearly broke him, and he was forced to concede defeat and restore the workers' wages. The successful strike set off a stampede to join the

Knights. Membership increased to approximately 700,000 and the Knights of Labor reached its zenith of power.

From this pinnacle of power, the labor movement, and by association the Knights, suffered four general defeats and one eroding trend which caused an ebb in labor's power. The Knights of Labor supported a reduction in the workday from 10 hours to 8 hours (independent unions also supported this cause with the Knights). On May 1, 1886, labor organizations all over the United States called a nationwide strike in support of the 8-hour day. Over 300,000 workers heeded the call, and 80,000 people in Chicago alone marched in support of the demand. This was a potentially explosive situation, because workers had been striking the McCormick Harvesting Machine Company since February to protest pay cuts and the firing of union organizers. McCormick had hired strikebreakers to keep his plant running. On May 3, police and strikers clashed at the plant. On May 4, approximately 300 workers confronted 180 police officers at a rally in Haymarket Square. A worker threw a stick of dynamite into police ranks, killing eight police officers. The police opened fire into the crowd, killing two workers and injuring many others.

The Haymarket Incident was a damaging blow to public opinion regarding the labor movement. A large segment of the U.S. population blamed the violence on the labor movement in general. Fears that the labor movement was merely a front for European anarchists and socialists arose again.

A second incident in 1886 further weakened the movement. In March 1886, the Knights of Labor called a second strike against the Gould railroads. This time, however, Gould held firm, and on May 4, the Knights called off the strike without winning any concessions from Gould. In addition, most of the striking workers lost their jobs.

Another crushing blow to organized labor occurred in the summer of 1892. On June 29, the Carnegie Steel Company of Homestead, Pennsylvania, cut wages. The Amalgamated Association of Iron and Steel Workers promptly struck the company. The company hired guards to protect property and strikebreakers. A battle between the union and the guards resulted in many deaths and injuries, and the Pennsylvania state militia was called out to restore order. The union was broken and most of the former union men returned to work.

The final damaging blow to the organized labor movement, and to the Knights of Labor in particular, was the Pullman strike of 1894. Once again, a wage dispute was at the core of the unrest. The American Railway Union, headed by Eugene V. Debs, struck the Great Northern Railroad in a sympathy strike, and refused to handle Pullman railroad cars. This refusal was predicated on the fact that Pullman employees were striking the Pullman Company because of a wage controversy. The strike spread to other railroads in the Chicago area. The police and strikebreakers battled the workers, and more than $80,000,000 in damage to property occurred. The mails were interrupted, and using this as a premise, a federal court issued an injunction against the strikers to stop their strike. Debs refused to honor the injunction, and federal troopers were sent to Chicago to break the strike and restore order. Debs was found in contempt of court and received a lengthy prison sentence.

Although the Knights of Labor was not directly involved in several of these actions, it was indirectly linked. The Knights had become involved in political-reform activities, the nemesis of the early labor union movement. Eugene V. Debs was an avowed socialist, although he was not a member of the Knights of Labor. The terms "labor," "socialist," "anarchist," and "violence" became linked and embedded in the public consciousness. The Knights association also battled the craft unions, which were more acceptable to the general public because of their emphasis on skilled labor, over the issue of unlimited membership in the association. The Knights of Labor lost favor with the public, and faded rapidly. By 1900, it had nearly disappeared.

While the Knights of Labor was reaching its zenith, a small rival organization began to rise. Originally formed in 1881 as the Federation of Organized Trades and Labor Unions, it reorganized in 1886 as the American Federation of Labor. Under its great leader, Samuel Gompers, the A.F. of L. finally found the recipe for success. It stressed the traditional factors of which the general public was in favor (craft union membership, higher wages, and the 8-hour day), while avoiding the major factors which had destroyed its predecessors (political reforms and association with perceived left-wing elements). Gompers' early philosophy was summarized by the following quote: "Our labor movement has no system to crush...nothing to overturn." The A.F. of L. prospered under this philosophy to grow into the largest and most powerful organization of its type in the United States.

Large strikes and labor unrest continued sporadically throughout the early 1900s. Coal miners, under the able direction of John L. Lewis, took the lead as one of the most militant factions of the labor movement. In 1902, over 145,000 miners in the anthracite fields of Pennsylvania struck over wages and working conditions.

Another militant labor movement started during this time period. The Industrial Workers of the World, an overtly socialist labor organization, was organized in 1905. It was founded on two basic principles: Whereas the A.F. of L. embraced the capitalist system, and sought benefits within the system, the I.W.W. opposed capitalism and sought to over throw it worldwide. Secondly, the A.F. of L. embraced only craft unions, while the I.W.W. wanted to bring all workers of each industry into one industrial union. The I.W.W. faced internal struggles between the socialists and the anarchists. In 1920, many I.W.W. members joined the Communist party, and the I.W.W. disintegrated. However, for a time, it posed a significant threat to the A.F. of L. as the voice of the American worker.

Massive strikes continued into the 1910s and 1920s. In 1919, the first nationwide strike of workers occurred, with 4,000,000 workers idled. These nationwide strikes were to occur throughout the 1920s. Also in 1919, the Boston police force struck, the first strike in American history by public employees. In 1921, miners in Mingo County, West Virginia, struck violently against low pay and harsh working conditions.

The worst strike of all was the coal miner's strike in Herrin, Illinois, in May 1922. Miners battled police and private guards during the bloody strike, causing twenty-six deaths. This strike, along with the paralyzing national strikes, forced the government into the realization that state control of the situation was not sufficient. The result was the series of great labor laws of the 1930s and 1940s.

Major Federal Labor Laws

The study of the great federal laws is of necessity tied to the history of the labor movement. In my studies of the labor laws, I found that passage of the major laws was almost always in response to major unrest in the labor movement. This is in keeping with the popular unofficial motto of American management: "The squeaky wheel gets the grease!" This is not so far from the truth. In a democracy, the interests of the majority of the constituents are the issues legislated upon. At the time of the passage of most of the landmark acts, labor unrest was a major concern of most Americans.

For example, specialized railway labor acts were passed in 1897, 1913, 1926, and 1934. These coincided with periods of great labor unrest in the railroad industry. We will be examining only the Railway Labor Act of 1926 in any detail, for this is the only one of the railway acts which has some applicability to general labor-management relations at large.

The Clayton Act of 1914 was a part of the great "trust busting" legislation which began with the Sherman Act of 1890 and continued with Theodore Roosevelt's activities in the early 1900s. However, buried deep in the language was a somewhat obscure clause which organized labor immediately capitalized upon. The clause stated that injunctions should not be issued against strikes except to protect property. Samuel Gompers of the A.F. of L. hailed this clause as labor's "Magna Carta" (or labor's "charter of freedom"). Subsequent events were to prove this sweeping statement premature.

The Railway Act of 1926 was one of the acts formulated to ease labor unrest in the railway industry, as mentioned above. There was one provision in this specialized legislation which served as a model for other, more generalized labor legislations, however. A clause in the Act set up the first federal industrial-labor relations council, called the National Mediation Board. Although this board was intended solely for use in railroad labor-management negotiations, the innovations of forming this board helped pave the way for similar boards in other pieces of legislation. Examples of legislation including similar boards include the "Wagner Act of 1935" and the "Taft-Hartley Act of 1947."

The massive national strikes of the 1920s, which idled millions of workers at a time, forced the government into action. The Clayton Act had sought to limit the power of the government to issue injunctions in strike situations. Matters had not quite worked out that way. Numerous injunctions had been granted in the 1920s, and many blocks had been placed in the path of collective bargaining. The "Anti-Injunction Act of 1932," also known as the "Norris-LaGuardia Act," sought to readjust the balance of power. It was the first of the great federal activist legislations of the 1930s, which truly gave labor its "charter of freedom."

The "Norris-LaGuardia Act" had three main clauses which had a major impact on labor-management relations. The first clause strengthened the "Clayton Act" and expanded upon it by prohibiting the courts from issuing injunctions against strikes, peaceful picketing, or boycotts. The second clause guaranteed the rights of workers to enjoy full freedom in organizing unions and demanding collective bargaining.

The third clause outlawed a practice which was universally condemned by labor as unfair – the "yellow dog" contract. A yellow dog contract was an agreement in which a worker was required to promise not to join a union once he or she was employed by a company. If a worker would not give this promise, he or she would not be hired. The "Norris – LaGuardia Act" formally outlawed this practice.

The next, pioneering act of Congress in labor-management relations, much broader than any that had come before it, was the National Labor Relations Act of 1935 (also known as the "Wagner Act"). This act had four main clauses generally affecting labor: two specific rulings, one clause defining definitely unfair labor practices, and a fourth setting up an administrative agency. The first clause authorized the "closed shop." The closed shop is an agreement between management and a specific labor union representing the workers at that company. It states that the company will not employ any worker who is not a member of that particular union. The second clause re-emphasizes the 1932 "Norris-LaGuardia Act" rules allowing workers full freedom to organize unions and bargain with employers, plus the additional right in the 1935 Act to choose their designated bargaining representative.

The third clause defined three specifically unfair labor practices by management:

1.) Employers could not penalize workers for belonging to unions.
2.) Employers could not interfere in the administration of the workers' union.
3.) Employers could not give money to a union, thus compromising the union's impetus to fairly represent the workers of the company.

The administrative agency created by the "Wagner Act" was the National Labor Relations Board (NLRB). The Board was invested with the power to investigate employers or unions which are suspected of unfair labor practices. If the employees' complaint is found to be true, the Board can order the employer to stop interfering with the employees' activities. The Board has the right to use the federal courts to enforce any rulings it issues.

I mentioned earlier that the "Wagner Act" gave employees the right to choose their bargaining agent. The Act, through the NLRB, also provides the machinery to decide which union organization the workers want to represent them. The NLRB prepares the structure for the orderly process of collective bargaining on wages, hours, and working conditions.

The "Wagner Act" was a truly groundbreaking piece of legislation. It prepared a fertile field for the massive "Taft-Hartley Act" of the next decade.

The final comprehensive labor law of the 1930s was the Fair Labor Standards Act of 1938, also knows as the "Wages and Hours Act." Once again, this legislation had three broadly applicable clauses which changed labor-management relations. The first clause stated that persons working in interstate commerce or in an industry producing goods for interstate commerce must be paid not less than a minimum wage. This section of the law has been progressively updated as inflation has been taken into consideration. The current minimum wage (as of April 1, 1990) is $3.80 per hour for most employees. A current innovation in the last update was the institution of a sub-minimum wage for teenagers. Teenagers starting their first jobs can be paid a 90-day "training wage" of $3.35, but firms cannot replace other help or cut pay to hire trainees. The minimum wage increases $4.25 in April 1991.

The second clause of the original 1938 statute stated that workers cannot be employed for more than 40 hours per week unless they are paid time-and-a-half for overtime. Thus, labor's long-standing goal of the 8-hour-day and the 5-day-week was institutionalized by the "Wages and Hours Act."

Finally, another of labor's long-standing dreams was realized with the passage of the "Wages and Hours Act." The Act prohibits the employment of children under the age of fourteen years. It permits the employment of children ages fourteen to sixteen in all industries except mining and manufacturing under conditions specifically detailed in the Act.

World War II created a break in the pace of labor legislation. However, the strains of war and the resultant recession shortly afterward created a need for additional laws to codify all of the interpretations of and corrections to the sweeping laws of the 1930s. This need resulted in the National Labor-Management Relations Act of 1947, popularly known as the "Taft-Hartley Act." The "Taft-Hartley Act" is the major statement of law that governs labor-management relations to this day, and is basically a continuation of the 1930s activist legislation. The following paragraphs give the major features of this massive piece of legislation. Where clauses (assigned for his report) in the following paragraphs are restatements of previous laws, this fact will be noted with an asterisk (*). The section numbers of the original law follow the clause numbers assigned for his report.

CLAUSE 1* [Section 7] Employees are generally recognized as having the right to form a union and to require their employer to deal with their union as their bargaining agent.

CLAUSE 2* [Section 8(a)] The federal law declares that it is an unfair labor practice for an employer to interfere with unionization or to discriminate against any employee because of union activities, or to refuse to bargain collectively.

CLAUSE 3a* [Section 8(a) (3)] The "yellow dog contract" by which the employer specifies that an employee will be discharged if he (she) joins any union, is invalid.

CLAUSE 3b [Section 8(a) (3)] In addition to Clause 3a above, the federal law prohibits a contract by which an employee must belong to a particular union, except to the extent that a "union shop" is legalized.

CLAUSE 4a* [Section 8(a) (3)] A "closed shop," in which the employer agrees with a particular union that he (she) will not employ anyone who is not a member of that particular union, was authorized by the 1935 Wagner Act.

CLAUSE 4b [Section 8(a) (3)] The 1947 Taft-Hartley act prohibits a "closed shop" and permits only a "union shop," when agreed to by the employer and the union. Under this plan, the employer is free to hire whomever he (she) pleases but, after a trial period of not more than 30 days, the employee cannot keep his (her) job unless he (she) joins a union.

CLAUSE 5* [Section 8 (b)] The federal law declares it to be an unfair labor practice to interfere with employees forming their unions or refraining from joining a union; to cause an employer to discriminate against an employee because he (she) belongs to another union or no union; or to refuse to bargain collectively. Additionally, in the 1947 law, it is unfair for a union in certain circumstances to stop work or refuse to work on materials or to persuade others to stop work or to refuse to so work.

CLAUSE 6 [Section 8 (c)] The Taft-Hartley Act preserves for the parties the right of fair comment. It provides that "the expressing of any views, arguments, or opinions, or the dissemination thereof, whether written, printed, graphic, or visual, shall not constitute or be evidence of an unfair labor practice under any part of the Act, if such expression contains no threat of reprisal or force or promises of benefit."

CLAUSE 7 [Section 8 (d)] The Taft-Hartley Act provides that in the case of industry-wide collective bargaining, the duty to bargain collectively shall also mean that neither party to the contract shall terminate or modify the contract without giving the other party 60 days notice, and the parties must then meet to negotiate a new contract while both sides continue in operation during the 60-day period.

CLAUSE 8a* [Section 9(a)] Whatever union or person is selected by the majority of workers within the unit becomes the "exclusive representative(s)" of all the employees in such unit for the purposes of collective bargaining in respect to rates of pay, hours of employment, or other conditions of employment.

CLAUSE 8b* [Section 9(a)] Whether all the workers are members of the representative union or not is immaterial, for in any case, this union is the exclusive representative of every employee.

CLAUSE 9 [Section 10(c)] An employee can neither be reinstated nor rewarded back pay if he (she) was discharged for cause.

CLAUSE 10 [Section 13] Although a strike is deemed an unfair labor practice under certain circumstances, the Act does not outlaw strikes generally but provides that "nothing in this Act, except as specifically provided herein, shall be construed so as either to interfere with or diminish the right to strike, or to affect the limitations or qualifications on that right."

Additionally, the "Taft-Hartley Act" subjects unions to a civil suit for damages for certain strikes or secondary boycotts that might in themselves be regarded as illegal conspiracies.

The final "activist" legislation dedicated specifically to labor-management relations was the Labor-Management Reporting and Disclosure Act of 1959. This legislation was a reaction to charges of corruption within organized labor and widespread fears that organized crime had infiltrated some major unions (the Teamsters had been expelled from the AFL-CIO in 1957 for allegedly unethical activities).

The Act is far-reaching and specific. The following is a summary of ten major clauses in the Act.

The Act has clauses which specify that:

- unions must adopt constitutions and bylaws.
- each officer and key employee must file conflict of interest.
- employers must report payments to union officers.
- national unions are limited in their ability to control local unions.
- unions must protect individual members' equality, right to vote, and right to information on union matters and contracts
- Communists and persons convicted of major crimes are barred from office for a specified period.
- union assets must be protected from fraud and/or embezzlement by specific means delineated in the Act.
- loans to officers are specifically limited, and unions are barred from paying fines imposed on officers or employees.

The Labor-Management and Reporting Disclosure Act of 1959 expands the definition of unfair labor practices. The Act specifically delineates four unfair labor activities:

1.) The Act prohibits and makes it a crime to picket to extort money.

2.) The law makes it an unfair labor practice to picket for recognition when a rival union is lawfully recognized and no representation issue can be raised.

1.) Agreements between unions and employers that the latter shall not use nonunion materials ("hot cargo agreements") are made void and an unfair labor practice, except in the construction and garment industries.

2.) Secondary boycotts and coercion of neutral employers thereby are generally made unfair labor practices.

The Labor-Management Reporting and Disclosure Act of 1959 was the last of the dedicated labor-management laws. It was also the last of the great 1930s-style activist legislation.

A Condensed Review of Labor and Labor Law in the Past Thirty Years

With the passage of the Labor-Management Reporting Act of 1959, the basic labor-management laws, which govern labor-management relations to this day, were in place. Yet, clauses in legislation since that time have had a profound impact in certain areas.

The first of these recent laws was the Civil Rights Act of 1964. This act forbids employers to discriminate as to compensation, privileges, and conditions of employment against any person because of race, religious creed, color, sex, national origin, or age. This final criterion, age, was further strengthened by the Age Discrimination Act of 1967, which prohibits discrimination against workers aged 40 to 65.

The period of the middle and late 1960s was marked by the passage of President Johnson's "Great Society" legislation and by an escalation of the Vietnam War. Because Johnson and the U.S. Congress were hesitant to increase taxes sufficiently to cover the huge costs associated with these two very expensive activities, inflationary pressures increased. When this was coupled with a long period of economic expansion (1961-'69), these pressures were magnified, and inflation grew alarmingly.

Richard Nixon was elected President of the United States in 1968 partly due to a platform including planks outlining economic reform. The economy experienced a short, sharp recession in 1969-'70. Due to the enormous federal financing needs, which kept inflation high, and the economic recession, which lowered productivity and job creation, the country suffered the onset of "stagflation" (simultaneous economic stagnation and inflation). Organized labor increased wage and benefit demands substantially during this period to compensate for inflation and the rising unemployment of its members.

As a result of the above phenomena, Congress passed the Economic Stabilization Act of 1970. Nixon used the mandate provided by the language of this law to institute wage and price controls on August 15, 1971. This was a multi-phase process, of which two phases were actually implemented. Phase I was a 90-day freeze on wages, prices, and rents. This was an attempt, among other goals, to hold labor wage demands to 7% per year. Phase II established a bi-partisan "Cost of Living Council," with two subcommittees: The "Pay Board," to limit inflationary wage increases, and a "Price Commission," to restrain prices and rent increases. Almost universally condemned by both labor and management, the wage and price controls were nevertheless somewhat successful in abating the rise in inflation for a time in 1972 and early 1973. They did, however, cause serious disruptions of supplies and certain commodities. We will never know the long term effects of this legislation, for the first "oil shock" in October 1973 caused huge inflation, beyond the Council's control. The recession it spawned enhanced and deepened "stagflation," and the Council was formally disbanded in 1975, being considered ineffective. The wage and price controls of the early 1970s were the most ambitious attempts in the nation's history to "micro-manage" the economy, and by association, labor-management relations.

The recession of 1969-'70 caused the failure of a good number of businesses. When these businesses failed, the pension plans for the workers also failed in many instances, leaving workers without retirement benefits. In response to this need, Congress passed the Employee Retirement Income Security Act of 1974 ("ERISA"). ERISA mandated complicated guidelines for the establishment of pension rights and protections for pensioners of insolvent firms.

The trend in bargaining demands changed over the period of thirty years. The demand for much higher wages was dominant in the 1960s and early 1970s. However, it became obvious that the economy had shifted from a national basis to a global basis in the late 1970s. No longer did the U.S. simply make the goods that the rest of the world bought, at whatever price the U.S. charged. The fact of the "world economy" was brought home by the sharp recession of 1981-'82, when many of the affected industries simply didn't recover, due to foreign competition. This fact was not lost on the labor unions, and as the '80s continued, the dominant bargaining issue shifted from wage demands to job security. Although the abatement of inflation had an impact, the pinch of foreign competition certainly was the major catalyst for this change in tactics. By the end of the decade of the '80s, the U.S. was less the dominant economic force and more simply one of the major economic players in the world economic market.

Conclusions and Recommendations

We have now completed a short review of labor history and the resultant laws which were enacted to protect both labor and management. The obvious question becomes, "Why did the need for labor laws arise?" Why couldn't the two sides work together for the mutual benefit of themselves and the country?

As I worked through my analysis of labor law, I came to the conclusion that much of the blame must be placed at the feet of management. I have identified several main factors which I believe account for the bulk of the problem which management has created for itself. Charlie Brown's twist on Commodore Perry's old adage is uncomfortably true: "We have met the enemy, and they are us!"

The first factor is management's original disregard for the "special needs" of labor. Abraham Maslow's "Hierarchy of Needs" identifies "social" needs as the second level in the hierarchy. For many years, especially in the years on either side of the turn of the century, organizational managers paid little attention to the social needs of people. It was assumed that the economic reward of "a fair day's pay" would elicit a fair day's work and that worker needs required no more attention. "A fair day's wage" was an example of attention to "safety" (or "survival") needs, a lower level need. According to Maslow, this need would be deactivated when met. The next higher need, social needs, would be activated and demand satisfaction at that time. This aspect was often denied by turn-of-the-century managers.

Over the years, it has been determined that workers' productivity is usually governed to a great extent by their social relationships. When these relationships are permitted and the physical environmental factors do not constrain it, social contact will make itself visible. It was tempting to treat all social behavior as counterproductive, and to recommend a hardline approach to eliminate it. Yet, as Maslow's theory shows, this attitude not only overlooks the significance of social behavior to productivity, but counters the very foundation of human needs.

Closely related to the concept of "social needs" is another social phenomenon known as the "norm of reciprocity." The norm that it is obligatory to "pay back" roughly what one has "received" is almost universal and operates between individuals, groups, organizations, and even societies. The norm of reciprocity serves to stabilize relationships, brings them into a steady state, and allows predictability and continuity.

It is clear from our review of labor demands over the past century of so that labor has not felt this norm was working properly in its relationship with management. A common thread in contract negotiations from 1880 to 1980 was a call for increased wages and reduced working hours in return for higher productivity. This was heavily resisted by management. In cases in the 1800s, management even <u>reduced</u> wages in times of increasing productivity. Obviously, little attention was paid to the norm of reciprocity.

A third "social" phenomenon creating conflict is "professional identity." Sociologists have discovered there are very fundamental differences in how different professions view themselves, their priorities, their importance, and the qualities of other groups. When these views collide, there is <u>inherent conflict</u>; conflict that is a reflection of the background factors of the parties involved. Traditionally, it has been management's job to balance these views in ways that benefit both the organization and labor's position. The history of success in this balancing act has been a mixed bag at best. Often, the attention and skill needed on the part of management to keep things from deteriorating in "win-lose" or "lose-lose" situations had been lacking. Frequently, labor-management strife has been the result.

Moving from the social area, we progress into problems which "interaction styles" may present in labor relations. It appears from my observations that many laborers have a limited concept of their abilities, and therefore seem to prefer strict task relationships. This is evidenced by desires for wage structures, strict interpretations of job descriptions, seniority hierarchies, and resistance to "merit" increases in wages. On the other hand, management has traditionally seen themselves in the role of "boss," and has had difficulty in developing a "collaborative" (or "colleague") type of relationship with labor. This superior-subservient mentality, combined with low self-esteem on labor's part, had created a simmering caldron which erupts in the form of strike violence.

Another related type of problem has been the unsuitability of some management types for the job of interacting with labor. Especially in the last forty years, "financial types," with a heavy emphasis on "analysis," have risen to the top of major corporations. Traditionally, their education in interpersonal communication has been sketchy. In the earlier stages of their careers, as they concentrated on "number-crunching," they have had little need for interaction beyond the "minimal task" level. Suddenly, they are thrust into the arena of multiple negotiations with various diverse stakeholders. These managers simply are not up to the task. They make careless, unempathetic statements and moves, and suddenly a labor crisis is at hand.

Finally, we come to the historic, base, driving force of simple greed. Corporate history is full of such "robber barons" as Jay Gould, Thomas Durant, and George Francis Train, who pursued wealth, power, and material goods regardless of the cost in human suffering.

Yet, over the years (especially in the last thirty), this mentality has changed somewhat. Janet Axelrod, vice president of Lotus Development Corporation, discusses her company's aversion to executive perks as follows:

"None of us had any kind of interest in being people who lived in ivory towers and traveled around in limousines. It's not just that it wasn't in our lifestyle, it wasn't what we wanted to be. It seemed to be an awful money sink, and artificial separations among people. Status-related differences between people are an unnecessary division, and none of us wanted to be divided in that way. A lot of big, heavy industry in this country was born out of this kind of robber-baron mentality, and we're not in that anymore; it's just not the way we do business."

What is the solution to these long-standing problems? I am not a starry-eyed idealist, so I don't believe one hundred and fifty years of more or less controlled animosity will be cured with a magic elixir. However, I do believe the path in the right direction was blazed by Douglas McGregor in the 1950s with the formulation of Theory "X" and Theory "Y," and blended in the early 1980s by William Ouchi with his development of Theory "Z.".

The famous Theory X states that a manager who subscribes to this type of thinking views his subordinates as by nature:

1) Disliking work
2) Lacking in ambition
3) Preferring to be led rather than lead
4) Resistant to change
5) Irresponsible

These perceptions can cause managers to be overly directive, very narrow, and control-oriented in their approach to people at work. This fosters discomfort, and directly leas to labor unrest.

By contrast, theory Y assumes subordinates as:

1) Willing to work
2) Willing to accept responsibility
3) Capable of self-direction
4) Capable of self-control
5) Capable of imagination, ingenuity, and creativity

Perceptions in the Theory Y model encourage managers to allow subordinates more participation, freedom, and responsibility. This fosters more opportunities for self-esteem and self-actualization needs to be met.

William Ouchi built on McGregor's pioneering work in 1981. As can be seen from Exhibit I, Theory Z conceptualizes that American and Japanese attitudes and practices toward employees differ along seven factors. This theory borrows one factor from Theory "A" (American "individual responsibility") and three factors from Theory "J" (Japanese "collective decision making," "slow evaluation and promotion," and "holistic concern"). It also takes a middle-of-the-road stance on the three remaining factors ("long-term employment," "implicit, informal control with explicit guidelines," and "moderately specialized career paths").

In my opinion, the participative style of management which results from adherence to Theory "Z" is the only way to close the riff between labor and management. Indeed, this theory is beginning to be adopted even as I write. Douglas Fraser, head of the United Auto Workers, sits on the Board of Directors of the

Chrysler Corporation. He was present, sitting cheek-by-jowl with GM's chairman, Roger Smith, in the first "Saturn" automobile to roll off the new Spring Hill, Tennessee, assembly plant. I applaud such visionary efforts, and hold them out as the way to keep the government from being forced to pass legislation to mediate labor and management's historic dissention.

Exhibit I

ORGANIZATION TYPE "A"
(American)

1) Short-term Employment
2) Individual Decision Making
3) Individual Responsibility
4) Rapid Evaluation and Promotion
5) Explicit Control Mechanisms
6) Specialized Career Path
7) Segmented Concern for Employee as an Employee

ORGANIZATION TYPE "J"
(Japanese)

1) Lifetime Employment
2) Collective Decision Making
3) Collective Responsibility
4) Slow Evaluation and Promotion
5) Implicit Control Mechanism
6) Non-specialized Career Path
7) Holistic Concern for Employee as a Person

ORGANIZATION TYPE "Z"
(Modified American)

1) Long-term Employment
2) Collective Decision Making

3) Individual Responsibility
4) Slow Evaluation and Promotion
5) Implicit, Informal Control with Explicit, Formalized Measurement
6) Moderately Specialized Career Paths
7) Holistic Concern, Including Family

Source: Adapted from William Ouchi, *Theory Z*, 1981, Addison-Wesley. Reading, Mass., P. 58. Reprinted with permission of the publisher in Ricky W. Griffin, *Management*, 1984, Houghton Mifflin Company, Boston, Mass., p. 59.

Selected Bibliography

Anderson, Ronald A., and Walter A. Kumpf. _Business Law_. 9th ed. Cincinnati: South- Western Publishing Co., 1972.

Cohen, Allan R., Stephen L. Fink, Herman Gadon, and Robin D. Willits. _Effective Behavior in Organizations_. 4th ed. Homewood, IL: Richard D. Irwin, Inc., 1988.

Estey, Martin. _The Unions – Structure, Development, and Management_. 3rd ed. New York: Harcourt Brace & Jovanovich, 1981.

Griffin, Ricky W. _Management_. Boston: Houghton Mifflin Company, 1984.

Miller, Bernard S., Kenneth W. Lund, and Kenneth L. Peters. _Prosperity and Panic, 1921 to 1932_. Vol. 12. Chicago: Davco Publishing Company, 1962.

In Defense of the World War II Allied Strategic Bombing Campaign

A Critical Analysis of Airpower in the War

By

John Eric Vining

Many have commented that the World War II Allied Strategic Bombing Campaign was not a success because Germany's production of war materials continued, even increased, during 1944, at the height of the Allied strategic bombing campaign. I think it is important to note certain facts associated with the West's strategic air campaign against Nazi Germany. Much of the Nazi's increased production late in the war was due to the genius of Albert Speer, whose Herculean efforts to mobilize and disperse manufacturing assets during the crisis of the Third Reich were crucial to this feat. Those same commentators usually state that it was the *tactical*, rather than the *strategic*, bombing campaign that was truly useful in facilitating the victory in the West. Tactical bombing destroyed Nazi transportation and communication systems on continental Europe; thus the tactical air campaign paved the way for the Allied ground invasion of Europe, and ultimate victory in the European Theater.

To quote an expert, *"The story is a lot more complicated than that."*

We have to look at the weapon systems that German production genius Speer was producing in 1944. At least in the case of airpower, this production was centered on increasingly obsolescent types such as the Messerschmitt 109 day-fighter, the Junkers 88 and Messerschmitt 110 night-fighters, and the Heinkel 111 medium bomber. These airplanes were being produced in record quantities because the replacements for these systems, the Messerschmitt 262 jet day-fighter, the Heinkel 219 night-fighter, and the Dornier 335 fighter-bomber, could not be placed into production. True, the Nazi aircraft administrative leadership (the "RLM") made a series of huge blunders in the 1940-'42 period in not adopting and placing these systems into production when they could have done so. But by 1943 the RLM leadership had seen the light and was pushing for the development of these modern systems. By then, it was too late. At significant points during 1942, '43, and '44, new aircraft prototypes, engineering specification drawings, and initial machine tool setups for these new systems were destroyed in their embryonic stages, thus preventing their move to full production status. This destruction was accomplished by the *strategic* bombers of the RAF and USAAF.

It is important to note that in the fall of 1943 (in the case of the USAAF) and the early spring of 1944 (in the case of the RAF), the German Luftwaffe nearly brought the Allied strategic bombing campaign to its knees with the elderly weapons outlined above, still at its disposal. The Me 262, He 219, and Do 335, with proper administration in 1940 to '42, all could have been in production and present in the air in significant numbers by the fall of 1943, manned by talented and experienced pilots. All these weapon systems were markedly superior to the Allied aircraft opposing them, and almost certainly would have ensured the destruction of the Allied strategic bombing campaign by late-1943. If the air 5 to 6 miles up over the continent could not be secured (the strategic bombing arena), then the air a few thousand feet up (the tactical bombing arena) could not be secured against these superior weapons either. The Allied tactical air campaign of early-1944, and thus success in the Allied invasion of Europe in mid-1944, would have been seriously in doubt.

It was *intransigence of the Nazi administration* - the *RLM* and Adolf Hitler - in the crucial 1940-'42 period and the *strategic bombing campaign* over Western Europe in 1943-'44 that played a huge role in the Allied victory in the West during World War II.

A 150-Year Evolution: Mounted Militia to Mechanized Infantry - 1790 to 1940

1997

By

John Eric Vining

An interesting progression can be developed, linking the mounted militia of Wayne's advance to Fallen Timbers in the Woodland Wars of 1790-'95 all the way up to the storm troopers of the German World War II "blitzkrieg". In the campaign leading up to Fallen Timbers, one of the main problems had been how to accumulate a force sufficient to guarantee a knockout blow to the British-backed Native American confederacy. Wayne had built a hard-core Legion of the United States, composed of approximately 2100 infantry and 400 cavalry, but potentially this total could be matched by the Miami Confederacy in the Ohio-Michigan-Indiana tri-territory area.

Unreliable militia forces had been substantially responsible for the defeat of both Harmar's and St. Clair's campaigns of 1790 and 1791, respectively. However, Wayne called on a mounted militia force, partially trained by him at Legionville and Hobson's Choice in 1792-'93, to supplement his Regulars in the 1793-'94 campaign.

Mounted militia offered potentially unique flexibility if it could be harnessed. Large numbers of short-term recruits could be raised quickly. They brought their own mounts, giving them the ability to move quickly – perhaps up to 50 miles per day, compared to 20 miles for foot troops. They also brought their own weapons. These usually consisted of a Kentucky longrifle, with a range of 150-200 yards, and which could be fired approximately 2 times per minute (as opposed to a musket which had a range of 60 yards and could be fired approximately 3-4 times per minute). They sometimes carried 1-2 flintlock pistols and a war hatchet/tomahawk. They had the ability to use all these weapons from the ground or from horseback.

Militia's downfalls could be several and severe. Not being professional troops, they exhibited a definite lack of military discipline. They could not be consistently depended upon to serve dismounted in a European-style line of battle, and particularly to withstand a disciplined and determined enemy bayonet charge. They could be unruly in camp life, not always fortifying an encampment on the march, or disrupting the rest of the more disciplined contingents of the army. Finally, they could not always be depended upon to execute orders with the discipline and precision needed to maintain formation integrity in battle.

However, if employed properly, mounted militia had certain definite advantages. They could be employed less expensively than regular volunteers – they brought their own mounts and weapons, so horses and firearms did not need to be procured and purchased for them. They represented the ability to bring a large amount (big numbers) of accurate, long-range firepower to any sector of the battle in which they were employed. They could fight mounted or on foot, adding great flexibility in usage. Being mounted, they could range far afield, giving an increased ability to project power away from the line of march or field of battle.

Militia's lack of military discipline and knowledge meant that it must be employed carefully. Specific and detailed orders must be drafted for them, since in many cases their officers had little more knowledge of military science than the rank-and-file. They must not be employed in a European-style line of battle; their lack of discipline, bayonets, and rapidity of fire would prove fatal. However, by employing them as shock troops (as in The Battles of the Thames and Horseshoe Bend, and potentially at Fallen Timbers), they could be decisive. Also, for use to ride to battle as dragoons – then to dismount and either defend or attack in heavy cover - they could be very successfully employed.

George Washington decried the value of militia in the Revolutionary War, and as noted they were mainly responsible for Harmar's and St. Clair's defeats. Anthony Wayne was successful with mounted militia because he insisted on training them before battle, he insisted in fortifying his camps ("Roman Camp"-style each night, to lessen the chances for a surprise to his raw militia), and he insisted on a protected, realistic route (to make sure the large number could be supplied from Fort Washington [Cincinnati]). Wayne then employed them in battle under a strong leader (General Charles Scott).

Mounted militia was indispensable to William Henry Harrison in the Western Theatre of the War of 1812. Harrison faced the need to gather great quantities of material at forward bases to attack Detroit, Fort Malden, and Sandwich, yet he could not base troops close to these strong points because of the difficulty of supplying *his* adjacent base, Fort Meigs. Because it was so difficult to accumulate quantities from his forward commissaries of Piqua, Urbana, and Franklinton (Columbus) to Fort Meigs (basically because of Meigs' inaccessibility due to the Great Black Swamp and the meandering St. Marys River), essentially basing troops at Meigs caused them to eat up all the food accumulated there without spare supplies to move forward and attack!

Thus, we come to the indispensability of mounted militia to Harrison. They could be called up quickly, in large numbers, for short periods; being mounted they could move far and quickly (in the War of 1812, from Kentucky to Fort Meigs), and wield massive (due to their numbers) and effective (due to the long rifle and militia's ability to fight either mounted or dismounted in rough country) firepower.

Harrison was able to succeed for three basic reasons: 1) He was a master of logistics, able to accumulate and protect sufficient numbers of rations in Northern Ohio to prepare for the northern offensive. 2) He chose to use mounted militia in their element: traveling mounted from a distance into heavy cover to where they could fight in this cover either mounted or afoot. Finally, Harrison utilized strong western leaders who were trusted by the militia.

Because these western leaders were not particularly adept in military science, 3) Harrison was a master of detailed orders. All three of these characteristics were crucial to his success.

Andrew Jackson, in the Creek War of 1813-'14 and the War of 1812 in the Southwest, was successful with militia for a combination of several of both Wayne's and Harrison's characteristics, but added a defining quality of his own: A fiery will and personal intimidation. He knew how to raise and supply his men; he knew how to fortify his supply line, and he knew how to pick leaders for the militia. On top of this, he added the dimensions that he simply would not give up no matter what the situation; he simply would not be beaten; and he would move his men forward to defeat the enemy via domination of both friend and foe with his own personal will.

In the years between the War of 1812 and the Civil War, several expedients were attempted to replicate the characteristics of mounted militia, which was increasingly too undisciplined and unsophisticated for modern warfare. The problem was how to develop similar firepower of large numbers of inexpensive militia in more expensive (training, arming, mounting, and maintaining), less numerous regular soldiers.

During 1836, Colt came out with a small, 5-shot revolving pistol, the *"Paterson."* In 1847, Captain Sam Walker, of the Texas Rangers and Taylor's U.S. Army in Northern Mexico, suggested improvements in the basic revolver. This resulted in the Colt *"Walker,"* a mighty .44 caliber handgun weighing 4 lb., 8 oz. It became known as a "horse pistol" because it was carried in holsters strapped to the pommel of a saddle. It fired six shots (i.e.: increased firepower), and at short ranges (up to 100 yds.) had the muzzle velocity and hitting power of a contemporary rifle. The first step toward developing the mobile firepower of the mounted militia had been taken.

Colt continued to improve its "cap-and-ball" pistols (like the M-1836 *"Paterson"* and the M-1847 *"Walker"*) into the M-1851 *"Navy,"* the "1st, 2nd, and 3rd Model *'Dragoons,'"* and the ultimate cap-and-ball pistol, the M-1860 *"New Army."* The 3rd Model

"Dragoon" came with a detachable shoulder stock which pointed toward turning multiple shot weapons into carbines. However, the shortcoming of all these weapons was the percussion cap, along with loose gunpowder loading, wad, and ball, which were essentially "muzzle-loaded" into the cylinder. In 1848, an inventor and gunsmith named Christian Sharps invented a rifle (also available in carbine) into which one eventually could breech-load a self contained shell (a bullet, powder charge, and percussion cap all in one). Although only available in single shot, the Sharps set the stage for the repeating carbine, the key to true mobile firepower.

Mid-way through the Civil War, the combination of weapons and organization came together to finally build a replacement for mounted militia, and point the way toward blitzkrieg. The Spencer 7-shot and the Henry 17-shot lever-action repeating rifles appeared and went into action. A professional cavalry trooper could now go into battle with a Spencer carbine (the preferred weapon because it could be produced more rapidly and its magazine was more protected than the Henry), two Colt M-1860 six-shooters, and a cavalry saber. (Note the resemblance to mounted militia in weapons type – a long arm, two side arms, and an edged weapon for close combat.) The firepower of large numbers of mounted militia could be approximated or improved upon by professional soldiers armed with repeating weapons, who were amenable to orders and direction. Large cavalry armies could ride long distances into enemy territory with tremendous small-arms firepower and wreak havoc with enemy production and communication systems.

Basically, the method of arming light troops was set by Sheridan's Civil War cavalry armies for the storm troopers of the German blitzkrieg. The horse was replaced by an airplane (paratroopers) or a tank/halftrack/motorcycle (mechanized infantry). The 7-shot Spencer repeating carbine was replaced by the 32-shot Schmeisser submachine gun; the 6-shot Colt revolvers were replaced with 9-shot Luger automatic pistols; and the sharpened cavalry saber was replaced by the jagged edges of shrapnel from exploding hand grenades. The line of descent from Wayne's mounted militia to Guderian's mechanized infantry was complete.

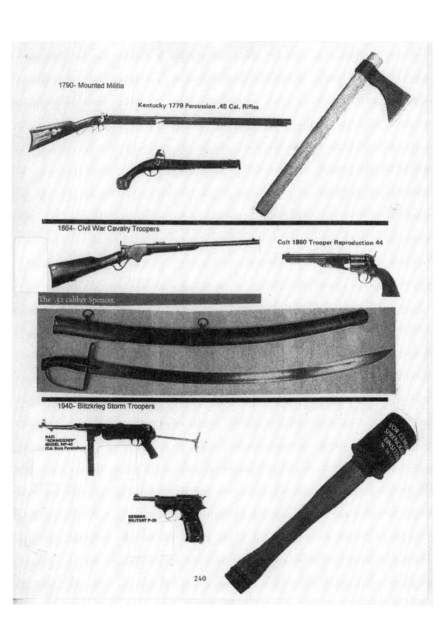

1790- Mounted Militia

Kentucky 1779 Percussion .45 Cal. Rifles

1864- Civil War Cavalry Troopers

Colt 1860 Trooper Reproduction 44

The .52 caliber Spencer.

1940- Blitzkrieg Storm Troopers

NAZI "SCHMEISSER" MODEL MP-40 (Cal. 9mm Parabellum)

GERMAN MILITARY P-38

240

American Super-Frigates

2005

By

John Eric Vining

Ever wonder where the early 1900s British concept of the "battle cruiser" came from? A battle cruiser was a hybrid ship that was more heavily armed than anything faster than it, and faster than anything more heavily armed and armored than it. Its fatal weakness was that to get high speed and heavy armament, it had to sacrifice armor. If it could be shadowed by a pack of regular cruisers (which were faster and could avoid contact at will) until cornered by incoming battleships, a battle cruiser could be destroyed (the German pocket-battleships were "in the same boat" – pardon the pun).

Where did the British come up with the idea for the battle cruiser? If you think about it, the British really had no major sea battles between the Trafalgar (1805) and 1900 (the advent of the battle cruiser) – except the American War of 1812. In that war, the American super-frigates (like the USS *Constitution*) were supreme – they defeated many British frigates and generally avoided destruction by British ships-of-the-line. How? They were faster and more heavily armed than the contemporary British frigates, and considerably faster than the much more heavily armed British ships-of-the-line (sound like a battle cruiser?).

Thus the last true battle experience the British had for nearly 85 years (1815-1900) was against the American super-frigates. However, the British made one crucial mistake in developing the battle cruiser concept from this experience. The American super-frigates were very heavily bulwarked internally with stout oak beams, and their external planking was very heavy – thus, they were also highly protected as well (hence the nickname *"Old Ironsides"* for the *Constitution*). They developed their superior speed from superior hydrodynamics, and also used this overall superior hydrodynamic design to crowd more sails onto the masts.

But by the time the British used this experience to build battle cruisers, ships had moved from wood to steel and sail to coal-fired steam. The only way to carry superior armament at high speeds while carrying enough coal to enable battle cruisers to get anywhere was to sacrifice armor – and hence the ultimately fatal weakness of the battle cruiser.

Setting the Stage for "Fiction"

John Eric Vining

"Sometimes ya just gotta cut loose!"

Bob and John spent most of their lives writing about history or quasi-political subjects – "factual stuff." While this writing was interesting (perhaps only to them!), it was of a relatively narrow focus. Once again proving that "blood is thicker than water," both tried a little different tack (unknown to each other) at about the about same stage of their lives (their late 40s and 50s)…they decided to try fictional writing.

John, given his fascination with military history, decided to focus on drawing up a word picture of a charismatic Civil War cavalry leader, perhaps in the mould of Nathan Bedford Forrest. His *"The Lion of the West"* does that, and a little more – it attempts to vividly recreate the emotion of fear that a cavalry charge must have engendered in both the cavalryman charging and the infantryman receiving the charge.

Bob seemingly went off the deep end with his farcical fiction *"Get a Good Look at the Basket."* If you read it on the surface, you might come away with the idea that you just have wasted a half-hour of your time on a silly, nonsensical story. However, if you "peel the onion," you might find just below the surface an example of Bob's biting satire about the absurdity of grown men playing a kid's game. About the ridiculousness and self-importance of coaches, who turn into ranting, petty tyrants for the sake of "improving" players' performances. About supposedly educated athletes who can barely speak complete sentences when describing their game. About the cynicism that performing for money and fame introduces into playing an innocent game.

Here, then, is Bob's and John's move into a new arena – fiction!

The Lion of the West

THE LION OF THE WEST

(Set in The Civil War, circa 1862)

By

John Eric Vining

We sat on the hilly mountain glade and peered at the battle lines nearly one-half mile away. From this elevated vantage point, the tiny figures scurrying back and forth along the opposing battle lines looked like miniature toy soldiers. However, each member of the Forty-first Ohio Volunteer Cavalry Regiment, of which I was a member, knew the lethality of the weapons those seemingly tiny Confederate soldiers possessed.

If we all were inwardly shuddering at the looming specter of death, our commander, Colonel Rex Moore, certainly did not display such emotions. Standing nearly 6'4", and weighing around 240 pounds, Moore sat erect and alert upon his horse at the far right flank of the regiment. The overall impression one drew of him was that of massive athleticism. A huge head, crowned by glistening salt-and-pepper-colored hair that covered his ears when not flowing in the wind, featured solid, impassive facial features and a dark countenance. Thick shoulders and upper arms which supported tight, sinew-like forearms and giant, gnarled hands – not unlike those of a blacksmith – maintained an authoritative control of the reins. Taut, heavily-muscled legs, sheathed in thigh-high black cavalry boots and capped with sharp, cruel-looking spurs, added to the awe-inspiring aura which surrounded Moore.

Even the horse upon which he was mounted enhanced this impression. No Kentucky quarter horse could long withstand the size and vigor of this officer. Instead, the colonel was mounted on a huge gray-white Percheron. Any other officer in the Union Army mounted upon a draft horse would have inspired derision among his troops, yet such was Moore's standing and presence within the

Federal Army of the Tennessee in this year of 1862 that none dared scoff at him. Indeed, the Percheron seemed to sense its master's strength and charisma, for in the countless charges which Moore had led against the Western Theater Confederates, not once had the lean, sleek mounts of the various troopers which charged with Moore been able to overtake him. Such was the measure of the man and his horse.

I will never forget my first and only personal encounter with Colonel Moore. A group of us were making coffee around a low campfire one evening. The colonel rode past and stopped for a cup with us. In the regular army, such fraternizing between officers and enlisted men would be strongly frowned upon. However, in the volunteers, where the officers were elected by the rank-and-file from their own number, the distance between officers and men was much less pronounced.

After a short round of light banter, I finally worked up enough courage to ask a question of my commanding officer:

"Begging your pardon, sir, but why do you risk your life so in our charges? You are always so far out in front of us. No disrespect intended, sir; but after all, you are one of us!"

In a voice which greatly contrasted with my image of him as a true hell-bent-for-leather cavalryman, Moore softly said, "I realize I am a dry-goods store manager in Cleveland in my real life. But you have elected me as your commander. As such, I will do all in my power to break the enemy – his spirit as well as his body. This might require the sacrifice of my life for a cause greater than my own existence."

In carrying out this mission, Moore had a flair for the dramatic as he prepared his troops to charge. Invariably, in full view of his enemies, Col. Moore would gallop to the head of his command, flinging his hat heavily to the ground as he dashed forward. Silver hair gleaming in the sunlight, black eyes burning malevolently like coals in a hellish locomotive firebox, he would grasp his sword and viciously slash it from its scabbard. Brandishing the glinting, razor-edged instrument of destruction menacingly above his head, Moore would cause the tremendous Percheron to rear high onto its back legs as he leaned into the horse's mane to maintain balance. For a split-second, man and horse would freeze in a picturesque pose, while from the ranks of his men arose a tremendous, hoarse, primal shout; the kind heard down through the ages as warriors prepared to fight and die. Above the din would come a deep, resonant roar from the lion-like soul of Col. Moore, and as the Percheron regained its legs, it would spring forwarded with a massive leap of adrenaline. In a rush of wind and a shower of spinning turf, colonel and horse would hurl forward, his men unhesitatingly galloping behind – minds melded together as one toward the goals of victory or death.

I tried to imagine what the Confederates must feel as this mountain of a man, his luminous white charger, and his furious, screaming shock troops thundered toward them. I imagined the enemy saw the flowing silver hair, felt the pounding of heavily-shod hooves, and sensed the prospect of cold steel death emanating from the massive man and his tremendous horse, as rider and steed bore mercilessly down upon them. If they were religious, Revelation 6:8 must have filled the enemies' terror-stricken minds: "And I looked, and behold a pale horse: and his name that sat on him was Death…" Fingers fumbled for triggers as cold sweat cascaded into fearful eyes. Suddenly, he was among them, the flashing saber at the end of the powerfully muscled arm sowing death and destruction among the masses.

I was jolted back to reality by a rising crescendo of cheers which approached like a tidal wave from my right. From my position in the ranks, I caught a flash of streaming silver hair as I sensed, rather than felt, a pulsating rush of energy moving over me. Trembling fingers clutched my carbine as cold sweat clouded my eyes and trickled down my back. Soon would come the rearing stallion and the flash of hooves. Would today be his day…or would it mine?

Get a Good Look at the Basket

By

Robert E. Vining

Edited by

John Eric Vining

Player-Coach Jason Victor slammed the newspaper down on the desk at which he was sitting and jumped up. He clenched his fists. "How could he do this to me?"

Coach J, as he was commonly called, paced back and forth in his den, his mind deep in thought over the article he had just read in the sports section of the Ft. Wayne *Herald*. He glanced at the mantle clock located on the wall. 3:45 PM. "He" would be home in 15 to 20 minutes.

"What am I going to do now?" he moaned. "How am I going to handle this?"

Coach J continued to pace while watching the clock. For years, he and his Ft. Wayne Vipers semi-pro basketball team had come close to winning it all only to be turned back by the Muncie Wolverines. Jason quickened his pace as he gritted his teeth. Just the thought of losing to the Wolverines' coach, Sam Bowen, made his blood boil. Bowen delighted in humiliating the teams he beat, especially the Vipers. His mean, sarcastic comments struck home, really getting under Coach J's skin.

All of this wouldn't be so bad if Coach J hadn't tried so hard. For years – no decades – he had striven to be just like his hero, Bobby Knight. Why, Jason even practiced throwing chairs across the basketball court, and had a Puerto Rican police doll he beat up on and choked, all in an effort to become just like Coach Knight. And it worked! Coach J was now as good as Bob Knight, and in one way even better. Nobody could scream at his players like Coach J. Nobody! Not Bob Knight; not Gene Keady; not P.J. Carlisimo; not even Pat Riley with his quadruple X-rated tirades were better than Coach J. He was the best. But it was all for naught. He couldn't win the big one; he couldn't be the champ.

However, this was supposed to be the Vipers' year. *"Big Gun"* Smith, the Wolverines star player, was out with an injury. Without his scoring, the Wolverines were vulnerable. But now, because of "him," Coach J's hopes were dashed.

Jason glanced at the clock again. 4:05 PM. He heard the car door slam. Moments later, "He" walked into the house. Coach J opened the door to his den and looked out. "Morris! Could you come in here?"

Morris looked up and saw the glare in Jason's face. He looked down; his shoulders slumped. "Yes, Dad."

Morris strolled into the den. Coach J slammed the door behind him. Jason's eyes narrowed; his lips curled. "I want an explanation about that article in the paper!"

Morris turned around and looked his father straight in the eye. "I did it for the money!"

Jason pointed his finger at Morris, and he gritted his teeth. "I thought I raised you better than that!"

Morris glared back at his dad. "I'm sick and tired of busting my butt for you and the Vipers for $19.95 a game. When the Wolverines offered me a five-year, $10,000 contract, I took it, and I'm glad I did!"

Jason looked away, his face red, his blood boiling. "This is the worst stab in the back I've ever received. How could you leave the Vipers for mere money?" His eyes bore in on his son like drill bits. "Is a few dollars that important to you?"

Morris looked away, his head down. Jason resumed his pacing. "I'm not going to say another word about this, but come Friday night when I and the other Vipers step on that basketball court, we're going all-out to win, and we're coming after you!"

Morris stomped toward the door. "Good! And I'm going after all of you – it's the only way to play the game!" He slammed the door on his way out.

Jason plopped down into his recliner. He leaned over, putting his elbows on his knees and cupping his hands around his head, staring at the floor. "What am I going to do?"

The door to the den swung open. Jason looked up; his faithful, overweight assistant, Thomas Rhoades, walked in. "Are you okay?"

"No," sighed Jason.

"What happened between you and Morris?"

"He quit the Vipers to join the Wolverines. All for money! Now what am I going to do? Where am I going to find a replacement for him at this late date?" Coach J had built the Vipers around himself, as player-coach, and his four sons. Morris, *"The Rifleman,"* was at one forward position. Albert, *"The Bombardier,"* was the other forward. Coach J, *"Mr. Clutch,"* was the man in the middle. Alphonse, *"Mr. Mechanical,"* was the shooting guard. Elrod, *"The Ramrod,"* was the point guard. He got his nickname for his almost supernatural ability to be at the right place at the right time to do whatever was needed to keep the team running smoothly. Rounding out the Vipers was Jason's nephew, Kory Fuqua, called *"Klondike"* because of his rough, Dennis Rodman-like style of play. No threat on offense, he was an animal on defense – absolutely fearless.

Coach J hopped up and paced again. "We'll never whip the Wolverines without a first-rate offensive player. We'll never score enough points. And this is my last chance against Bowen. The board of directors has told me if I don't win this year, I'll be fired. Gone will be my $10,000 a year salary." Jason stopped pacing a stared at Thomas. "What am I going to do?"

"Don't worry," answered Thomas. He put his arm around Coach J's shoulder and punched him playfully. "I have a solution." He pulled away and looked straight at Coach J. "I don't know how to tell you this, but I can play for the Vipers."

Jason stuttered, "You! You're way too fat and out of shape."

"I can play," insisted Thomas, "because I'm Nofoola Widabdula."

Coach J, wide-eyed, stepped back. Could this be true? Jason, of course, knew the story well. Nofoola Widabdula was the former superstar of the Albanian national team. Nicknamed the *"Terror of Tirana"* and the *"Muslim Monster,"* he led his team to one European title after another. Then after a game in Olso, Norway, he defected to the West, fleeing the communist tyranny of his home country, and seemingly disappeared from the face of the earth.

"I know this has to be a shock for you," said Thomas, "But it's all true. After I defected, the CIA searched its databanks worldwide to find someone who looked exactly like me. They eventually found that Thomas Rhoades was an exact look-alike. I let my hair grow out some and put on eighty pounds so we were identical. I came here and found a job; no one knew the difference. The real Thomas Rhoades is married, lives in Oregon and has fourteen kids."

Jason shook his head. "This is too much for me!" He staggered to his recliner and flopped down. "I can't believe this is true."

Thomas stood directly in front of him. "It's all true. All these years I've had to watch you and the boys play basketball, wanting to play so badly, but knowing I must keep my secret. But now the Cold War is over; there's nothing more to fear. I will play for the Vipers."

"You're gonna have to prove it to me," said Jason. Coach J and Thomas went out to the paved driveway which led to the garage. Over the garage door was a rim and backboard. Jason flipped on the lights and passed the ball to Thomas. He whirled and launched the ball high in the air toward the basket. SWISH! Thomas then proceeded to swing around the three-point arc, drilling the ball through the basket time after time. Coach J stood still, wide-eyed and dumbfounded. He had always considered his assistant a clumsy ox, incapable of walking and chewing gum at the same time. How wrong he was! With a basketball in his hands, Thomas was "Superman."

Thomas flipped the ball once more toward the basket. SWISH! The terrific backspin he put on the ball caused it to bounce back toward him after it went through the basket. He grabbed it, dribbled hard toward the bucket, hoisted his bulk high in the air, and with both hands slammed the ball through the hoop. He hit the ground, whirled, and faced Coach J. "Have you seen enough?"

"More than enough," answered Jason, his eyes still wide. "Let's go tell the rest of the guys."

"No. We've got one more topic to discuss. No way am I going to play for the lousy $19.95 a game you pay the boys and the miserly $14.95 you pay Kory."

Coach J's eyes narrowed; he frowned and snarled. "What? You know the rules! $19.95 is tops!"

Thomas shook his head. "Not for me, it isn't"

"I can't believe this! The love of the game should be enough of a reward, let alone the *extra* $19.95 I pay." Jason emphasized the word *"extra."*

Thomas shrugged and partially turned away. "No way! If you want me to play, you're going to have to fork over some big bucks!"

Jason clenched his fists and looked away. "Except for Kory, you modern ballplayers are all the same. You never hear him squabble over his $14.95 per game. That's because he loves the game. He has the heart...the soul...of a ballplayer. Don't you want to be like Kory?"

Thomas shook his head. "Nope. If I bust my butt, I want paid and paid well. Understood?"

Coach J hesitated for a moment. "I'll tell you what I'll do. The $19.95 will be your base salary. But if we win, I'll give you a bonus of one-tenth of one ten-thousandth of my salary. Fair enough?"

Thomas's eyes glazed over, deep in thought as he mentally tried to figure out how much that would be. Thomas had mastered the American language, but the mechanics of Western finance had escaped him. He finally threw his hands into the air. "I guess so."

With his long basketball experience, Coach J was terrific at overcoming problems, devising strategy, and putting together winning combinations. He was worth every penny of his $10,000 salary.

The week passed quickly. Even though relations were strained between Morris and the rest of the Victor family, they remained cordial toward him. True professionals, they would even the score with him on the basketball court, where it should be. Coach J and Thomas practiced together every night. Jason wanted to keep his new superstar a secret, not wanting to give Sam Bowen any time to prepare for the tornado that would soon engulf him and his Wolverines. Every minute he spent on the basketball court, Nofoola Widabdula got better. His good stuff was coming back. He was every bit as awesome as he was twenty-four years earlier when he fled Albania. Although just thinking about Sam Bowen made him wretch internally, Coach J many times had read Bowen's classic book on basketball strategy, "*Winning in the World of Semi-Professional Basketball.*" Sam was a master at the mental side of the game. Jason was looking forward to how Bowen would react when confronted with the *Terror from Tirana*.

Game time neared. The Vipers were in their locker room at the Muncie arena, changing into their blue uniforms with gold trim. As usual, Klondike had not yet arrived. Thomas sat quietly on a chair by the door. Albert, The Bombardier, looked around. "Dad, there are only four of us."

Coach J pulled on his blue jersey with the number 23 on it. "I know. Don't worry." Klondike was pulling another one of his pranks. It irritated Jason to no end, and he hoped there wouldn't be a repeat of the incident last year. Coach J was administering a verbal reprimand to Klondike – screaming at him at point-blank range, when Klondike lost all control. He grabbed Coach J around the neck, flipped him over his back, and slammed Jason onto the basketball court. Then Klondike jumped on him and began beating Coach J to a pulp, stopping only when Elrod politely asked him to stop. Coach J staggered to his feet, and in no mood to take this "Latrell Sprewell-like" outburst, promptly slapped a $.50 cent fine and a ten-minute suspension on him. That put Klondike in his place, and until now, he had been an angel.

Coach J walked to the door and peered out. "Where is he?"

"Don't worry," said Thomas. "He'll be here."

Coach J walked back into the locker room. "I can't wait any longer. Gather 'round me." He motioned to the boys and Thomas, circling with his arm.

The boys and Thomas grabbed chairs and sat down in a semicircle around Jason, who paced back and forth in front of them. "I don't have to tell you the importance of this game." He clenched his fists. "For the last three years, we've come close to beating the Wolverines, only to lose in the final minute of the game. Now we're up against it. The Rifleman, for money, has deserted us and gone over to the Wolverines. It's time for revenge and we're gong to get even!"

The Vipers jumped up off their chair. "YEEEAAAHHH!" they screamed.

"But how?" Alphonse, Mr. Mechanical, asked. "We don't have enough players."

Coach J glanced at his assistant coach. "I've go a surprise for you boys. Show 'em, Thomas."

Thomas jumped up and whipped off his sweats, revealing his blue and gold uniform with the number "00" on it. Thomas's nostrils flared; the sides of his lips curled downward forming an upside-down "U;" his face reddened; and a piercing glare burned from his dark, menacing eyes, radiating throughout the room. Thomas had disappeared, and in his place…

"May I present to you," roared Coach J. *"Nofoola Widabdula!"*

The boys, wide-eyed, silently looked at each other, then stared at the snorting, salivating Thomas Rhoades. Could their mild-mannered, overweight assistant coach really be Nofoola Widabdula, the greatest European basketball player ever? All of sudden, they all burst out in side-splitting guffaws, the thunderous laughter only subsiding moments later when Klondike stumbled into the locker room.

Coach J, upon seeing him, began jumping up and down. "Where have you been?" he screamed at the top of his lungs.

"Sorry I'm late," whined Klondike. "I was passing a house with smoke and fire pouring out of it, and there was an old couple hanging out of the upstairs windows. I stopped to save them. I thought the couple's lives were more important than…"

"No excuses," Coach J interrupted loudly. "This is going to cost you another $.50 cents!"

"Oh please, don't!" pleaded Klondike. "I need the cash for my kids' school milk money!"

"No!" screamed Coach J. "You need to learn that when I say, 'Be here on time,' I mean – 'BE HERE ON TIME!'"

Klondike's head dropped; his shoulders slumped. "I'll try to do better next time." Tears formed at the corners of his eyes.

"Okay, everyone, gather around me," said Coach J. "We need to go over some strategy."

The team huddled around Jason. "On defense, we're going to play a box-and-one. Mechanical and Ramrod will play out front; Bombardier and I will play underneath the basket. Nofolla will stick on the Rifleman like cold on ice. Got it?" Nofoola and the boys nodded.

Klondike scratched the side of his head while he tried to hide the traces of tears in the corners of his eyes. "What am I supposed to do?"

Coach J purse his lips. "Sit on the bench until we need a hatchet man."

Klondike brightened up right away. "I can do that!" he shouted enthusiastically.

Coach J paced in front of his team. "Now on offense, Nofoola will play the low post; the rest of us will play on the perimeter. Feed the ball into him. If they don't double-team you, Nofoola," said Coach J, zeroing his eyes in on him, "Take it to the basket."

Nofoola nodded his head again.

Jason paced once more. "If they do double-team, which I think they will once they realize who Nofoola is, you are to pass it back out to the perimeter. Someone will be open. Pass to the open man, get a good look at the basket, and shoot. Is that clear?" roared Coach J, emotionally rising to the moment and making eye contact with each of his players in turn. "When you get a good look at the basket, SHOOT!"

Everyone nodded, the adrenalin rising in their veins.

"One more thing," bellowed Coach J, while jabbing his palm with a clenched fist. "Don't give the Wolverines any easy baskets – foul 'em and foul 'em hard! Make them beat us at the foul line if they're going to beat us." Coach J thrust his hand into the middle of the huddle. "OK, WHO ARE WE?"

"VIPERS!" screamed the team as they broke huddle and tore out of the locker room.

Up on the court, the Vipers warmed up by shooting lay-ups. While waiting for his turn to shoot, Coach J looked around the Muncie arena. The place was packed with screaming Wolverine fans. On the other end of the court, the Wolverines also warmed up. Jason saw Morris, the former true blue (and gold) Rifleman, dressed in that awful brown Wolverine uniform. "How could he stoop so low?" Jason mumbled.

In front of Jason stood Nofoola, waiting for his turn. Bombardier flipped him the ball; he exploded toward the basket, dribbling the ball between his legs, then he jumped high in the air as he crossed the foul line. WWHHUUMMPP! Nofoola slammed the ball through the basket with both hands.

"AAUUHH!" moaned the crowd. "Who is that Viper guy?"

Coach J whirled around to see the Wolverines reaction. The Rifleman stood frozen, like an ice statue, not believing what he had just seen his ex-coach do. Jason then saw Bowen standing along the Wolverines' bench. His hands were on the sides of his face, his eyes wide open; his mouth had dropped open and formed an "O." He knew his team was in for a real battle. Perspiration poured off his bald head. His fat body quivered. He shook his head and his big ears flopped back and forth. It was easy to see how he had gotten the nickname "The Elephant Man."

The Wolverines front line consisted of three tall, tough, but rather slow defensive players with the nicknames of Buck, Butch, and Bull. Well built, these blond-haired, blue-eyed giants could be depended upon to keep the Wolverines in most games because they rebounded so well.

For offense, the Wolverines depended on their guards. Last year Big Gun Smith provided the outside shooting, but with him gone, the Rifleman would have to do the gunning from downtown. The other guard, Commando Kenton, was a quick, fast player with rockets for legs. He drove to the basket to score, trying for either lay-ups or foul shots. Coach already made up his mind: no lay-ups; The Wolverines would have to beat the Vipers at the foul line.

The referees walked onto the court. Jason smiled. The Vipers had really lucked out. The league had assigned referees' whose nicknames were Mr. T and Captain Hook. Both were normally tough and very fair, able to control any situation. Mr. T got his name because he wouldn't hesitate to call a technical foul. To remind the players who he was, he cut his hair in the form of a bushy T. Captain Hook got his name from his reputation for kicking players out of games. He kept the index finger on his right hand in the form of a hook, ready to fling it in the air and send some player to the showers. Both of these men were rugged, no-nonsense referees most of the time, but in the presence of their wives, they turned instantly into disgraceful wimps, cowering down in dread fear of the punishment their wives often slapped on them.

Coach J peered around the stands, searching for the referees' wives. "Ah, there they are," he grinned. Both already had on their mean glares and sour faces that made them so special. Their names were Miranda Fields and Rebecca Vance. What made Coach J so happy is that both thought Alphonse, Klondike, and Elrod could do no wrong; the refs wouldn't EVER call anything on these three players. They also thought the world of the kind-hearted assistant coach, "Thomas."

Coach J scanned the scorers' table where the officials were taking their seats. Sitting next to them were Bob Cook and Bill Williams, who would be broadcasting the game to a regional audience. Floor analyst Amber Ricks walked past them and waved to Coach J, and he trotted over and stood next to Amber; the cameraman moved in for a close-up.

Amber spoke into her microphone. "Coach J, what do the Vipers have to do to beat the Wolverines?" She then put the mic close to Jason's mouth.

Coach J's eyes narrowed, zeroing in on the camera. "Well, you know, we need to play our game. We're focused, you know, and uh, you know, we're really up for this game. The Wolverines, uh, you know, are good…uh; you gotta give them credit, you know. They can beat anybody when they play focused, you know…"

"Well said, Coach!" intoned Amber. "What exactly is 'your game?'"

"Well, you know, Amber, on offense, we've got to move the ball around, you know, and, uh, take high-percentage shots. Then on defense, you know, we've got to keep the Wolverines bottled up; make them take, uh, poor shots. If we can score more points than they do, you know, uh, we've got a really good chance to win the game."

"Always informative to hear your incisive analysis of the game, Coach," returned Amber seriously. "How do you feel about the Rifleman signing with the Wolverines?"

Jason shook his head. "There's no loyalty, you know, in semi-pro sports anymore. The good old days when players played for the thrill of the game are gone. You know, uh, now days, money talks. Money, you know, got to the Rifleman. It's sad, you know, real sad," finished Coach J, wiping a tear from the corner of his eye.

"Good luck to you and Vipers tonight, Coach," concluded Amber.

Coach J nodded and trotted back to the Vipers' end of the court.

The buzzer sounded; both teams moved to their benches. Many in the crowd were still murmuring, "Who is that Viper player?"

"Ladies and gentlemen," roared the PA announcer. "Welcome to tonight's game between the Fort Wayne Vipers (a low, sinister-toned booing drifted through the arena) and your *MUNCIE WOLVERINES* (an ear-splitting "YEAAHH" raised the rafters)!"

"First, for the Vipers, starting at wing, Viper Player-coach: Jason Vance. Also at wing: Albert Vance. At '2-guard:' Alphonse Vance. At 'Point:' Elrod Vance, and the big man in the middle, from Albania, the former *"Terror of Tirana,"* the *"Muslim Monster:" NOFOOLA WIDABDULA!"*

A blanket of silence descended over Muncie Arena. The crowd was in shock…disbelief. Could this be true? Their beloved Wolverines were in for a long, long night!

While the introductions of the Wolverines were being made Coach J gathered his Vipers for some last minute instructions. "Now remember, Nofoola is our go-to guy in the low post. Nofoola," said Jason, looking him straight in the eyes, "If they double team you, flip the ball back out." Coach J looked at his other players. "Pass the ball to the open man, get a good look at the basket, and shoot. Got it?" The Vipers all nodded.

Tweeeeet!!! Mr. T blew his whistle. The Wolverines and the Vipers positioned themselves at center court for the tip off. Nofoola lined up with Butch in the center circle. Mr. T held the ball between them, then threw the ball up into the air. Nofoola jumped first and easily controlled the tip, flipping the ball to Ramrod. He then raced to the basket. Ramrod dribbled the ball up the court, easily out maneuvering the slower Wolverines. Mechanical zipped to an open position along the baseline. Ramrod whipped the ball to him. Mechanical grabbed the ball and set to shoot, drawing the Wolverine defenders to him. The shot fake worked; Mechanical drilled a precision pass to Nofoola, who fought for position under the basket with Buck. He caught the ball, whirled toward the bucket, and WHUMP! He slammed the ball home as the outmuscled Buck held on.

Tweeeeet!!! Captain Hook pointed at Buck. "Foul's on Number 6." Nofoola walked to the foul line, dribbled the ball twice and shot the ball through the hoop, easily completing the three point play. The Vipers hustled back on defense.

The Wolverines' "Three Bs." Butch, Buck, and Bull, took up positions along the baseline. Commando dribbled the ball up the court and then side to side. The Three Bs set a series of picks, trying to pry the Rifleman open; but Nofoola, so quick and powerful, stayed right with him. The 24-second clock ticked down to zero. Commando slashed into the middle of the lane, trying for a lay up, but CRUNCH/BAMB! Mechanical came in low while Ramrod hit up high and – SMACK! – Commando hit the court spread–eagled, with a black-and-blue right eye.

Tweeeeet!!! Mr. T pointed to Mechanical.

"Who, me?" he whined.

Commando sank both free-throws. The Vipers grabbed the ball, rushed it down the court, and fed it to Nofoola, who immediately slammed it home again. Vipers–5; Wolverines–2.

The Wolverines, now on offense, were determined this time to get the Rifleman open. One good look at the basket and he'd drill it for sure. The Three Bs set a triple pick. The Rifleman sped past them and into the open. Commando whipped the ball to him. The Rifleman caught it, turned, looked, and fired all in one motion – but WHAM! – Nofoola crashed through the pick; his arms outstretched skyward, he leaped and smacked the ball out of the air, blocking the shot. Then, like a raging bull, Nofoola knocked over the Rifleman and anyone else (on either team) who was in his way as he went for the ball. As bodies flew everywhere, Nofoola dived into the crowd, at the last second flipping the ball backwards directly into the Ramrod's hands. Ramrod raced down the court, passing the ball to Mr. Mechanical. Mechanical passed the ball back to Ramrod. The Rifleman, who had regained his feet and raced to a defensive position directly in front of the basket, watched the ball movement intensely. Suddenly, Nofoola, who had disengaged himself from the crowd, now trailed the play, while also watching the ball movement intently. Ramrod looped the ball up toward the rim, where a rampaging Nofoola leaped up for an alley-oop jam, slamming the ball with a mighty crash and alighting heavily on the waiting Rifleman. Nofoola's upraised knee struck the Rifleman squarely in the midsection.

"OOOOOPH!" moaned the Rifleman as he collapsed onto the floor, curling into the fetal position.

Captain Hook had raced down the court with the play and got a good look at the obvious charge. He raised his hand and was about to slap it on the back of his head, the signal for an offensive foul, when out of the corner of his eye he caught a glimpse of Rebecca in the stands. She was jumping up and down, her eyes full of fire. She pointed, wiggling her index finger at him. His shoulders slumped. He put both hands on his hips, the signal for blocking. "Foul on Brown, Number 10!"

The Rifleman, writhing in agony, looked at the one, zero on his brown jersey. He made his way to his feet as best he could, screaming at Captain Hook: "You have *GOT* to be kidding! Are you blind?"

Coach Bowen, pacing along the sideline, also chimed in: "You *idiot*!"

Captain Hook glanced at Bowen then back at the Rifleman. He raised his hand with the hooked finger, ready to kick both of them out of the game.

But Mr. T, realizing the importance of the game (and perhaps weighing the officials' chances of getting out of Muncie Arena in one piece if Captain Hook ejected Bowen and Vance), intervened and pulled Captain Hook's hand down. Mr. T whirled, pointed to both Bowen and the Rifleman, and made the T-sign twice: two technical fouls.

The Rifleman, unsteady on his feet, pleaded with Captain Hook. "Our coaches always taught us that referees would call a fair game!"

Captain Hook glared the Rifleman straight in the eye: "Your coaches taught you wrong!"

Bowen had seen enough. He called time out to settle his team down and devise a defensive strategy. When the time out was over, the Ramrod, a 99% free throw shooter, calmly sank all four technical fouls.

The Vipers took the ball out of bounds and lobbed it again to Nofoola. This time, the Three Bs surrounded him, a triple-team. Nofoola fired the ball back out to Ramrod. Smothered by a Wolverine defender, he zipped the ball to Mechanical, who made a precision pass to the Bombardier - wide open and already set to launch a long jumper just outside the three-point arc. The Bombardier grabbed the ball, cocked, and fired a high, spinning jumper that came cascading down into the basket for three points.

The Bombardier's bucket was a demoralizing knockout punch. The Wolverines staggered up court, made a few half-hearted passes, and then lost the ball to a 24-second violation.

The Vipers, sensing the kill, roared down court, again took advantage of the triple-team on Nofoola, and got the ball to the once more wide-open Bombardier, who immediately put three more points on the board.

Commando grabbed the out-of-bounds pass and, determined to get the Wolverines back into the game, raced up the court to score a lay-up before the Vipers could set up their defense. He zipped into the paint and, wide-open, flipped the ball to the bucket. But WHACK, Nofoola rotated over from the weak side, slapped the ball back in Commando's face and broke his nose. Blood squirted everywhere. Commando wobbled and crashed face first onto the floor. But he hopped up, ran to the bench, grabbed a towel and wiped his nose before hustling back onto the court.

Mechanical drilled another three-point bomb. Bowen, screaming profanities along the sideline, called time out.

Coach J, grinning from ear to ear, gathered his Vipers around him for the time out. He peered down at the Wolverines' bench. Sam Bowen was going spastic…berserk…waving his fists while screaming at his players.

Coach J looked back at the Vipers. "We've got them really shook up, but watch out for some special play, something to get them back into the game – okay?"

The Vipers broke and trotted back onto the court. Ramrod brought the ball up the court, as usual flipping the ball to Mechanical who lobbed it on to Nofoola.

But the Rifleman jumped in front of him and stole the ball. He roared down the court looking for an easy slam dunk.

The Ramrod had anticipated the Rifleman's move and had fallen back on defense. Both players raced to the Wolverines' basket. They reach it at the same time; Ramrod tried to get set, but was still moving just a bit when the Rifleman ran straight into him - then up and over him for a mighty slam dunk!

Captain Hook had followed the play and was about to call a blocking foul on Ramrod. But this time he caught Miranda Fields out of the corner of his eye. She was jumping up and down, screaming, pointing he finger at him with one hand and clenching her fist with the other. Gritting her teeth, her look had changed to pure venom. It was too much for Captain Hook. He waved off the two points with one hand while slapping the back of his head with his other hand, the signal for charging on the Rifleman.

The Rifleman was horrified and angry beyond words. But knowing the futility of arguing with Captain Hook, he merely raced back on defense, a new determination etched all over his face.

The rest of the first half continued to be a blow out, with the Bombardier and Mr. Mechanical zeroing in with one three pointer after another. Coach J jumped for joy as he led his team off the court. This is what he had long been waiting for. The Vipers' defensive strategy, however, had put them deeply into foul trouble.

Both teams soon returned to the court and warmed up for the second half. The Vipers practiced shooting the ball, but Nofoola stood at the top of the key, bent over…panting. He had played his heart out in the first half, and without much time to get in shape, was worn out. Coach J jogged over to him. "What's wrong?"

Nofoola stood up, but his head was still down. "I'm tired. Maybe you should start Klondike for the second half."

"No way! We've got the Wolverines on the run and I want to keep the pedal to the metal." Jason was no longer interested in just winning. He wanted to run up the score to both teach the Rifleman a lesson and humiliate Sam Bowen.

The second half started out like the first with the Vipers in control, but within two minutes Nofoola, exhausted, could hardly make it up and down the court. He called a time out, hobbled to the Vipers' bench and plopped down heavily. He put his head between his knees and closed his eyes.

Coach J, frown on his face, rushed over and stood in front of him. "What do you think you are doing?" he screamed.

Nofoola, gasping for air, raised his head. "I can't do it anymore…I can't go on!"

Coach J gritted his teeth. "You've got to suck it up and get out there," he pointed to the court, "Regardless of how you feel!"

"I can't…It's too much!"

"Look, you wimp," Jason bellowed. "You've got to get the lead out of your behind and get out there, now!"

"Me? Why don't you get your head in the game and do something? You haven't done a thing all game but yell at us!"

"What? You either get out there or you're fired!" Coach J raged.

"Fired? I quit!" Nofoola whirled around and stomped up the stairs to take a seat next to Miranda and Rebecca. Coach J, realizing what a mistake he had made, followed him, begging Nofoola to come back. Nofoola crossed his arms and stared moodily at the court, paying no attention to Jason's ranting. Finally, Nofoola lifted his stare directly into Jason's eyes. "No!" he shouted resolutely. "I'm through with you and the Vipers!"

Coach J had learned to late that you don't fool with Abdul.

Coach J returned to the bench and told Klondike to report in at the scorer's table. Klondike took his position as the chaser in the box-and-one defense. The other Vipers, all in foul trouble, wouldn't be able to help him much; Klondike would pretty much have to contain the Rifleman all by himself.

The Wolverines were quick to seize the opportunity. They whipped the ball around the perimeter of the defense as the Rifleman came off screen after screen. Finally, he caught the ball, aimed, and cocked all in one motion. He fired away before Klondike could catch up with the play. The ball spiraled toward the basket and Whump…careened off the back of the rim, straight up, then directly through the basket, a three-pointer.

The Wolverines quickly converted to defense. With Nofoola out of the middle, they were able to extend their defense outward. The Vipers whipped the ball around with laser-like precision, but to no effect. The Bombardier and Mechanical, unable to get open, couldn't get good looks at the basket. The 24-second clock ticked down. The Bombardier forced up a wild shot from thirty feet away. WHAM! The ball bounced off the back of the rim; the Rifleman grabbed the rebound.

Coach J looked up in the stands at Nofoola. He raised his arms from his sides, pleading. Nofoola shook his head. Coach J gritted his teeth once again and hustled back on defense.

Commando, realizing the Viper defense was now weak down the middle, dribbled up the court, then slashed into the paint towards an easy lay up. The foul-plagued Vipers let him go, but not Klondike; shoving the Rifleman out of his way, he lunged at Commando, leaping high into the air. While going for the ball, of course, Klondike delivered a mighty smash into Commando's mouth while popping another slap across Commando's shooting arm. They crashed together, their legs becoming entangled. As Commando fell, he tried to pull Klondike around him to cushion the fall. Not falling for that old move, Klondike delivered a tremendous elbow to the torso of Commando.

Klondike disengaged himself from the bruised, bloody mass that just a few seconds ago had been recognizable as Commando Kenton. Commando remained on the floor, shaking and whimpering. Captain Hook slapped his hand on the back of his head: "Offensive foul on Brown, 3-2!" (Commando).

An enraged Sam Bowen leaped from his chair on the sideline and raced out of the coach's box. "You *MORON!*" he shouted at the top of his lungs.

Mr. T whipped his hands in the form of a "T," then yelled, "Technical foul!" Hook flipped his crooked finger into the air. Bowen was gone, kicked out of the game.

Meanwhile, Coach J had run over to Commando and knelt by his side. "Are you okay?"

Commando murmured, "I'll be alright, I think. Tell Klondike that was a cheap foul and I'll see him next season!"

Coach J then trotted to Klondike, who was bent over, supporting himself with his hands on his knees and gasping for breath. He patted Klondike on the back. "Don't let this affect your game, okay? You did what you had to do. Basketball is a tough game at times."

The Wolverines' trainer finally got around to looking after the stricken Commando. "Both arms broken. Several teeth knocked out." He waved for a stretcher.

The Wolverine managers put Commando on the stretcher, wheeled him off, then returned to clean the floor. Without further ado, both teams were ready to resume play.

Klondike tore after the Rifleman with renewed energy and determination. However, the Rifleman was too quick for him. Time after time he gave Klondike the slip, got a good look at the basket, and fired home one three-pointer after another.

The Vipers watched the progress of both the clock and the scoreboard. One was moving far too slow for them, and the other was mounting far too fast. On every possession, the Vipers ran off as much clock as they could, but the Rifleman was on one of his patented tears. The Vipers' lead melted. With 28 seconds left in the game, the Rifleman pumped in a three-pointer than made the score 61 to 58, the Vipers still in the lead. Coach J called a time-out.

In the huddle, Coach J went over his final play…one that would seal the victory. "We'll run the shot clock down to seven seconds. Then Klondike and Mechanical, you set a low double pick for me. You other two, get me the ball. I'll put this game out of reach for the Wolverines."

The Vipers returned to the court. This was the moment for which Coach Jason Victor had played basketball his whole life. This is why he earned the big bucks; this is why he was called Mr. Clutch.

The Vipers took the ball out of bonds. The Ramrod dribbled the ball at center court while the clock ticked down. With seven second left, Klondike and Bombardier set their picks. Mr. Clutch flew by. Mechanical bulldozed Bull, setting him squarely on his tail, but the Rifleman squeezed by Klondike and rushed at Clutch. Klondike whirled and lunged desperately at the Rifleman, just getting enough of him to trip him. The Rifleman spun to the floor.

The Rifleman looked up at the refs, pleading for a call, but both Mr. T and Captain Hook looked away; no call.

Meanwhile, the Ramrod whipped the ball to Coach J, "Mr. Clutch," who got a wide open look at the basket. Aiming carefully, he launched the last shot, but CLANG; he had misfired and thrown up a brick. The ball careened off the backboard and out of bounds. Wolverines' ball.

The Rifleman called the Wolverines' last time out. In the Vipers' huddle, Coach J anticipated a three-pointer to tie the game and send it into overtime. "Whatever you do, don't foul outside the three point line. Understand?" He looked at each of the players in turn, and each nodded yes – all except Klondike, who had a strange look of determination written on his face.

The game clock showed three seconds left. The Rifleman would inbound the pass at the center court line. Klondike moved right up on him, determined to deflect of steal the inbounds pass.

"Oh, NO!" gasped Coach J. He immediately attempted to call a time out, but it was too late. The Rifleman faked a high pass, causing Klondike to leap up. He then bounce passed the ball to Buck, who immediately set a screen. The Rifleman slashed by, getting the ball back. Klondike followed, zeroing in on the Rifleman like a bulldozer run amok. He slammed into Buck, knocking him out of the way. But the Rifleman had time to get a good look at the basket. He started his shot just as Klondike lunged at him, hitting him with a vicious cross-body block. Both of them tumbled to the floor. Somehow the Rifleman had been able to launch his patented jump shot, arching it high into the rafters from long range.

The ball spun toward the basket. In mid-flight, the game-ending buzzer blew. The ball descended, seemingly from the heavens; coming from so high it nearly had ice on it. But no matter; it tracked unerringly through the middle of the hoop and hung the net as it *SWISHED* sweetly!

And then…*a late whistle.* Everyone in the house looked to mid-court. Captain Hook stood nearly inside the center circle, arm straight in the air and fist clenched. "Foul on Blue, Number 7!"

Klondike looked down at his jersey. "That's my number! You can't call that foul! *NOBODY* calls a foul with three seconds left on the clock!

The Rifleman trudged slowly to the foul line. He was all by himself at the line; every Wolverine eye was on him, enamored with their new hero. Every Viper eye was on him as well, glaring with all the vitriol that a traitor engenders.

The Rifleman stood trembling slightly at the foul line. Just as Captain Hook prepared to bounce-pass the ball to him, Coach J ran to Mr. T, screaming "Time out! *Time out! TIME OUT!!!*"

Both teams headed to their benches. As they approached theirs, Mechanical scratched the side of his head and asked, "Why did we call time out?"

Coach J grinned, "To ice him. I want him to think about the importance of this shot. I don't think he has a snowball's chance of making it!"

The stadium horn blew and both teams made their way onto the court – nine players at the mid-court line and one – the Rifleman – standing alone at the free throw line. He was shaking so badly he could barely catch the ball as it was passed to him from the official. The Rifleman took a deep breath, bounced the ball twice, aimed, cocked, and let 'er fly. The ball looped up, came down, clanged sharply off the back of the rim, went straight up, and fell directly through the basket. The delirious Wolverine fans rushed the court. The Wolves win! The Wolves win!

Coach J fell to his knees, bowed over with his face to the court and pounded the floor with both fists. He had never been known as a good loser. In fact, one of his key sayings for years had been, "Show me a good loser, and I'll show you just that…a loser!" Let's face it, the old saying 'it's not whether you win or lose; its how you play the game' is bull. And Coach J had lost – again – this time having been gunned down by his own son.

Elrod, "The Ramrod," trotted over and knelt by his father. "Come on, Dad, you gotta get your act together. It's only one loss. We'll come back from this and get 'em next year."

For once, the Ramrod was not able to accurately foretell the future. There would be no "next year" for Coach Jason Victor. The board of directors of the Fort Wayne Vipers had lost to the Muncie Wolverines one time too many under Coach J's watch. Although he had been a dedicated player and coach with the Vipers for years, boasting a winning percentage of .814 over a seventeen-year career, he was canned as the team bus made its way back to Ft. Wayne from Muncie (receiving the news via text message on the bus). That's the way it was in the cut-throat world of semi-professional sports.

Nofoola consoled Coach J on the bus. "Hey, Coach, it's just a game – it's not the end of the world." But Nofoola was also wrong. For Coach J, losing the game and his job was the end of the world.

Later that evening, Coach J rested in his recliner in the den. Still in shock, he held his face in his hands. He had had it all right there – *right there* - in the palm of his hands: Victory! Revenge! A renewal of his $10,000 contract! Now all was lost – gone forever.

There came a knock at the door. The Rifleman walked in. "Dad, I need to talk to you. You were right. The money isn't worth it. I've given up my big contract with the Wolverines. I'd like to come back to the Vipers, if they'll have me. What do you think?"

Coach J rose from the recliner and patted Morris on the back. "Yes, I'm sure the Vipers will want you back. I'm proud of you. You did the right thing!"

The rest of the Victor family came into the den and joined Jason and Morris. United, they were a family again, the way it should be and the way it remained for the rest of their lives.

PART III

Growing Old in the Rural Midwest:

"At 60, you realize *nobody* was thinking about you."

The Beauty and the Beast

2012

By

John Eric Vining

I'm a long-time Harley Davidson Sportster fan – so much that I have two of them sitting in my garage. The tale of how I acquired these two is a story unto itself.

I first became a Sportster nut in the spring of 1972. I was sitting at a local ice cream shop when a friend rode up on a brand-new cream-colored '72 Ironhead Sportster. It was love at first sight. This love went unrequited for nearly 40 years until the spring of 2009. I drove past a nearby barnyard and there, with a "for sale" sign on it, was a rough but nearly complete 1974 Ironhead Sportster. I decided at my age it was now or never: I whipped out my checkbook and purchased it on the spot!

After spending some coin to get it road-worthy, the Ironhead sat quietly in my garage as my last son finished high school, with all the attendant rush of activities this involves. Fast forward to the spring of 2012. Harley Davidson introduced the Sportster *Seventy-Two*: 2.1 gallon "peanut" gas tank; laced spoke wheels; small front/ large rear tires; metal-flake paint. Hey, I got one-a-those in my garage already! Out came the wax and touch-up paint!

In the meantime, my wonderful wife realized I was going through some personally rough times. One evening, out of the blue, she blurted, "I've located a pristine '03 Harley Sportster; let's get in the car – I'm going to buy it for you." Home we came with a beautiful "One-Hundredth Anniversary" Evolution Sportster!

This is a comparison of the two Sportsters, built twenty-nine years apart. First, let me make clear that I'm not a mechanic and have no pre-conceived notions about the two machines. I've just began to ride both relatively extensively in 2012. This essay is basically the impression of a novice Harley Davidson Sportster rider who is starting to ride the two bikes almost simultaneously.

The first indication of my impressions of the two bikes is the unofficial nicknames I've given them: the "Beauty" (the 2003) and the "Beast" (the 1974). Let's get the raw statistics of the '03 out of the way: 1,200 cc Evolution engine; 5-speed transmission; 58 horsepower; 72 lb/ft of torque; and 562 lbs in weight. The '03 has the appearance of a refined street cruiser: relatively tall, not a large apparent disparity between the front and rear tires, magnesium wheels, classy black and silver "anniversary" paint job, and comfortable stepped saddle.

It rides as beautifully as it looks. The starting sequence is easy and the electric start is smooth. Controls come easily to hand and foot. Moving onto the road, acceleration is swift and sure, the 5-speed transmission providing a smooth and steady progression to a comfortable 55 miles per hour. That 5th gear really feels nice at about 2,400 rpms.

Speaking of the tachometer (and speedometer), the electronic revolution had arrived by 2003 and the gauges smoothly and accurately portray what is happening inside the 74-inch Evo engine. The Evolution purrs richly from (almost) unmodified exhaust pipes. Deceleration is sweet with outstanding disc brakes front and rear.

The only somewhat surprising feature is that at its rated 72 lb/ft of torque, the Evo seems very slightly balky as you complete the downshift to second gear, make a turn, and begin acceleration once again. There is a little bucking and the slight sensation of stalling until the rpms pass 2,000, then the sure acceleration once again takes hold.

All-in-all, the '03 Evo is a perfect machine for a Sunday afternoon cruise around the neighborhood. This is very indicative of what the Sportster has become. It provides the sensation of riding a well-bred Tennessee Walking Horse.

Next, "The Beast." The first impression is what the Sportster really was in 1974: a rawboned streetfighter. It has the "Three L's" of appearance in spades: long, low, and lean. The basic statistics: 1,000 cc Ironhead engine; 4-speed transmission; 57 horsepower; 55 lb/ft of torque; and 485 pounds in weight. There is an apparent disparity between the relatively small front tire and the large, beefy rear tire. The spoked wheels and the generic flat black oil tank give the impression of lean functionality.

Now, to start the monster. The start sequence is similar to the Evo's until you go to press the "start" button - there is none. The Ironhead kicks like a mule because there is no compression release. If I complete the starting sequence exactly right, it takes 2 to 3 kicks - if I screw up, perhaps 8 to 10. The upper shock attachment is right above the kick starter; if I'm not extremely careful, I have an on-going "Harley tattoo" (i.e.: a dark black bruise) right behind my right knee throughout the riding season!

Upon starting, there is a rush of noise, rattling, and shaking! The raucous, blattering roar of the Ironhead through (who knows what is left inside of) the exhaust pipes pierces the air. The front wheel shakes. The seat vibrates. You sense the bike through every pore of your body – and it is not an unpleasant sensation! You feel you have mounted a tough, half-broken mustang. You thrust the Ironhead into first gear and it jumps slightly – the bike is rearing to go. Pull onto the road and the Ironhead's 1st gear devours the tarmac. Second gear: the aggressive gearing pushes you back and you feel the bike's power. Third: once again, the sensation of unleashed momentum. Fourth is the road gear. The Ironhead rumbles and races to cruising speed – where is fifth gear? You want to hunt for it, but you know there is none.

You glance down to get some indication of performance. The gauges bounce and dance – they were mechanical in 1974. You think you are turning about 3,000 rpms and 55 mph, but you can't be sure.

Deceleration: what a powerful sensation as you work down through the gears! The Ironhead sounds great as it growls down to turning speed. You press the foot/rear brake to assist: nothing happens. You press harder...and harder...finally the rear drum brake takes hold and enhances the deceleration. You pretty much have to use that anathema of Harley riders – the front disc brake – to get slowed enough to turn safely.

Despite its rated 55 lb/ft of torque, the 61-inch Ironhead feels "torque-ier" at low speeds than the 74-inch Evolution. It possibly has something to do with favorable "power-to-weight" and/or "gearing" ratios, or the more positive chain drive.

All in all, the two machines are perfect at what they were designed to be: the pleasant cruiser and the tough streetfighter. Despite similar appearances (and it *is* apparent they are generational relatives), they are very different machines. The friend and the fighter. The thoroughbred and the bronco. The "Beauty" and the "Beast."

TUX & OLIVIA

2010

By

John Eric Vining

That fateful day we as parents all must face finally came: my fourth son, Evan, left home for college. I had managed to put off this day for an extra year by more or less bribing Evan to attend a regional campus of our state university for one year; if he would go to the branch for one year, I would pay for it. He dutifully put in that year, but now he was leaving home to go to the main campus. I was officially an *empty nester*. I managed to fight off the tears (Dads aren't supposed to cry, you know) as we helped him set up his room in his "new" (to him, at least; it looked like *"Animal House"* to me) apartment. Now, as my wife and I drove home and the tears trickled unabashedly down my cheeks, I had to face reality. I loved being a dad, and while I still was one, it just was not the same. The boys essentially were on their own. *What was I going to do now?*

I went home, and for the next three months, I basically bounced off the walls as the silence in our home grew deafening. My wife saw how discomfited I was, and she became despondent that I was so upset. "You need something to love and take care of," she said with certainty. As usual, she was exactly right.

It's funny how sayings you learn when you are a kid stick with you even when you are old. Take for instance the phrase, *"Never say 'never'."* When I was younger, even when we first had been married, we had dogs around the house. Not inside dogs, though...always outside dogs, for hunting or working with the livestock on the farm. My mother had been a real stickler for a clean house, and dogs were not allowed inside. Thus, when my wife and I were married, I made the hard and fast statement: *"We will never have animals in the house!"* Famous last words on the subject…

On Labor Day weekend, 2010, my wife and two youngest sons sat me down at the dining room table and looked me straight in the eye. "Dad, there are boxer puppies for sale in the paper just a few miles from here. We are going to check them out, and you are going with us!"

"Well…okay," I countered. "We're just going to look, though… right?"

"Yeah, sure," they said. "We're just going to check them out."

We drove the 15 miles to the private breeder's home, and after greeting us at the door, he stepped outside. The young man said that while the advertisement stated he had two puppies left from this litter (a male and a female), the female had been placed in a home that very morning and there was only the male left. He was approaching 11 weeks old and had been passed over by some other buyers, so the breeder was willing to part with him at a discount if we were interested in him.

"Okay," I said non-committedly, so the breeder went back into the house to let the puppy out so we could see him. Suddenly, the back door flew open and out flew a tall, slender, gangly, fawn-colored boxer pup. He made a bee-line straight for me, leaped off the ground, onto my lap, and into my heart.

"Write the check," I told my wife.

The puppy had a tawny coat with a white breast and long white "tails" streaming back well onto his mid-section. Imbedded within the white breast was a virtually straight row of black pigmented spots. It was obvious – his name would be "Tux."

I was all set to be cool and collected with the new puppy. We purchased a dog crate for him to sleep in, placed the crate in a corner of the utility room, and went to bed. Tux was lonely, and it was not long before we heard a pitiful whining coming from downstairs.

"I'll go down and sleep on the couch," I said to my wife sleepily. "If I put the crate right beside me, he should be just fine."

I dutifully set up the living room just as I said, but no - that was not good enough. Tux looked at me mournfully through the bars of his crate and a few more lonely whimpers emerged.

"Okay, little fella," I said to Tux. "I understand. You miss your mommy. How would you like trying to sleep on my chest?"

I rearranged myself on the couch and pulled Tux onto my chest. He fell asleep immediately and a great friendship was born. I awoke once around 3:00 AM and there was little Tuxie, nestled on my shoulder with his nose right against my neck. It would have taken a cold, hard-hearted person to not fall in love with the little guy right then and there!

Tux and I became a team. He grew from a gangly, skinny-looking guy into a very tall, muscly, long-legged, handsome male. The muscles grew large on his skinny frame and his tawny coat looked like it was a size or two too small, so he looked like a finely-tuned athlete. And he was definitely an "alpha-male." While extraordinarily friendly and affectionate to humans, he was absolutely the opposite with other male dogs. While on our frequent walks with him along the river, virtually always, much larger dogs cowered and slunk away at Tux's approach. For those that didn't – well, let's just say it was all I (and the other alpha dogs' owners) could do to keep them apart! Several times I heard the other dogs' masters mutter (under their breath) words to the effect, "I'm glad that guy kept that boxer off our Rottweiler – did you see the muscles on that dog?") The skinny, gangly pup had come full circle!

But as big and tough as Tux became, he couldn't overcome one weakness: he was lonely. My wife was an OB nurse who frequently worked 12+ hour shifts, while I was working about 12-hour days myself at the time. Tux was a good dog and eventually was given the run of the house, but he needed a companion - just as he had become a companion for me.

We knew that animal shelters were bursting at the seams. However, we had grown to love the boxer breed, and wanted a full-blooded boxer female as a companion for Tux. Because boxers were so affectionate and beautiful, we despaired of finding one. Who would possibly give up such wonderful dogs?

Nevertheless, we began to scour the internet for boxers. We could not believe how fast we came up with one, only 35 miles away in a nearby city! The picture showed a beautiful fawn 11-month-old female boxer with a nearly completely white face, black eyes, and beautiful perky ears. Her name was "Olivia." We called the shelter: "Is Olivia still there?" we asked. Yes! "Can we bring our male with us to see how they get along?" Sure. We made arrangements to visit the shelter the next day.

When we arrived at the shelter, our hearts nearly broke. The air was filled with pain-filled barks of lonely dogs. This particular shelter made a point of never putting its wards to sleep, so they had to ration the available food accordingly. We went back to the kennels and our hearts continued to sink. Cage after cage of beautiful, healthy, but rejected dogs filled our eyes. They were skinny due to the rationing, but they were alive and eager for a home and someone – anyone – to love them. We came to the kennel of a very skinny, nearly full-grown, and anxious boxer – Olivia. She looked up at us with beautiful eyes, but eyes which had become old too soon.

We heard Olivia's story. She had been picked up on the streets of the city very alone, hungry, and dirty. Her masters had gotten a divorce. Olivia had been the ex-wife's dog, but her new apartment complex would not accept animals. So Olivia by default had been sent to the ex-husband, who did not care about Olivia in the slightest. One day Olivia got free of her loveless abode, and hit the streets. She spent weeks roaming and scrounging for whatever morsels she could find. She was finally picked up by county workers and taken to the shelter in very poor shape. The shelter caregivers had gotten her back into decent condition, but she was very thin. "She's a little sweetheart, though," said the keeper. He was right.

We took Olivia out to meet Tux, and let's just say there is definitely such a thing as love at first sight! The formerly listless Olivia came alive; her black eyes flashed. She danced like the puppy she still was, and made all the bouncy, flirty moves she could summon. Tux was just as taken with her – there was no sign of his alpha-dominance toward this little girl!

How could we say no? Olivia became a part or our growing family as well. It took some time for her to remember her house-training, and she had some (probably well-founded) anxiety issues that found release in some mild destructiveness. But after some time she was able to trust us, and open her heart to us as well.

But there was never any doubt that she loves Tux and Tux loves her. We've often jokingly commented that Olivia tolerates us, but really *loves* Tux.

And me...I have my new family to love and take care of. Some of my favorite times are now spent in the early morning darkness of our living room, sipping that first cup of coffee of the day, with two of the world's biggest lapdogs draped across me. I have youngsters back in my life again!

BUT, GEE, ALL I HAVE ON MY TEAM IS A BUNCH OF ROOKIES!

The Initial Evaluation Process of a Young Boys' Basketball Team: The Crucial "First Practice"

2003

By

John Eric Vining

Amazing as it may sound, *every* coach at *every* level of basketball must evaluate the talent he has on his team almost immediately in order to design a proper practice regimen. And I do mean at EVERY level! I feel the crucial importance of evaluating talent has arisen because of the astounding change youth basketball has undergone in the past 25 years. Ever since basketball legends "Magic" Johnson and Larry Bird transformed the college game into a media bonanza in 1979, kids of all ages have hit the courts earlier in their lives than ever, with impressive results.

I have been coaching boys' basketball at various levels for about 15 years – from the third grade level at the local YMCA to the junior varsity level in AAU. I believe the most interesting youngsters to coach are 10-to-12-year-olds. These boys are developing coordination at this point, they have watched a lot of basketball on television, and they are discussing the game with their friends on the internet. But while they possibly may know a lot about statistics and stars, they don't know as much about the overwhelming importance of the mechanics of the game as they think they do.

This is where the fun starts! This is a great time in a young man's life to show him that "doing it right" usually equates with "doing it well" in life as well as in basketball. In this article, we're going to take a look at initially evaluating the talent on the teams you may coach, which will be a key for developing a practice regimen for your team.

At this point in my life, I usually coach boys in the summer. However, my preparation for the summer team begins much earlier than the start of practice in April. I normally visit the YMCA winter leagues to see what is being taught and to determine the overall level of talent in the area. I work with the "Y" director and the local Junior High and High School coaches 1) to determine if there is a particular player they would like to see involved in a summer program, and 2) to see if there are definite offenses or defenses which they would like to see developed. It's surprising how much these coaches know about the young players in their systems!

Next, I select players for the team. With the background knowledge I've assembled by this point, it's not difficult to come up with ten or twelve players who want to play in the summer. One of the initial activities at the first practice is to sit with the group on the sidelines and talk to each of them. I get a peek into their personalities and an early idea on how I should handle each of them individually in a practice or a game. I've found one's first impression about a player's personality is rarely far off.

After I get to know the players initially, I query them informally about their experience in the game. Without their knowing it, they are providing important information on how their practices will be structured. If I've done my homework right, I have selected kids who have a feel for the basics, gained in organized winter "Y" leagues, "mini-varsity" programs (high school varsity players helping with the school's youth program), or other "coached" instructional leagues.

It's now time to hit the floor with simple drills. Our first drill is the lay up line for both left and right hands. I watch this drill very closely, and mentally note several items. Is each player comfortable with his "off hand"? If not, I will spend time reminding them in coming weeks of the importance of using both the left and the right side of the floor. Do they go hard to the basket, or exhibit some discomfort going inside? Once again, I will use this information to encourage them to become full "inside-outside," "left and right" players.

Second, I instruct the players to dribble to the lane "elbow" and take a jumpshot. I look closely at each player's mechanics. Does each bend his knees and use his legs to shoot, as opposed to being an "arm-shooter"? (An arm-shooter will never be consistent if allowed to develop this form of shooting.) Does each keep the shooting elbow in and follow through?

Next, I have each player dribble to the corner, pivot, set, and shoot. How comfortable is the player in changing hands while pivoting? Is he able to square-up and set for the shot immediately after pivoting and switching hands? Does he fade backwards or drift left or right after the pivot? All these questions will provide mental facts about the players in my mind so I can work with them to eliminate mechanical weaknesses throughout the summer.

Fourth, we move to a zig-zag dribbling drill. Has the player been taught to use his body to shield the ball? Does he have a cross-over dribble? Is it a forward cross-over, a between-the-legs cross-over, or a spin move? What is his level of ball control at the completion of the change of direction?

Fifth, a defender is placed on the ball handler. I look for basics in both the dribbler and the defender. Is the dribbler able to handle pressure relatively comfortably? Does the defender have a proper stance? What is the defender's level of pride and tenacity in stopping the dribbler?

Next, the players form two parallel lines and simply pass the ball back and forth. I look for proper passing technique: hands on the side of the ball, full extension and thumbs down upon release, backspin on the ball, and accurate placement of the pass to the receiver's chest. Does the receiver catch the ball in "triple threat" position?

Finally, there is one crucial activity left for the first practice. I always ask mom and/or dad to come in and pick up the player. This accomplishes several goals. Most importantly, it assures the player is returned to the parent rather than turning him loose onto the street. Second, I look for the level of enthusiasm from the parent toward his or her son's participation on the team. A well-supported player will receive positive reinforcement and will tend to be more successful. Third, an important reason for having the parent pick up the child is to see how tall the parents are. Young boys mature at different times, and the biggest 12-year-old on the team might be the shortest senior in high school six years from now. If the player is tall now but has short parents, I will encourage that player to develop his outside shooting and ball handling. Conversely, past observers have sometimes questioned why I use such a short 12-year-old at post. It's because when mom and dad came to pick up Junior from practice, mom was 5'10" and dad was 6'3"!

Coaching young players is not rocket science. The important thing is not to be overly concerned about winning or losing. It's more important to do what is right for each player individually; to work to ultimately develop that young man into the best player and person he can be. Attention to detail in the initial evaluation at the first practice can go a long way toward fulfilling this goal.

THE SUPERSTAR

2003

By

John Eric Vining

Sometimes, a special person comes into one's life. That person makes one feel that a little special compassion spent on his behalf really was worth the effort.

This is a story of how a young man went from being just another kid on the street to a celebrated local athlete. This story shows that each of us can make a difference in a young person's life not by being specially gifted, but just by being there for them.

1995

Head Coach Dave Eiker and I paused at the entrance to the gym, hesitant to enter. This was the final practice before cuts for the fifth grade basketball team. Of all the aspects involved in coaching little boys, this was the only part I disliked. It was at times like this I wished I had never let my friend and league organizer Jim Craft virtually draft me into coaching. Even though I was not head coach this year – Dave and I alternated each year so neither of us got burned out – I felt personally responsible for making the decisions. How do you tell a fifth grader his dreams of being the next Michael Jordan are over?

I gazed out onto the floor as sixteen little boys lined up for lay-ups. Fifteen all dressed neatly in clean, crisp basketball tops and shorts – one dressed in a faded tee-shirt and ragged cut-offs. All these kids are about the same – only twelve will make the team. Cal Jensen (a pseudonym), the one in the faded tee-shirt, was no different than the rest, really. Just a few less dollars in Mom and Dad's pockets, that's all.

I looked into the stands. Fifteen pairs of parents all sitting on the edge of their seats, intensity written all over their faces. High up in a corner, sitting alone, Cal's mom glanced at the lights, the floor, the banners – everything but the basketball floor below. Cal's dad… who knew where he was, I thought. Probably still sleeping it off from last night's round of the neighborhood bars.

"What do you think about Cal?" I asked Dave. "He only has average size and speed. He really doesn't do anything any better than any of the other kids. Yet, there's something about him. I really can't define it."

"I know what you mean," replied Dave. "It's just something about the way he moves on the court. Hey, the kid needs a break. Let's keep him on the team."

"OK, but we are setting ourselves up for trouble. He's kind of on the edge. Rumor has it he's been in some trouble around town and in school. Take a glance up in the stands – you can see what the body language of his mom is telling us – no support there. We've had experience with this sort of thing, you know."

"The kid needs a break," Dave repeated firmly. "Basketball might make THE difference to this one."

1996

It was a few minutes before the championship tournament game, and already my stomach was churning. Even with a sixth grade game, the adrenaline was coursing through my veins. For heaven's sake, I told myself. It's only an elementary school game. Besides, we had Cal on our team. When all else failed, we always had Cal.

What a difference a year made! In 1995, the question was whether to keep Cal on the team. In '96, the question was how was the best way to have him touch the basketball at least once every possession!

Cal did not disappoint himself, his coaches, or his fans in this game. Scoring with ease from every conceivable angle, he led his team to victory in the championship final. As I viewed his shining eyes on the championship stand, I had a feeling this championship would not be his last.

It was obvious basketball had made a major impact on Cal's life, and not just on the court. I noticed that as Cal arrived at the gym, the clothes he wore were old, but spotlessly clean. His hair was always neatly groomed. On the court, his old-style warm-up jersey and trunks were like everything else about him – spotless and pressed.

Yet, vaguely, I was uneasy inside. It was clear to me that Cal had spent endless hours honing his skills over the past year. I knew that Cal's mom and dad had split over the winter. Was basketball a crutch for him? Was he spending the hours in the gym that he would have spent with them? Was the sound of the ball swishing through the hoop an opiate for his pain?

1998

I checked in at the front desk at the local YMCA. It was 6:30 AM. Somewhere deep in the bowels of the "Y," a basketball pounded against the hardwood courts. Instinctively, I knew eighth-grader Cal Jenson was there. I hadn't heard that particular cadence of pounding for a couple of days, which was strange – Cal was always in the gym at the "Y." Early in the morning or late at night, no matter when I showed up at the "Y," Cal was there.

After checking in, I followed the sound of the pounding to the court where Cal methodically pumped shot after shot through the hoop – most touching nothing but net. As I stood in the gloom of the half-lighted entrance, I mentally noted that practice was no different than games for Cal – every shot was a perfect swish.

"Hey, Cal! 'Sup, dude? Where you been lately?

"I had a little trouble, Coach," Cal said with eyes averted. "I got caught slipping through a window at school. I just wanted to get in a little extra practice and work a little kink out of my shot!"

"Are you sure that's all there is?" I questioned him closely. "I can't believe you could get into THAT much trouble over a little extra shooting."

"Well, there's a little matter of some grades. I just don't read so well. I guess I should have paid more attention in elementary school. I have had to spend some time in detention for some bad grades. Everything is so hard now!" Cal said plaintively.

"Cal, there is much more to life than basketball," I said forcefully. "Basketball is just a vehicle: a means to an end. You are smart, and you are dedicated. Don't let your past dictate your future. Practice basketball, but focus on your schoolwork as well. Everyone has twenty-four hours in a day. How can you use yours to meet ALL your goals?"

Cal took my words to heart. As I read the list of honor students in the local newspaper during his freshman year, Cal's name would invariably be listed among the top students in his school.

2002

I sat high in the bleachers as the pregame presentation started. Tonight would be a special night for Cal Jenson. He was to be recognized before all his fans for breaking his school's all-time career scoring record with the awarding of a specially engraved gold-plated basketball. However, I knew his school planned an additional special honor for Cal that night. Waiting inconspicuously just off the court was a representative of the United States Naval Academy at Annapolis, Maryland. The representative was there to award Cal a full athletic scholarship to the academy. Cal would be playing basketball for the Navy for the next four years.

My heart burst with pride as I watched the ceremony. I thought back to the little boy in the faded tee-shirt. Wasn't that just yesterday? I was so proud to have had even a little part in Cal's success.

Months later, I had a few minutes to talk to Cal as he prepared for his college career:

"Basketball became the focus of my life," Cal told me. "It helped me build the strength I needed to face all the challenges in my life. I owe much of this to the youth basketball program back at the "Y". The team was so important to me at that particular time in my life, because it helped me have a positive focus at a time when things could have gone wrong for me."

Cal Jenson was just a little boy with a dream all those years ago. Yet, all it took to nudge him down the path to that dream was a little time and patience from a couple of guys who had been "drafted" into coaching a fifth-grade basketball team. How many other "Cal Jenson's" are looking for some help? How many other guys have some spare time a couple days a week to help a little boy reach out for a dream?

Setting the Stage for: "The End of One of Us"

2002

By

John Eric Vining

If you live long enough, you are virtually assured of losing a person that is close and dear to you. One that reminds you of your own mortality. For me this came in November, 2002.

I was at work late one afternoon when the phone rang. It was my sister, telling me that my brother, Bob, had had three massive heart attacks and was not expected to live. I made immediate plans to head to Florida, where he lived and was hospitalized, with our mother accompanying me.

The following two stories tell of Bob's miraculous survival, and his quest for redemption, conversion, and peace. It is also the story of the end of his life, and of another miracle, so that he could spend his last hours with us, his family.

These two essays are also the end of this collection of stories. Somehow, that seems right, now that Bob's pen is stilled forever…

GOD IS IN CONTROL

(Originally titled: *"Sweet Peace, The Gift of God's Love"*)

2002

By

Robert E. Vining

I lay motionless in a hospital bed with my eyes closed, semi-conscious, and wondering what had happened to me during the night. The sun rose, filling the room with light. I opened my eyes and peered at my long, thin body. Wires, tubes and IVs ran everywhere. A tube snaked down my throat, gagging me and making it impossible for me to talk. I looked to my left and saw my wife, Violet, standing beside me. I reached out and clutched her hand, then stared into her sparkling brown eyes. A short but stout woman, she squeezed my hand in return.

Violet put her other hand on my forehead, then brushed back my graying blond hair. "Can you hear me?"

I nodded.

"Do you know what day it is?"

I nodded again. It was the day before Christmas: December 24, 2002.

"Do you know where you are?"

I nodded once more. I was in the Intensive Care Unit at South Bay Hospital in Sun City Center, Florida.

Violet let out a sigh of relief. "The doctors told me last night you wouldn't live until morning because your heart attacks were so severe." I shook my head no.

Violet grinned. "I understand. I didn't believe them either."

Four hours later, two nurses removed the tube that snaked down my throat. I could talk.

Violet still stood by my side. "How are you?" she asked.

I grasped her hand again. "Very weak, but I'm going to live."

"How do you know you are going to live?" she inquired.

I gazed on her sad, oval face. "My eyes. When I woke up this morning and looked upon your face, my eyesight was sharp and focused. It hasn't been that way since I became sick last month. I'm supposed to live. God will heal me. I know it."

Later that day Dr. Rolando Rodriguez, a tall, dark, middle-aged man, stopped by to see how I was doing. He placed his stethoscope on my chest.

"How bad is my heart?" I asked.

Dr. Rodriguez lifted the stethoscope and looked at me, then at Violet. He shook his head. "Very bad. Your heart has only ten percent of its former capacity. We've put you at the top of the list for a heart transplant."

"There's no chance my heart will recover on its own?"

Dr. Rodriguez shook his head again. "It's possible, but don't get your hopes up; the chances of that happening are remote."

Dr. Rodriguez left. I glanced at Violet, who paced back and forth along side my bed. "Don't worry, Violet. Please don't!"

Violet put her hands over her face. "I can't help it. It's so sad what has happened to you."

"God will heal me! He healed my eyes. He will heal my shattered heart. Have faith. I know this will happen." I looked away and closed my eyes.

My mind raced over the events of the past seven weeks. I knew when I had my first heart attack. I was a truck driver for Dart Transit and had made a delivery at Pine Hill, Alabama, late on the night of November 8, 2002. I later fell asleep in the sleeping compartment of my truck. When I woke up the next morning, I was sick. My body was weak, my head drowsy, and my eyesight blurred. I thought I had caught a cold because I had no pain; years of diabetes had dulled my senses.

Beginning that day, as my dispatcher found loads for me, I began to crisscross the Deep South and Midwest. I headed for Lanette, Alabama, to pick up a load at Knauf Fiberglas, then to

Jacksonville, Florida, for the delivery. A pickup at Panama City, with delivery to Mobile, Alabama. Back to Pine Hill for another pickup, with delivery in Rockford, Illinois. Then on to Aurora, the Twin Cities, and Chicago.

My cold was growing steadily worse. I though I might have pneumonia and drove to the Petro Truck Stop at Rochelle, Illinois, because I knew there was a clinic there. The nurse at the clinic took one look at me and immediately sent me to the local hospital. The emergency room doctor there told me I had Hepatitis B. Stunned, I crawled into my truck and headed for my home near Tampa, Florida, nearly 1,300 miles away.

As I headed steadily south, my condition grew worse. I kept telling myself that hepatitis was not that serious, but while traveling south on U.S. 231 near Dothan, Alabama, I realized that I could meet my Maker at any time. I prayed and made things right with God by asking to be forgiven of my sins. The peace of God's love swept over me. I felt no fear. God was in control. What ever happened from that point on was okay.

The next day I arrived exhausted at Ruskin, Florida, and went immediately to my doctor, Betty Carter, a short redhead who resembles her cousin, the former President and Nobel Prize winner, Jimmy Carter.

"Put this mask on!" ordered Dr. Carter. I took the clear plastic mask and placed it over my face. I breathed deeply, drawing in the oxygen. *Oh my!* I thought. *This is exactly what I need.*

After a few minutes, Dr. Carter motioned for me to follow her. I felt like a new man and believed I had been healed. We entered a small room. "Please lie down on the bed," said Dr. Carter. I complied. Soon wires were attached all over my chest. Dr. Carter read the EKG and, as gently as possible, delivered the devastating news: "You've had a heart attack. You're very lucky to be alive." An ambulance was summoned and took me to South Bay Hospital.

Two weeks later, I was out of the hospital, but I knew I hadn't been healed. My vision was still blurred; I couldn't see the way I did before the heart attack. Then on December 23, 2002, I suffered two more heart attacks and was near death.

Now it was Christmas Eve. I lay in South Bay Hospital, a broken man, but I was alive and by the grace of God, a changed man. My minister, Reverend Ernest Howell, stopped by to see me. A short, stocky man, Rev. Howell had the faith of a saint. I didn't remember it, but Rev. Howell had been by my side during the night when I was dying. Rev. Howell had prayed God would revive my failing body.

"I'm here to minister to you," said Rev. Howell. "Perhaps-"

"That's exactly what I need!" I cut in. Rev. Howell placed his powerful hands on my right arm and prayed God would heal my shattered heart.

Four days passed. Wires, tubes, and IVs still covered my body. I spent most of my days staring at the ceiling. Dr. Rodriguez stopped by once again to check my heart.

After Dr, Rodriguez finished his examination, I looked away from the ceiling and into the doctor's eyes. I sighed. "Tell it to me straight. When can I leave the hospital?"

Dr. Rodriguez turned away, not wanting to look at me while telling me the truth. "I don't know. Your blood pressure is very low. You can't survive without the IV; you need a new heart."

I closed my eyes and shuttered. *Bad news! Really bad news!* Then I remembered that moment when my eyes had met Violet's. *No! It's not bad news! God will heal me! I only need to keep my faith strong!*

Ten more days passed. Violet and I sat across the desk from Dr. Carter. My blood pressure was up. I was off the list for a heart transplant. I could walk on my own.

Dr. Carter studied my folder. "Amazing!" she said. "Simply amazing! It's hard to believe you are alive and out of the hospital."

"What are my chances of living a long life?" I inquired.

Dr. Carter glanced at me out of the corner of her eye. "You don't want to know."

"Why not? I'm a big boy. I can stand the truth."

"Okay, I guess you have a right to know. You have had what doctors call a "Class Four" heart attack. Fifty percent of the patients in this category die within six months. Most die within a few years. However, I believe you are going to be the exception to these statistics."

I smiled. "So do I!"

I often ponder on these events that have transformed my life. I had always been a Christian but one with weak faith. Like most people, I feared death. But on the highway to Dothan, after the peace of God's love swept over me, I reached a new level of faith I never believed possible. I no longer feared dying and was filled with an overwhelming desire to become Christ-like. I was ready to die. I wanted to meet my Savior but knew my fate was not mine to choose.

God is in control. God decides who lives and who dies. My time to die has not yet come.

The Rest of the Story

(A Sequel to *"Sweet Peace, The Gift of God's Love"*)

2006

By

Marianna Fetters

The phone call we had dreaded came on Thursday, October 5, 2006. Our brother Bob was back in the hospital. He had had trouble breathing that day and had been admitted to South Bay Hospital again with congestive heart failure. I called the church prayer chain, thus initiating the beginning of many prayers for Bob. Almost four years (47 months) had passed since he had suffered three heart attacks, and had miraculously survived to live a fairly normal life with his wife, Violet. But Violet had died the year before and now Bob was alone in Florida.

Due to privacy laws, our phone calls to the hospital only yielded vague information about Bob's condition. We were only informed that he was critical. We asked if we, his family in Ohio, should come. No one would tell us outright to come. My brother John asked Bob's male nurse, "If that were your brother lying there, would you fly in to be with him?" The nurse said, "Yes," and John immediately made reservations to fly to Tampa. Our daughter's wedding was the following Saturday, so I couldn't go along.

John rented a car and drove to Sun City Center Saturday morning. He was not prepared for how he found Bob. He was completely on life support, a ventilator tube down his throat. He was ashen gray, unconscious, and very still. John was told that Bob had suffered a massive heart attack the day before and could not survive. Such devastating news! John sat faithfully by his bedside, comforting Bob who was very quiet except for his choking on that ventilator tube, which he had hated during previous hospital stays.

325

We had to give a "Do Not Resuscitate" order Saturday evening and we knew when the life support came off, Bob would die. He had told us many times that he didn't want to live like a vegetable on machines, yet the order to pull the plugs would be very difficult to do. Since Bob was completely unresponsive, we were prepared to do it. However, three days went by and his treatment stayed the same. Being told that Bob could go on like this for some time, John reluctantly boarded a plane back to Ohio.

Early the next morning (Monday), only six hours after John had arrived home, the phone rang. It was Bob's doctor, asking for permission to remove the life support. I was stunned. John had been at the hospital for three full days while nothing was done. Now Bob was alone. I told his doctor to please remove the individual components of Bob's life support system gradually, so if Bob could live on his own, he'd be given the opportunity. Over the next three days, the life support was taken away very slowly and Bob lived. By Thursday evening, I was even able to talk to him on the phone. Having had the ventilator tube in his throat for so long, his throat was raw and his voice was affected. Talking was difficult for him. I couldn't understand much of what he said, but I did get "I love you" loud and clear. I was elated!

That elation was short-lived, though. On Friday, another early morning call brought the request to move Bob to a hospice house down the street from the hospital. I decided right then: If Bob was going into hospice care in Florida, he could go into hospice care in Ohio with his family with him. I called his nurse to find out what orders had been issued. She told me there were no orders for him to be moved that day and she'd take very good care of him over the weekend. Now I had two days to come up with a plan to get him home.

During the week of phone calls and answering machine messages, the words "air ambulance" had shown up on the notepad beside our phone. Bob needed to be transported by air. How was I ever going to find a plane? That Friday evening when we were eating out, my friend Mary, who is a hospice worker, and I were talking about Bob. I mentioned that we needed an air ambulance to bring him home and then hospice care would be required. That was all Mary needed. She made many calls that weekend while my daughter had a beautiful fall wedding on Saturday. There was no news from Florida. Bob must be holding his own. I called John that evening to get his agreement to bring Bob home by plane. He told me we must be prepared for the expense involved, but to go ahead.

Sunday at church, Mary gave me the phone number of a dispatcher named Larry who arranged air ambulance flights. I called him that afternoon and he told me there was a family in Ohio who wanted to fly their loved one to Florida. Since two families needed a flight there and back, they would share the expense of the trip with us! The plan was to fly their patient down on Tuesday and then bring Bob back on the return trip. That night, however, Larry called to tell me the plans had changed. His pilot needed to take a liver, which is only viable for five hours, to Florida immediately. The plane would be in Florida tonight and bring Bob back tomorrow (Monday). He said the other family was still in the plan only the trips were now reversed. Larry told me his medical team would take over in the morning and transport Bob by ambulance to the plane.

Now I had questions for Larry: Since we live in a remote area of Ohio, the nearest airports are 50 to 60 miles away. Where would they land? Another ambulance would be needed to transport Bob the 50 miles to our hometown, the location of the hospice center: Celina, Ohio. Larry told me they would just land in Celina. I told him we didn't have an airport, but Larry said he had information in front of him that said Lakefield airport was in Celina. I was shocked! Lakefield is a very small airport a few miles south of Celina. I insisted they couldn't land there. Larry informed me that Lakefield's runway was long enough and assured me that his pilot could land there. He also told me he would take care of the ambulance to get Bob to the Miller House in Celina, where our mother was a resident and the hospice care would be administered. Bob was to be in the room next to hers. I had to trust.

Then Larry gave me my instructions. I needed to get to our bank in the morning and wire the money for the trip. He would

FAX the permission form/contract to the bank while I was there. I also need to call Bob's doctor and get him to release Bob to the ambulance personnel when they arrived. Things were moving fast!

In the night, Bob's nurse called to tell me that Bob's doctor would be coming in very early for rounds. I needed to call at 5:30 AM. Everything had to click just right to get Bob home. I made that early morning call to the doctor and he prepared the necessary release forms. All of the bank transactions went as planned. By early evening Bob was in the air!

Hospice had taken care of getting a hospital bed, oxygen, medical supplies, etc. set up in Bob's room. I was there Monday getting things ready for him. When I got home, only fifteen minutes before his scheduled time of arrival, my husband hurried me to the car and we rushed to the little airport. Would there really be a plane? Had all of this really happened? It was a dark, rainy night and as we drove into the airport, we looked up and saw the lights of the plane shining through the clouds! An ambulance was waiting by the runway. Our beloved brother was home-delivered to our doorstep!

Bob lived 26 hours after arriving back home in the Midwest. He was conscious part of the time and we were all together. What a gift! Bob entered Heaven Tuesday evening, October 17, 2006, at 10:16 PM, surrounded by the family who loved him so dearly. A Tuesday flight would have been too late! Once again, God showed me that He indeed is in control, and miracles still happen!

EPILOGUE

By

John Eric Vining

So there you have it...a collection of stories from the lives, passions, studies, and frivolities of Bob and John Vining. I hope you found something that you liked...perhaps something that made you think. You might even have found some things that you thought were a waste of your time. Hopefully those were few, but these too are part of the whole idea – to create a smorgasbord of writings to give you new ideas to sample...different thoughts to ponder.

If you have gotten this far, I'd like to thank you for reading this collection. For me, there are other writing projects needing completion, and new writing projects planned but not yet started. This compendium of stories marks just another chapter in the on-going journey that is my life – I hope you will stay along for the ride in the future!

Robert E.Vining was born on November 20, 1946, on a small farm in West-Central Ohio. He farmed there from the mid-1960s until 1985.

He eventually moved to the Tampa, FL vicinity. Based from this area, he drove a truck cross-country until his death on October 17, 2006. Bob was an unusually astute student of history and observer of the present, and commented on both at length. Some of his observations are contained in this volume.

John Eric Vining was born on this same small farm on March 6, 1955. He assisted his father and brother until the family decided to cease farming operations in the fall of 1985. John's destiny led in a different direction, and he managed departments for several local businesses from the 1980s to the 2010s. He, too, is a man of varied interests, and some of those interests are represented in this volume. John still lives in Northwest Ohio, and continues his studies of history and business right up to the present day.

Made in United States
Orlando, FL
27 May 2022

18229095R00209